School Calendar Reform

Learning in All Seasons

Charles Ballinger
Carolyn Kneese

Rowman & Littlefield Education
Lanham, Maryland • Toronto • Oxford
2006

Published in the United States of America
by Rowman & Littlefield Education
A Division of Rowman & Littlefield Publishers, Inc.
A wholly owned subsidiary of The Rowman & Littlefield Publishing Group, Inc.
4501 Forbes Boulevard, Suite 200, Lanham, Maryland 20706
www.rowmaneducation.com

PO Box 317
Oxford
OX2 9RU, UK

British Library Cataloguing in Publication Information Available

Library of Congress Cataloging-in-Publication Data

Ballinger, Charles, 1935–
School calendar reform : learning in all seasons / Charles Ballinger, Carolyn Kneese.
p. cm.
Includes bibliographical references.
ISBN-13: 978-1-57886-278-8 (hardcover : alk. paper)
ISBN-13: 978-1-57886-426-3 (pbk. : alk. paper)
ISBN-10: 1-57886-278-7 (hardcover : alk. paper)
ISBN-10: 1-57886-426-7 (pbk. : alk. paper)
1. Year-round schools—United States. 2. School improvement programs—United States. I. Kneese, Carolyn, 1941– II. Title.
LB3034.B26 2006
371.2′36—dc22

2006000389

™ The paper used in this publication meets the minimum requirements of American National Standard for Information Sciences—Permanence of Paper for Printed Library Materials, ANSI/NISO Z39.48-1992.
Manufactured in the United States of America.

Contents

Acknowledgments

I wish to express my deep appreciation for the support of staff at the National Association for Year-Round Education in the writing of this book: Sam Pepper, Shirley Jennings, and Peggy Logan. I also salute Mary Liebman, Ann Grooms, Don Glines, James Bingle, and Wayne White—all of whom have believed in and worked for the cause of school calendar change for many years.

Acknowledgment of the guidance of professional colleagues—Paul Klohr, Erven Brundage, Ted Dixon, David Pascoe, and Jerry Rosander, who have helped to shape my interest in K–12 education in general and year-round education in particular—is appropriate.

I also commend the patience of family members who have both endured and supported my efforts in this and similar endeavors over many years: my wife, Venita, and my parents, William and Mildred Ballinger.

—Charles Ballinger

This book is dedicated to the children of our country, who deserve the best education possible.

I wish to acknowledge and express deep appreciation for the long-term dedication of the staff of the NAYRE and those involved with and dedicated to educational endeavors, who believe in the cause of school calendar change.

—Carolyn Kneese

Introduction

> What will it take to reshape our care-worn system? Money, talent, and time. To do the job . . . will require year-round learning, which requires year-round teaching, which means, in turn, year-round schools.
>
> —Lloyd H. Elliott

Education has come a long way in America. Early in our nation's history a primary function of school was to enhance religious instruction. At one time it was a crime, according to law, to teach the enslaved to read and write. At another time, it was deemed acceptable for students to be segregated into separate, unequal schools. Over the years, there has been a persistent effort to reform and improve America's system of education, and that endeavor continues.

Today, there is a multiplicity of efforts to reform and restructure K–12 education. In his book *Spinning Wheels: The Politics of Urban School Reform* (1999), Frederick M. Hess marvels that so much recent reform effort has produced so little change, in effect maintaining a status quo. He remarks that no entity is reforming more, and changing less, than urban public schools, an assessment with which some may agree. If so, why has there been little change? Is there not enough reform, or not the correct reforms, or simply too much reform with little focus? More importantly, what type of reform is needed?

There is a big difference between *school* reform and *educational* reform (Sizer, 1994), a differentiation, which, properly understood, aids in the restructuring of the educational enterprise. *School reform* refers to extensive systemic and structural change, which, to date, has not yet been adequately addressed. *Educational reform*, consisting of multiple teaching and learning innovations, has been introduced into the educational system in a chaotic and disorganized fashion. Consequently, strategies for significant structural change have been almost impossible to implement and sustain.

Successful school reform will come from a clear understanding of *what it is that we want our children to know*. Subsequently, consideration about *how much time is needed* for students to learn and how that time is structured is required. Learning time will differ for different students. For example, those not proficient in English may require a different time structure than others. After considering what our students need to know and how much time it will take, only then can *decisions about financial resources* be made. Once the goals, time, and money required are known, educational reforms can be layered atop.

Reform, however, does require time for results. Until now, most change, such as that of restructuring the school calendar, has been considered in some circles a "quick fix"—a Band-Aid, if you will. The reader is asked to consider the proposition that restructuring the school calendar can be a basis for school reform, a view similarly advanced in 1994 by the National Education Commission on Time and Learning in its report *Prisoners of Time*. The commissioners wrote that an unacknowledged design flaw in American education is the structure of time in schools.

The purpose of this book is to review all aspects of restructuring the school-year calendar and the concepts and pertinent research pertaining to the impact of time on learning, as well as to take a fresh look at education year-round, in order that the general public, educators, and policy makers might comprehend the issues surrounding calendar reform and reflect upon the educational dialogue that such change merits.

The majority of this country's adults work 12 months of the year, with a small portion of that time for vacation. In contrast, students K–12 attend a school year of approximately 9 months, conforming to a calendar that was once a strategy fundamental for accommodating child labor, which seems quite unrealistic and unreasonable in today's economic and social environment. This school calendar, termed the traditional calendar, was never designed to be an educational calendar.

Increasing access to learning opportunities is imperative, for evidence indicates students need to learn more in order to attain the high standards that America demands. More likely than not, if students need to learn more, more time—and quality time at that—will be needed. Because the long summer vacation associated with yesterday's school calendar is known to be harmful to retention of information, most educators feel that the school year should be modified. In his study of 57 school districts, Hess (1999) selected five major reforms as the focus of his research, one being day and time measures. The most common responses from school districts were extending the day and moving to a year-round schedule. The authors are responding, therefore, to this recent interest in school calendar modification.

PART I: THE CONCEPT OF YEAR-ROUND EDUCATION AND CALENDAR MODIFICATION

This book contains two major sections. In the first part the merit of modifying the school calendar for educating students year-round is discussed, as well as the particulars that contribute to restructuring the school calendar. Chapter 1 is an overview of the various types of year-round education—balanced (single-track), multi-track, and extended year. Definitions of commonly-used terminology and a rationale for calendar modification are offered. Chapter 2 is a survey of the historical background, recent developments, and probable future of year-round education. The organizational context of the three types of year-round education, including commonly-used calendar designs, is presented in chapter 3. And finally, in chapter 4, responses to frequently asked questions pertinent to stakeholders are presented.

PART II: EVALUATING THE PROGRAM

In chapter 5 of this book current research and evaluation of restructuring the school calendar are reviewed, and would be particularly of interest to practitioners and school district professionals. Program evaluation and indicators of school quality are explained. Subsequently, research findings for student academic performance on the three types of modified calendars—balanced/single-track, multi-track, and extended year—from across the nation are reviewed.

Chapter 6 includes a discussion of the broad context of the American educational system, with implications for policy. In this chapter current issues in public and private schools that necessitate consideration of school reform are examined. Another consideration is whether or not the agenda of the schools—to provide efficiency, excellence, and equity for all—is being met in schools that have modified their calendars and whether, indeed, year-round education, also known as YRE, holds promise as a possible solution to meet these criteria. Finally, there is a summary in which the authors urge discourse about the efficacy of calendar modification as a basis for systemic reform in education. While the final decision is left to the stakeholders (the public, school district professionals, and policy decision makers), it is the intent of the authors to describe the issues that call for school calendar reform and to present expert opinions and data from educators who have been involved with and researched the effect of modified time on learning over many years.

Part I

THE CONCEPT OF YEAR-ROUND EDUCATION AND CALENDAR MODIFICATION

CHAPTER 1

A Rationale for Modifying the Traditional School Calendar

Our usage of time virtually assures the failure of many students.

[There] is the pretense that because yesterday's calendar was good enough for us, it should be good enough for our children—despite major changes in the larger society.

—from *Prisoners of Time*,
National Educational Commission on
Time and Learning, 1994

The National Educational Commission on Time and Learning has acknowledged what most educators instinctively know, but seldom give voice to: There is a disconnect between the way that students learn and forget and the currently-used school calendar, which has little relationship to that understanding. Since students can learn in all seasons and months of the year, educators and others might well consider whether or not a school calendar that is more closely aligned to student learning modalities can be developed (Ballinger, Kirschenbaum, & Poimbeauf, 1987).

The traditional school calendar is not primarily a learning calendar now, nor was it designed to be. Rather, it is an amalgam of responses to the economic and social needs of a nation both rural and urban. Original intents—to provide helping hands on the farms and ranches of a bygone era, to provide extended instruction in English for young European immigrants, or to offer special interest classes to children of wealthy urbanites—have long since been surpassed by events in the 20th and early 21st centuries.

Nevertheless, the traditional calendar persists in a majority of American schools. Buttressed by the strong force of doing things the way they have always been done and supported by the inertia of simply accepting what is and has been, the traditional calendar continues to be anchored, though rusting, in many communities. The policy issue that remains, however, is whether or not calendar stability is of a higher value than adoption of a new calendar designed to aid student learning.

Today considerable flexibility exists for creating time models that better serve students' educational needs. For example, almost all state legislatures require students to attend school fewer than half of the days each year (180 of 365). If schools were to publish and distribute a hypothetical calendar that alternated legislatively required in-school days (180) with out-of-school days (185), most members of the public would be astonished to realize that American students would be out of school every other day of the year! Viewed through this lens, it is quite clear that American students have not been asked, nor required, to make the time commitment to learning that other leading nations of the world have asked of their students.

With significant learning loss occurring year after year because of the traditional long summer vacation, which in turn requires substantial time each autumn for reteaching the previous year's lessons, American students are not reaching the goals and expectations of the larger society. They are not likely to meet them when, as the commissioners of the National Education Commission on Time and Learning wrote, time usage in school virtually assures the failure of many students. Consequently, a question to be posed is this: Of what value is there to a community of having most of its classrooms unused for fully 25% of the possible school days each year, when America's students need more, rather than less, education?

While some educational authorities have suggested summer school as a solution to reduce summer learning loss, others respond that it is well to remember that considerably fewer than half of American students are involved in structured summer learning programs of any kind, including non-school activities. Further, they point out, the American summer school, for the most part, is not well-connected to the school's ongoing curriculum, lacking sufficient focus to be of much remedial help.

Other educators believe that summer remedial instruction comes too late to be useful. For example, if a student misunderstands an algorithm in October, he will most likely have to wait until the following June for the remediation process to begin. That struggling student's 7 months of frustration, waiting for help, is hardly an energized prelude to successful summer remediation (Ballinger, 1995).

Now that educational research has verified what experienced teachers have known for decades—that students forget a considerable amount of information over the long summer—a pertinent question to be raised in each community is this: How long should a summer vacation be? Three weeks or four? Five or six? As long as 10 or 12? Summer learning loss is a significant policy issue that requires ongoing community consideration of how best to lessen the loss. A community's focus on that loss and its ramifications may well lead to calendar reformation.

Yet, to a larger extent than one might think possible, there are communities across the nation that have resisted even minimal consideration and discussion of summer loss. In those communities mere mention of summer loss is dismissed without an articulated rationale for the status quo other than it has always been that way.

To a certain extent, the notion of learning loss seemingly fades with the resumption of school each autumn. Rather than learning loss disappearing, however, its reality is simply camouflaged by the resumption of school. Summer loss accumulates over time. Eventually, students from disadvantaged homes—known to be especially vulnerable to summer loss—slip further behind their peers each year and increasingly struggle to catch up with other students, prompting them to eventually abandon school by dropping out.

Unfortunately, even some educators are reluctant to confront the seriousness of summer loss. It is, as Bracey (2002) informs his readers, the phenomenon no one wants to deal with. To raise the issue is to disturb the comfortable status quo. Without a political groundswell in the community to confront learning loss—a groundswell unlikely without raising the issue in the first place—there is little incentive to tackle the summer loss phenomenon. Most school board members and district administrators feel quite safe in accepting the status quo because they are keenly aware that the parents of the students most seriously hurt by summer loss are also the ones least likely to demand change. Nevertheless, if learning challenges and objectives set by state and federal governments are to be met, discussion in the community about calendar reform is overdue.

THE IMPETUS FOR CHANGE

Community discussions on calendar modification to date have generated six generalized reasons to change the calendar. The reasons follow.

1. *Modified, balanced calendars can effectively maintain student interest in learning.* Periods of teacher/student interaction in the classroom, followed by scheduled vacations, is a balanced way of learning. Interest remains high throughout the learning period because students can, in their more difficult moments, contemplate a vacation just a short time away. The vacation period, however, is not so long that students seriously lose skills previously taught. A balanced year-round calendar provides a logical pacing of instruction, followed by regular breaks. Refreshed by the breaks, teachers and students return ready to work. Students thus learn to pursue work intensively, to rest and regenerate during short vacations, and then to work diligently again—a rhythm more like real life.

In contrast, the traditional school calendar begins its year after a nearly 3-month layoff. It lurches through the year by almost, but not quite, finishing the first semester before a 2-week winter holiday period. The semester resumes for just 3 weeks after the holidays and then is completed. Once the first semester ends, teachers typically are given 2 or 3 days to grade semester final exams, record the grades, and plan—with negligible time available for thoughtful revision—the beginning of the second term.

The second semester has its quirks as well. Teachers, staff, and students begin the semester with a rush. A short spring break of 1 week or less is scheduled about halfway through the semester. After the break there is a long slide in student interest in learning as the student contemplates the long summer vacation ahead.

2. *Students, learning differently, require different time configurations.* While affirming this truism in both community forums and edu-

cational seminars, many educators and community leaders actually adhere to another quite opposite learning principle when it comes to the school calendar. In practice, these educational leaders subscribe to the thesis that all students learn in the same way, at the same time, and that one calendar fits all. Further, there is often a clear pattern of denial about summer learning loss. Consequently, these school leaders ignore the warning of the National Education Commission on Time and Learning that there is an unacknowledged design flaw in school time schedules that can be corrected with provisions of time options for learning.

3. *Intersession classes provide faster remediation and advanced enrichment.* After several weeks of class work in modified-calendar schools, students have a scheduled vacation—the length of time of which depends on local calendar choices. The vacation is called *intersession*, during which remediation can occur or enrichment can be offered. If an elementary student is struggling with fractions, or a secondary student with algebra, intersession becomes a welcomed opportunity to take immediate corrective action. If the action is successful, struggling students have the opportunity to resume class work at a level comparable to that of their classmates when instruction begins anew.

Intersession also is a fertile period for enrichment and creativity. Year-round schools have developed exciting 1- to 3-week classes in the arts, sciences, computers, and independent study units, as well as the standard basic subjects. Once parents understand the possibilities inherent in intersession learning units, they tend to support calendar change all the more readily.

4. *Students learning a second language can benefit from the balanced calendar.* Students are arriving at schools with more diverse backgrounds than ever before. Consequently, a greater variety of languages is brought from the home to the school. A long summer away from language instruction is not helpful to students learning English as a second language. Indeed, the absence of formal language instruction is not helpful to any student learning a second language. Improving the school calendar can make a great difference in language acquisition for these students.

5. *Cocurricular and extracurricular activities can take place throughout the year and can reinforce previous learning.* Research

indicates that students remember most when they have an opportunity to apply what they have learned. A modification of the school calendar, with its intersession periods, can allow students creative avenues to apply recent learning. For example, intersession programs that incorporate in-depth science projects, independent science study, or science camp can add to what students have learned previously in their science classes.

Intersession intervals can also be excellent times to prepare for music events, Scholastic Aptitude Test (SAT) or American College Test (ACT) exams, or academic decathlons. For high school students, fall and winter intersessions can be desirable times to visit prospective college campuses. Student athletes can utilize intersession in at least two ways: 1) a significant portion of the sport's season is free of exam and homework requirements, allowing increased concentration on the sport; and 2) student athletes experiencing academic difficulty can use the intersession to correct the problem and retrieve good standing.

6. *Teachers can take advantage of year-long opportunities for staff development.* In a balanced calendar school, staff development is continuous and available throughout the year rather than available largely in the summer months. This in-service schedule is similar to that in professional fields such as medicine, law, and engineering.

Teachers' fears that an alternative calendar will prohibit them from pursuing advanced degrees have not been realized. Graduate schools live by the law of supply and demand. When teachers need in-service or graduate training, universities provide it. In areas where several teacher institutions vie for graduate students, the institutions compete vigorously to provide classes at times convenient to teachers.

RATIONALE FOR SINGLE-TRACK, BALANCED CALENDARS

Schools that choose to move to a single-track, balanced calendar generally do so with high purpose. They want to reduce—not eliminate—the long summer vacation of the traditional calendar to reduce the forgetting that accompanies it. They also want to establish to a greater degree than heretofore possible a school calendar that mirrors the way students learn: continuously. Thus, they adopt a single-track calendar in which all students and teachers follow the same schedule, but one in which there are periods of learning followed by periods of vacation (called intersessions).

Schools considering calendar modification for learning reasons only have the luxury of choosing among many schedules, unlike those schools facing or experiencing heavy overenrollment. The former may choose among a variety of structured calendars such as 45/15, 60/20, 60/15, 90/30, or variations of these common four. They also have the opportunity to develop and implement a design of instructional delivery of their choice: quarter, semester, trimester, or continuous. In those schools favoring a philosophy of meeting student needs by personalizing instruction, parents and students may choose among personalized calendars, which are designed to respond specifically to individual student needs and parental schedule(s).

The single-track's schedule is flexible enough that staff and parents can include an extra day or two, or an extra week, around legal holidays to take advantage of lower traveling costs or more quality family time. There can also be consideration of special days set aside for community festivals, local events, and county fairs, all within the context of vacations no longer than 8 weeks and most no longer than 6 weeks.

There are other reasons to consider implementation of single-track, balanced calendars. Utilizing scheduled vacation periods of 3 to 5 weeks, classroom teachers have time to reflect upon what has previously transpired in the teacher/student interaction and to plan future instructional strategy.

Because of the intermittent, scheduled vacations, there is reduced teacher and student burnout. For both, there is a period away from classroom tensions and personality conflicts that are so often present when humans interact. Because of this period of recuperation, some single-track schools have reported better attendance on the part of both teachers and students. Other schools have reported fewer student disciplinary referrals, which they attribute to the scheduled vacation intervals and the opportunity to dampen negative feelings toward the school on the part of some students.

REASONS GIVEN TO AVOID CALENDAR MODIFICATION

At the same public forums that generated reasons to implement a single-track modified calendar, there were reasons offered not to proceed with modification. Eight of those reasons are reviewed here. Three are linked to issues of family life, three are linked to school district administrative or operational concerns, and two are linked to non-school experiences. None of the eight are linked to instructional concerns.

All of these concerns are real to those who raised them. All have been addressed in other communities that have implemented a balanced calendar. All have been resolved or rendered non-threatening to the satisfaction of most families.

Parents were initially concerned about possibly having their children on differing schedules, if, for example, the local elementary school were to move to a modified calendar plan, while the feeder high school remained on a traditional schedule. Likewise, parents raised the matter of family vacations if calendar change were to occur. Both of these concerns have been, and can be, ameliorated to a large degree by printing and distributing to parents well in advance both the modified and traditional calendars. Parents quickly realize that there is a common in-school schedule most of the year and that there are usually 4 to 6 weeks of common vacation time in the summer, 2 weeks at Christmas/New Year's, and 1 week in common during spring vacation. That is a total of 7 to 9 weeks of common vacation each year. Since most families rarely take more than 3 weeks of vacation time together annually, including the winter holidays, this issue of separate schedules ceases to be a major one.

Parents were also concerned about whether or not child care would be available when students were on their scheduled vacations/intersessions. Experience in other communities has shown that child care is a service responsive to parental needs and follows the law of supply and demand. If child care organizations do not offer service at the times parents demand it, the organizations quickly go out of business. Thus, when the school schedule changes, the child care schedule follows quickly.

Parents also wondered whether or not students could still find and hold jobs after calendar modification. Concerns about student employment are usually allayed by the experiences over the past 3 decades of high school students in modified-calendar schools. A pertinent fact for consideration is that the vast majority of high school students do not have jobs affected by a change in the school schedule. For example, only on occasion do freshmen and sophomores have work especially sensitive to calendar change, if indeed they hold jobs at all. Even among 16- to 18-year-olds it is not common to have a job affected by calendar change.

Students holding jobs have actually been helped by balancing the calendar. Most employment of high school students is in the fast food, grocery, and service industries, jobs which are usually part-time and available in all months and seasons of the year. Because of the nature of these jobs, experience has shown that students in modified-calendar high schools are available to work in the above businesses at times when other high school and college students are in class and not available. By not having to compete with every other high school and college student for all-too-few jobs in the summer, modified-calendar students do very well indeed during their several vacation periods.

There is one job-related circumstance that merits special attention. Organized opposition to calendar change in some communities has come from the summer recreation industry. Fearful that minimum-wage labor will not be available at certain peak times, the industry has suggested to parents and others that a community's economy will be greatly damaged if minimum-wage labor is not available and local resort businesses fail.

This perceived threat to summer recreation sites can be viewed two ways. On the one hand, local summer resorts pay taxes, which is the lifeblood of all government agencies, including public schools. Consequently, no harm to business is wanted nor intended when a school changes its calendar. Rather, modification of a calendar is activated to attain the purpose of schools, which is to help students achieve the highest degree of learning possible. That is what taxpayers, including summer resorts, expect for their money. School districts in resort communities should work with local businesses to determine the number of students, if any, needed for successful business operations. It may well be that a summer vacation of 6 to 8 weeks may provide ample workers during the peak season. Work/study programs may supplement resort personnel needs. Discussion should include whether the resort(s) will be employing college or high school students, and if the latter, whether any will be below the age of 18.

On the other hand, the active opposition to calendar modification by the summer recreation industry is mystifying to many, since 99.9% of America's K–12 students are not employed nor eligible to be employed by this industry. Is it sound public policy to respond solely to the .1% that may be employed in the summer recreation industry, at the expense of the 99.9% who are not?

Parents also worried whether or not their children could be involved in activities such as Little League or high school sports. Activities such as these continue as before, experience has shown. They are affected little to none by balancing the calendar.

Other stated concerns revolved around air-conditioning during warm weather, building cleaning and maintenance, and having some schools out of sync with others in the district on such circumstances as teacher in-service and graduate work.

School administrative and operational challenges are easily taken care of in the single-track format. Maintenance and cleaning of school facilities continue as before. Since there are several scheduled vacations each year, maintenance and deep cleaning are actually enhanced by the single-track arrangement. No longer do the school facilities need to wait until summer for cleaning and maintenance.

Air-conditioning of any school functioning in all seasons of the year is an ongoing discussion with educational, physical, and financial implications far broader than first realized. If students cannot learn because of heat in a non-air-conditioned school, then is the value of classes held in May, June, and September suspect, as well as any summer classes held in that school? Yet hundreds of non-air-conditioned schools hold classes in warm weather each year. On the other hand, if students can learn in summer school despite the heat, then why would they not learn in a year-round school as well?

Most schools built in the past 20 years are built with air-conditioning in mind. Many older schools have been wholly or partially air-conditioned in the past 2 decades. Over time, this issue will dissipate as more schools move into some kind of climate control. In the meantime, balancing of the school calendar should be approached on its own merits first in a community's discussion, and once that decision is affirmed, then additional consideration can be given to climate control in the classroom.

The content of teacher in-service does not change because of a change in a school's schedule. The timing of the in-service may change in those districts that offer two or more calendar options to students and parents; however, districts offering a choice of calendars have found common times when all staff are available for in-servicing. More discussion of these issues is found in chapter 4.

RATIONALE FOR MULTIPLE-TRACK YEAR-ROUND EDUCATION

As noted previously, a single-track year-round calendar is one in which a school, or a school district, functions on a schedule in which all students and school staff follow the same days in school and on vacation. Single-track calendars are adopted to provide a more balanced and enriched educational program, to reduce the reality of learning loss over the long summer vacation of the traditional calendar, to accommodate the needs of a particular community, or a combination of these. It is not intended to provide additional space, promote additional efficiency of resources, or to solve administrative or logistical problems.

Multi-track year-round education (YRE), on the other hand, is implemented to do what single-track does not do: provide additional capacity to house students, maximize the efficient use of resources, solve one or more administrative or logistical problems, or do a combination of these three. A multi-track schedule provides more classroom space by having a portion of the student body on vacation or "off-track" at any time during the year. It is one in which the instructional and vacation/intersession periods of each track (or group) are alternated throughout the entire year. Thus, not all enrolled students are in school on the same days. Multi-track calendars provide shorter vacation periods, as do single-track calendars, thus reducing forgetting and advancing student achievement. Nevertheless, the primary intention of implementing a multi-track schedule is to solve and rectify a prior problem, such as overcrowding. (A fuller explanation of multi-track calendar configurations can be found in chapter 3.)

Multi-track is not the only way to solve overcrowding. Educational administration authorities usually advance 10 options as solutions. They are:

1. Bond levies for new construction
2. Use of portable buildings/relocatables
3. Redrawing community school boundaries
4. Double sessions
5. Extended day
6. Busing students to nearby underutilized schools
7. Use of other community spaces
8. Increasing class size
9. Redesignation of special-purpose classrooms
10. Multi-track year-round education

Each of the 10 solutions to overcrowding has supporters and detractors. Each has advantages and disadvantages. Some have savings, and some have costs. All are challenged by opponents when implementation is suggested. All are responses to a previously-identified problem: too many students for seats available. Sometimes more than one option is selected simultaneously. A review of these options follows.

1. Bond Levies for New Construction

This option is significant after the problem of overenrollment is identified and publicized. Its success or failure controls the usage of the other options. Voters determine whether or not bond levies proposed by public authorities, usually a school board, succeed by choosing whether or not to tax themselves additional amounts of money to build new schools or additions to existing ones. When voters affirm educational bond measures, new schools, new rooms, or refurbishing can proceed. Even when a bond measure is affirmed, other options may be temporarily implemented for immediate relief from crowding because 3 to 4 years may elapse from the time a bond measure is proposed until the new/refurbished structure is ready for occupancy. When voters do not affirm a levy, construction is abandoned, and the other nine options are reviewed for selection as the best means to manage overenrollment.

2. Use of Portable Buildings/Relocatables

This option has been used to a very large extent in growth areas across the nation, both to house students and to lower class size. Relocatables have become a quick fix when additional space is needed. Critics of this option contend that portable buildings are neither cheap nor cost-effective because preparation costs associated with their use are considerable. A site has to be located and prepared; water and electrical lines to the new facility have to be established; blacktop and concrete poured; steps and ramps have to be built. Portables require a high degree of maintenance. Others lament the loss of playground space to accommodate the portables at elementary sites and disparage their presence at the secondary level as an afterthought.

Despite their costs, portables/relocatables are common sights on campuses. Common though they may be, and more permanent than promised, the housing dilemmas of many neighborhood schools have not been solved by this option. Indeed, many of the nation's schools and nearly all of California's schools, whether traditional or year-round, have made use of portable/relocatable buildings, without fully dissipating student housing needs.

3. Redrawing Community School Boundaries

It is possible in some instances to redraw community school boundary lines to shift some of the overenrollment into underutilized nearby schools. Because of the ease of redrawing boundary lines on a map, some school district decision makers select this option for implementation. There is often a price to pay for its suggested usage. When a redrawing of boundary lines is proposed, there are almost always threats of legal or political action against the district and/or school board members. Homebuyers often include the quality of the neighborhood school as a factor in deciding to buy a home in a specific locale. Redrawing a school's boundary line causes these homebuyers to charge fraud and deception on the part of school board members and school administrators, with resulting acrimony and recrimination.

When an entire school district is impacted by enrollment growth, it is quite likely that all schools in the district may face a space squeeze.

A redrawing of boundary lines may be of very limited, to non-existent, help in some communities.

4. Double Sessions

A school's capacity can double very quickly when double sessions are implemented. In this circumstance, one half of the student body would arrive at 7:00 a.m. and stay until noon. Another group of students would arrive at 12:30 p.m. and stay until 5:00 p.m. A high school originally built to accommodate 1,500 students can easily enroll 3,000 students, with half enrolled in each of the morning and afternoon sessions. Since there is a 30-minute interval between the departure of the first group and the arrival of a second, the common areas (library, lunchroom, hallways, restrooms, and gymnasiums) are not impacted to the degree they might otherwise be.

While double sessions can quickly relieve the impact of severe overcrowding, there are obvious drawbacks. Two large groups of students and two separate teaching and support staffs are using the same facilities daily. There would be strong irritants among faculty. Two teachers using the same room daily leads to differences about decor, seating arrangement, cleanliness, and similar factors that make up a classroom. Double loads of students mean double messiness in the classroom. Double sessions intensify all of the usual problems that come with being a school.

Parents are likewise resistant to the use of double sessions because their children, particularly the youngest, may have to wait for school buses in the dark winter hours as early as 6:00 a.m. or be returned to their point of pickup in afternoon hours as late as 6:00 p.m. Parents fear for the safety of their youngest children in such circumstances.

5. Extended Day

Extended day is a variation of double sessions. There are separate morning and afternoon groups. Unlike double sessions, extended day has an overlapping of time. The morning group may remain on campus through lunch until 1:00 or 1:30 p.m. The afternoon group may arrive at 11:30 a.m., before the dismissal of the morning group. The primary feature of this arrangement is that in the middle of the day, when both groups are on campus, singleton classes (specialized classes offered just once in a semester, or year, such as band, chorus, advanced trigonometry) can be offered with an adequate enrollment to sustain the effort and cost(s) of the class. This option is not often chosen because the problem of overcrowding has not been solved during the middle of the day. The common areas of usage—cafeteria, library, gymnasium, restrooms, hallways—are still severely impacted, causing the usual discipline and behavior problems associated with overcrowding.

6. Busing Students to Nearby Underutilized Schools

When a school site is faced with excessive enrollment, one option is to cap enrollment and bus students to another school in the district. In some communities the ride to a less-utilized school is relatively short; in others, the ride is quite long.

While this option has support in some financial quarters, it is an opposite of the neighborhood school concept, one of the strongest values among parents of elementary and middle school students. There is a feeling of safety and protection when the child is "near." Even in those states where parents are given the option of enrolling a child in another school or school district because of a parent's work station, the parent will invariably want the child placed in a school as "near" to the parent's work as possible.

Busing students away from the home campus is not cheap. The costs of operating buses twice a day, plus the labor costs of drivers, supervisors, and loading/unloading attendants result in an option that is not favored by parents and not often favored by school board members and administrators.

7. Use of Other Community Spaces

School does not necessarily have to take place on campus. Other learning venues are available in most communities. Among these possibilities are rooms at public libraries, youth organizations, churches, community colleges, and other worthwhile organizations.

While in some communities these spaces are utilized, there are significant legal obstacles to overcome. In California, for example, most parents want their children to be housed in buildings that meet earthquake and other safety standards associated with the Field Act, a measure passed by the California legislature seeking to prevent a catastrophic collapse of buildings housing children. In other states similar requirements of health and safety prohibit the use of otherwise available buildings.

Additional problems arise in non-school community space: proper water connections for drinking fountains; separate male/female toilets; an absence of sinks for science/art/technical classes; an abundance of religious symbols and trappings in rooms used for instruction; and spaces that are not conducive to learning, such as those fronting busy streets, those lacking blackboard (whiteboard) and map facilities, and those lacking control of entrance and exit of non-school personnel who might be in the area.

Finally, while community space is sometimes used on a short-term basis, it ordinarily is not available long-term because the organizations that own the space want to use that space occasionally, on the organization's, rather than the school's, schedule. Since community space is limited and not always available in sufficient quantity to meet a school's need, it is not a strong option to handle the hundreds of students beyond capacity with which many school districts have to deal.

8. Increasing Class Size

Small percentages of overcrowding can be ameliorated by an increase in class size. If the crowding is in the range of 6% to 10% over capacity, the crowding may be relieved temporarily, at least on paper, by increasing class size by 6% to 10%. A class of 25 would become a class of 27 to 28, while a class of 30 would grow to be 32 to 33.

There are legal and administrative limitations to use of this option. If a school is overcrowded by 25% or more over capacity, simply raising class size within a classroom may not provide much, if any, relief from the overcrowding. Many states have legal caps on class size that may also hinder implementation. There are educational considerations, as well. Most educators argue strongly for lower class size if instructional efforts are to be effective, an exact opposite inclination from the effect of this option.

9. Redesignation of Special-Purpose Classrooms

Some schools over time have designated certain rooms as special-purpose rooms: computer lab, reading lab, special education room, science lab, and the like. All such rooms, used well and with purpose, can add to the overall quality of the instructional program. However, many schools have no more than two or three such rooms.

Astute administrators, anticipating enrollment growth, sometimes redesignate special purpose rooms as ordinary classrooms at the beginning of a new school year. While a small measure of growth can be assimilated in this way, significant growth is beyond a school's capacity if only room redesignation is available as an option.

10. Multi-Track Year-Round Education

The use of multi-track year-round education to alleviate overcrowding in a school or school district is an option that has been chosen hundreds of times across the nation, although it is not the most commonly-chosen option. It is flexible, cost-effective, and academically sound. Sometimes multi-track is implemented in conjunction with other options to solve overcrowding, such as use of relocatables, redrawing of boundary lines, and busing to other schools, when overcrowding is particularly severe.

Implementation of multi-track year-round education has an immediate impact on the problem of overcrowding. It is a solution that delivers its intended outcome immediately, because it considerably lessens the number of students on campus at any one time. Depending upon the multi-track calendar chosen (see chapter 3 for calendar options), from one-fifth to one-third of a school's students will be away from school during a given period, enjoying their scheduled vacations.

Multi-track delivers on its promise—relief from overcrowding—while at the same time it gives financial relief to school districts unable to provide, for a variety of reasons, adequate space and seats for a burgeoning enrollment. It is cost-effective because it lowers the cost of educating students, on a per pupil basis, by building on the economic principle of shared costs, or what is known as an economy of scale.

The cost-effectiveness of multi-tracking, demonstrated repeatedly by districts choosing this option, is little understood and often lost on educators and community alike. By being able to provide seat capacity for up to 50% more students than a building's originally-rated capacity suggests, multi-tracking is the king of cost avoidance.

Extensive use of multi-tracking avoids the costs of constructing new buildings (or as many new buildings), buying land, paying architects, preparing the site, buying equipment for the building, staffing the building, and assuming the daily costs of operating the avoided building such as utilities and repairs. The matter of cost avoidance is frequently and regularly overlooked in professional journals, leading to inadequate or erroneous conclusions about the savings and costs of multi-tracking.[1]

When comparisons have been made about the savings and costs of the various options to alleviate overcrowding, multi-track actually fares quite well. The passage of a bond levy (or levies) means that multi-millions of dollars will be required to complete the tasks of buying land; hiring architectural competence; constructing the building or buildings; outfitting the new structure(s) with all the things that are required for school (maps, gymnasium equipment, desks, lockers, and so on); staffing with administrators, counselors, and classroom teachers; and operating the structure(s).

The use of portables requires the purchasing or leasing of the portables as well as the costs of preparation of each site, transportation and moving of each portable, and the daily operating costs of each. The options of double sessions and extended day have considerable savings, since the cost avoidance of construction is considerable. There will be increased administrative costs with two distinct schools, costs that pale in comparison to construction costs. The option of busing students to underutilized schools, and the redrawing of community school boundaries which may also require busing, have transportation-related costs that are appreciably smaller than the costs of the options discussed earlier. However, the degree of relief from overcrowding is appreciably smaller as well.

Increasing class size has minimal financial cost, since adding a few pupils to an existing room would not likely add personnel or facility costs, other than provision of additional desks and similar equipment.

This option faces more philosophical and educational than financial considerations when its implementation is being considered.

The savings of multi-tracking are easily misunderstood and are often overlooked. By avoiding the costs associated with construction of new buildings, multi-track savings can be in the multi-millions of dollars. It is true that when a school operates 12 months of the year, rather than 9 or 10, there will be additional costs. However, the costs of operation of 2 or 3 extra months in a multi-track school have to be compared to the costs of building and staffing new buildings, or purchasing/leasing/operating portables for a full school year, a major point that escapes or is not accepted by critics of multi-tracking. When fully understood, the savings of multi-tracking are indeed considerable.

Costs are not the only factor in the education of students, of course, though it is a major one. The learning outcomes from selection of the various options are also important. Multi-tracking is a viable learning option because of the shorter vacation periods reducing forgetting. Moreover, there is no educational research that indicates harm to student achievement because of its implementation. A longer discussion of multi-tracking and student achievement can be found in chapter 5.

Multi-tracking has been in use in the United States continuously for 36 years at the time of this writing. While it is almost always implemented because of overcrowding, there have been a few occasions where a school, technically not overcrowded, elected to implement multi-tracking to free space to use as specially designated learning rooms: reading lab, computer lab, arts rooms, and the like, a reverse of the room redesignation option discussed above.

CONCERNS OF THOSE HESITANT ABOUT IMPLEMENTATION OF MULTI-TRACK

Multi-track year-round education is a sophisticated arrangement for handling overcrowding. Consequently, there are those for whom multi-track is a mystery of operation. To some it seems complicated and therefore suspect. Unfortunately, in the process of considering its use, many forget which is the problem—overcrowding—and which is the solution—multi-tracking. Five concerns are raised most frequently.

They are 1) overcrowded and large schools; 2) truncated instructional time; 3) limited access to courses and specialized programs; 4) ill-timed breaks and limited access to activities and programs; and 5) academic performance. Each of the five points merits a full discussion.

1. Overcrowded and Large Schools

It is true that multi-track schools are sometimes large. Multi-tracking greatly reduces the largeness and subsequent overcrowding of those schools by having a portion of the student body away from campus at a given time. However, largeness is not exclusive to multi-track schools. There are thousands of traditional calendar schools that are both very large and overcrowded in the United States. In California alone, there are 311 elementary schools in the state with over 1,000 students in enrollment, 124 middle schools with over 1,500 students in enrollment, and 240 high schools in the state with over 2,500 students in enrollment, according to 2004–2005 census data.[2] This same pattern occurs in other states as well. Largeness, then, is an unfortunate, common trait in American schools, whether they be traditional, single-track, or multi-track in calendar configuration.

There are educators who maintain that an ideal high school should be from 400 to 800 enrolled students, and that elementary schools should ideally be in the 300 to 400 student range. While these numbers may well be ideal, and a result to be hoped for, consideration of them leads to two questions: 1) Since meeting this ideal would require the building of a minimum of 1,075 new high schools and 2,253 new elementary schools in California,[3] for example, to what degree would one expect that state's schools to advance toward this ideal over the next decade? and 2) Since smaller high schools of 400 to 800 students cannot possibly offer all of the class options that larger schools can offer, and since, as will be seen later in this section, some educators criticize large multi-track high schools for supposedly not offering a full range of courses on each track, a question arises: Are smaller high schools that necessarily offer far fewer course selections than larger high schools the better option, and if so, won't each track of a multi-track high school be large enough to offer students a quality education?

2. Truncated Instructional Time

There are educators who hold that there is truncated instructional time in multi-track calendars. By truncated they are referring to two scheduling situations where the annual calendar is shortened slightly to accommodate severe overcrowding. In those instances, each scheduled day has been lengthened slightly so that the total number of instructional hours annually is the same as that of a school utilizing a traditional or single-track schedule. In a fulsome discussion on the rearrangement of instructional time, one critic dismisses the idea of adding a few minutes to the end of the day by referring to a newspaper quote from a chemistry teacher that 62 minutes is a long time for high school students to concentrate (Oakes, 2002). It is a remarkable observation, in that many high school chemistry teachers would gladly accept longer classes so that more time could be available for understanding the lesson and/or for doing laboratory work.[4] Furthermore, one has to believe that if 62 minutes is a long time to concentrate, then time rearrangements such as block scheduling, adopted by many high schools across the nation,[5] one major thesis of which is that longer blocks of time allow more focused learning, are quite harmful to students, a view not shared by all educators.[6] The policy question to be raised and answered is whether or not there is a standard number of days required to meet student proficiency standards set by a school board, state government, or federal legislation. To date, there is no fixed number of instructional days annually that will guarantee student proficiency.

Minnesota is the only state to have no legislatively defined minimum school year. Interestingly, Minnesota is usually near the top of the ranking of states in overall achievement results,[7] a remarkable achievement since a common Minnesota year is of 170 instructional days. On the other hand, there are several states with a mandated school year of from 180 to 184 instructional days per year that are not ordinarily found near the top of any ranking of the states. A reasonable conclusion is that a small differential in the number of instructional days, *by itself*, has little effect on the overall achievement of students.[8] Lost instructional time in traditional, single-track, and multi-track schools is more a result of the school's and teacher's lack of focus on time on task than the operational calendar of the school.

3. Limited Access to Courses and Specialized Programs

Some of those hesitant about multi-tracking suggest that multi-track calendars limit student access to courses and specialized programs, more so than do traditional calendars. It is true that multi-track secondary schools do not offer every possible course and specialized program on each of their tracks, but neither does any traditional calendar high school of equal size to one of the tracks, which is the proper comparison gauge.

A values dilemma is recognized at this juncture of the discussion, a dilemma faced by high schools of any calendar across the nation: Is a small high school of no more than 800 students, offering a more limited number of courses, a value in its own right, or is it more important to have a larger high school offering more choices of instructional courses? The answer is an important one in deciding whether or not large high schools utilizing a multi-track calendar can offer quality instruction on each of the tracks of a multi-track schedule.

If a high school of 3,600 students implements a three-track calendar, each of its tracks would have approximately 1,200 students on that track. Obviously, a high school of 1,200 students will not offer as many courses and specialized programs as a high school of, say, 2,400 or 3,600 students on a traditional calendar. In total, however, the three tracks will offer as many courses and specialized programs as would be expected of a high school of 3,600 students, and each of the tracks would offer courses commensurate with expectancies of a school of 1,200 students. To expect each track of 1,200 students to offer what a school of 2,400 or 3,600 would offer is unreasonable. To expect a school to offer a full range of AP courses to every student on each track is also unreasonable. However, multi-track high schools offer as many instructional offerings as they possibly can, including a system called cross-tracking, which allows a student needing a specific course to jump to another track for that course credit.

If only mega-sized high schools can offer access to a full range of credible courses and specialized programs, then one would have to ask whether a public or private high school of 750 or fewer pupils (of which there are hundreds) automatically offers a subpar education? Further, can a private or public high school of 300 students offer any education that would qualify as quality instruction? If the answer is no to these two questions, most of the private high schools and many of the public high schools under 750 enrollment ought to be closed because of their limited course offerings. Thus, it is important to understand that if one really believes in the ideal of a small high school, then any criticism of limited course offerings in a multi-track high school rings hollow indeed.

4. Ill-Timed Breaks and Limited Access to Activities and Programs

Some opposed to multi-track year-round education suggest that students on certain tracks have ill-timed breaks. One need only to look at the traditional calendar to observe ill-timed breaks. For example, the traditional calendar has a summer break of 10 to 13 weeks, which is clearly a summer of forgetting. From a learning interest, the long summer break of the traditional calendar is an ill-timed break.

There are other obvious ill-timed breaks. With a semester usually beginning around Labor Day, the traditional calendar's schedule from Thanksgiving through the end of January is a calendar in awkward disarray. First, there is the Thanksgiving holiday break, not a major break in itself, but it is followed by a period of minimal instructional focus over the next 3 to 4 weeks as holiday enthusiasm builds, followed by a 2-week holiday, after which time students come back to prepare in 3 weeks for important first semester exams. This semester's schedule is a classic example of ill-timed breaks.

Further, the first semester of the traditional calendar usually ends on a Thursday or Friday, with the second semester beginning the following Monday or Tuesday. Over one long weekend of 3 to 4 days, teachers are expected to grade final first-semester exams, record the grades for placement in permanent record files, and initiate a corrected course outline for the second semester. Opting for the traditional school calendar is not a way to avoid ill-timed breaks, since all calendars, traditional and year-round, have ill-timed breaks. Moreover, because some holidays "float" from year to year, there will always be ill-timed breaks, irrespective of the calendar a school district chooses to implement.

There can be a minimizing of these ill-timed breaks, however, by balancing the school year calendar with one of the year-round calendars. One has but to look at Figure 1.1 to see how disjointed a traditional calendar is when compared to the regularly scheduled breaks of a modified annual schedule.

Whether or not students in multi-track schools have limited opportunity to be involved in extracurricular activities and enrichment programs may be more in the eye of the beholder than actual fact. While a student in one track of a multi-track calendar may be on vacation between Thanksgiving and Christmas, such circumstance does not necessarily indicate a deprivation of holiday activities. Students are ordinarily invited to participate in any holiday activity the school offers, either as an active participant, or as an audience member, irrespective of the calendar track. There are scores of community holiday pageants available to students off-track, if they wish to participate, without the restriction of needing to hurry home to go to bed because of the next day's classes or class assignments. Indeed, a student off-track may actually enjoy the winter holiday period more thoroughly, without the worry of papers due, exams to be taken, and parties/church services to attend. Since holiday time between Thanksgiving and Christmas has never been known in educational circles as a high time for concentrated learning, one wonders how this supposed ill-timed break can be an issue.

Some critics of multi-tracking point to summer primarily as a time when multi-track students are missing out on extracurricular activities. However, if the activity in question is summer school, year-round advocates simply point out that summer school would not be needed if the school calendar was organized in the first instance to fit a coherent plan for learning. Also, year-round's intersessions are in reality summer school rescheduled. If the issue is summer camp experiences, year-round advocates point out that no more than 15% of America's students have camp experiences and that autumn and spring camps are more useful learning experiences as nature prepares for the two more extreme seasons. Many students, particularly students with disabilities, are not likely to be involved in summer experiences such as long-term summer camps or lengthy out-of-state trips. For them, summer is unorganized and troublesome. Moreover, advancing the idea of a lazy, hazy summer of endless beach time patently ignores the abundant research

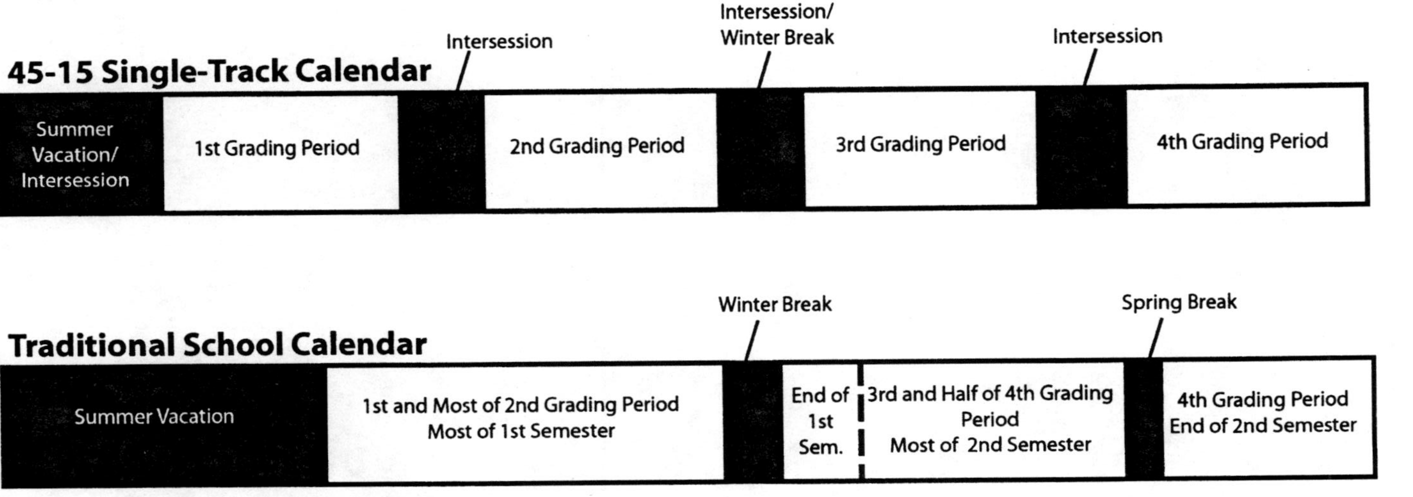

Figure 1.1. *Balanced Calendar Versus Traditional Calendar*

on summer learning loss, which is particularly hurtful to those students with learning or physical disabilities.

There are important experiences available to students off-track (on vacation) that are not available to students on a traditional calendar schedule. For example, the most significant programs in the arts fields do not occur in the summer, but rather in the winter. It is a common circumstance that traditional calendar students do not have the opportunity, because of schedule conflicts and calendar limitations, to take advantage of lower-cost theater or musical matinees, or free museum admission days/hours throughout the high point of the arts season. Off-track students, if they are interested, can do so.

Likewise, off-track students can be active in youth activities conducted by youth-serving agencies in all seasons of the year. Recreation is not just a summer activity. Work experience is just as available in autumn, winter, and spring as it is in summer. Entry-level jobs for 16-, 17-, and 18-year-olds (primarily fast-food and grocery operations) are available all times of the year. It makes little sense, from a job-seeking perspective (noted previously), to have all high school and college students, ages 16 to 21, to be seeking the same all-too-few jobs in the months of June, July, and August only. So for every experience that an off-track student may miss, there is another experience that students in school may miss, a circumstance not unlike the lives of all humans, adults as well as students.

5. Academic Performance

A full discussion of academic performance of students enrolled in schools utilizing modified/balanced calendars can be found in chapter 5 of this book. Only a brief response to those hesitant about implementation of multi-tracking is warranted here. Simply put, there is no credible evidence available indicating that multi-tracking is harmful to the academic well-being of students. Indeed, there is recent evidence of improved performance on the part of students following a multi-track calendar, particularly students who are educationally disadvantaged. In short, this concern is allayed by the evidence available.

THE PROCESS OF DECISION MAKING LEADING TO IMPLEMENTATION OF MULTI-TRACK YEAR-ROUND EDUCATION

Decision makers are faced with the dilemma of what to do when overcrowding—that is, when there are more students enrolled at a school than there are seats available to them—becomes a major problem. If voters are willing to pass bond measures, new schools can be built to house additional students. If they are unwilling to do so, other alternatives to cope with the problem of overcrowding have to be considered.

A political reality is that the voting public is often unwilling to pass bond measures for additional facilities until there is a clear, demonstrable need for new money. Illustrating to the public at large the need for additional facility space is difficult at best and may require a sense of crisis about overcrowding before an affirmative vote is granted.

As enrollment increases, decisions are required for housing students safely, comfortably, and equitably. When enrollment reaches capacity at existing schools, all options may need to be considered to meet the challenge of overcrowding.

Even though a bond measure may be offered for a vote by the electorate, acknowledged realities are that 1) an approved bond levy still requires time of 3 to 4 years before new facilities are ready for utilization, thus requiring other interventions to contain the problem of increasing enrollment leading to severe overcrowding; and 2) a failed bond measure will lengthen the timeline before new facilities are available to ease the student housing crisis. Thus, a prudent process of decision making explores the options for adequately housing students beyond the obvious alternative of new facilities.

SELECTING AN APPROPRIATE MEANS OF MEETING THE PROBLEM OF OVERCROWDING

Earlier in this chapter, 10 options were listed to ease overcrowding. One of the 10 would provide expanded facilities. Nine of the 10 are options when bond measures are not approved.

The option of multi-tracking will allow an increase in the numbers attending a neighborhood school, up to 50% more students than the school was originally built to house. Moreover, multi-tracking has an educational component that other options do not have. By reducing the long vacation of the traditional calendar, there is the likelihood of reduced forgetting, with more time available for new teachings and learnings. Since school boards and school administrators are in the business of education, is it any wonder, then, that multi-tracking is an option favored by many as the preferred solution to overcrowding?

NOTES

1. An example of erroneous cost calculations about multi-tracking can be found in Ready, Lee, and Weiner (2004). A fuller discussion of the costs/savings of modifying the school calendar can be found in chapter 6.

2. Data comes from the California Department of Education website: http://data1.cde.ca.gov/dataquest/content.asp.

3. Data comes from the California Department of Education website. The CDE website lists (for 2004–2005) 1,130 high schools in the state enrolling 1,763,918 students. The calculation used above goes like this: 1,763,918 (high school students) ÷ 800 (maximum ideal for high school enrollment) = 2,205 high schools. Since there are currently 1,130 high schools, an additional 1,075 high schools would need to be built. The CDE site indicates there are 5,556 schools enrolling 3,123,571 elementary students. The calculation used above goes like this: 3,123,571 (elementary students) ÷ 400 (maximum ideal for elementary school enrollment) = 7,809 elementary schools. Since there are currently 5,556 elementary schools, an additional 2,253 elementary schools would have to be built.

4. An example of teachers utilizing longer science periods to strengthen instruction can be found in Stenvall (1996).

5. For example, growth in block scheduling jumped from 6 high schools (2%) in North Carolina in 1992–1993 to 254 high schools (65%) in 1996–1997. Information located at the website of the North Carolina Department of Public Instruction at this address: www.dpi.state.nc.us/block_scheduling/1997.

6. In a research project designed to quantify the effect of lengthening the class period and reorganize the school calendar, Cabat found that there was a statistically significant preference for block scheduling among the non-white population. The block time periods were 90 minutes in length. Cabat, *Student*

Satisfaction Related to Year-Round Education and Block Scheduling, abstract, 1996.

7. There are several indicators of Minnesota's high standing among the states. For example, in a listing of ACT average composite scores (2004) there is this ranking of the states. Data found at www.act.org.

ACT	*State*	*Composite Score*	*% of Graduates Tested*
1.	Vermont	22.7	12
2.	Maine	22.6	9
3.	Washington	22.5	15
4.	Oregon	22.5	12
5.	New Hampshire	22.5	9
6.	Massachusetts	22.4	12
7.	New York	22.3	16
8.	Wisconsin	22.2	68
9.	Minnesota	22.2	66
10.	Iowa	22.0	67
National Average		20.9	40

8. The number of instructional days annually may be less important than other factors surrounding time. Aronson, Zimmerman, and Carlos (1998) have put it succinctly this way: "There is little or no relationship between allocated time and student achievement. There is some relationship between engaged time and achievement. There is a larger relationship between academic learning time and achievement" (3).

CHAPTER 2

Efforts to Modify the Calendar: Past, Present, and Future

> Year-round education: moving from nine-month discontinuous schooling to twelve-month continuous learning.
>
> —Don Glines

EARLY ATTEMPTS AT CALENDAR MODIFICATION

Always a major component in the American story, education in the United States has changed over the past two centuries in response to shifts in American society's needs and interests, a better understanding of the learning process, events that resulted in a reformulation of educational philosophy, and practical matters of school governance. As understanding of the educational enterprise grows, so too come adjustments to the way things are done.

The American school calendar has likewise evolved and changed over the years. From the 1840s onward, schools in America's largest cities were open 11 or 12 months of the year. New York City offered classes for 245 days annually; Chicago, for 240; Detroit, 259; and Philadelphia, 252.[1] This length of school year, advocated today by some educational and business leaders as essential to America's future competitiveness, but resisted skeptically by many American parents, was an accepted calendar arrangement earlier in the nation's history, notably at a time when air-conditioning was not an option nor even conceivable to most.

In contrast, the school year was considerably shorter in rural areas. With up to 85% of a state's population engaged in agriculture, young people, particularly those in their teens, were needed on the ranches and farms of that era for economic survival. School for some of the oldest students in sparsely populated rural areas might be as little as 3 months; for others it could be 6 or 7 months. In contrast, children in America's small cities and towns might receive 7 to 9 months of classroom work, a compromise between urban and rural school calendars.

As changes unfolded in the nation's economy and social fabric, a movement toward some similarity of annual school schedule ensued. City schools began reducing the length of their school year to 10 months, in partial response to affluent parents' request for more time for their children to travel or engage in outside-of-school experiences. Rural schools began increasing their time to approximately 8 months of classroom work. Finally, a consensus emerged during and immediately following World War II that school time should consist of 170 to 180 days of teacher/student contact annually, usually from around September 1 to around June 1, or from around Labor Day to Memorial Day. Notwithstanding this developing consensus, however, there continued to be significant variations in the beginning and ending dates of the school year among districts within states and sometimes even within counties. Despite the movement toward greater uniformity of the length of the year, there has never been a standard national calendar dictating the annual starting and ending times of America's schools, setting the United States apart in this regard from some other countries.

BEGINNINGS OF YEAR-ROUND EDUCATION

While some scholars advance the thesis that the origination of year-round education was the advent of summer "vacation" schools in the 1870s, others hold that these schools really were the forerunner of present-day summer schools, not year-round education (YRE). If those in the latter group are correct in their historiography, it would seem that little has changed in the nature and structure of summer school for over a century. Summer schools are still in large measure thought of as vacation schools. Their instructional programs are often only incidentally connected to the regular curriculum of the school.

More likely the forerunner of what is known today as year-round education began in 1904 in Bluffton, Indiana. William Wirt, superintendent of schools, initiated a voluntary four-quarter system to alleviate an overenrollment problem, as well as to provide a better quality of education. In 1907 Wirt became superintendent of the Gary, Indiana, schools where he implemented an extended year calendar, an arrangement that lasted for 30 years. From 1907 to 1937 Gary schools were open 50 weeks a year, 12 hours a day, 7 days a week.

From the start of Wirt's program in 1904 until 1940, various arrangements of the school year calendar were devised to improve the quality of education, to provide space, to implement programs for "laggards," to provide vocational training, or to assist immigrant children in learning English. Newark (New Jersey) developed a four-quarter program, 1912 to 1931, intended for immigrant children. Nashville (Tennessee) adopted an extended year calendar in 1928, solely to offer better learning opportunities and to "break the iron-cast system of education," in the words of the then superintendent, Henry Weber (Glines, 2002).

The first known districtwide, mandated calendar program to increase space was the four-quarter, rotating schedule implemented in Aliquippa, Pennsylvania, from 1928 to 1938. However, by the time of World War II, all year-round education programs of any kind had ceased. World War II dictated cooperation and uniformity to bolster the nation's resolve to win the war. It took more than 2 decades after the war to break away from calendar similarity before year-round education was implemented again.

However, the philosophy of year-round education was not extinguished by the war. From the late 1940s into the 1950s and early 1960s, there were individuals proposing the initiation of year-round calendars in Minneapolis, Los Angeles, McHenry (Illinois), Albany (New York), and Clarion (Pennsylvania). In 1968 the first year-round school in the modern era (post–World War II) was implemented at Park Elementary, Hayward, California. Park operated a 50/15, single-track schedule in which staff and students were in school for 50 days, followed by 15 days (Monday–Friday days) of vacation. Thus, each student at Park was eligible for 200 instructional days a year.

The following year (1969) two noteworthy events of year-round history occurred. The Wilson Campus School at Minnesota State University, Mankato, launched a personalized, K–12, continuous-year calendar, whereby students could elect to attend any 170 of the 240 instructional days offered, as well as vacation time as desired. The Wilson program commanded nationwide attention because of its innovations and total escape from rigid calendars of any kind. Led by Dr. Don Glines, indefatigable champion of student-centered learning, the school was remarkable for putting into practice oft-stated, but seldom implemented, educational and philosophical tenets.

It was also in 1969 that the first multi-track school in the modern era opened in St. Charles, Missouri, a suburban community of St. Louis. St. Charles had experienced rapid growth during the 1960s, with new subdivisions sprouting throughout what had been a semi-rural area. Becky-David Elementary School adopted a four-track schedule (or four-cycle, as it was called in St. Charles), with students attending school for 9 weeks, then vacationing for 3 weeks. With 25% of the students on vacation at any one time, the pressure of overenrollment was eased, while at the same time generating up to a 33% growth in enrollment capacity.

Multi-tracking was a novel idea for its time, but one welcomed by districts facing or experiencing overenrollment. It was a practical solution that came to be utilized in more than 1,500 schools over time. In the early 1970s an exceptionally large increase in student enrollment, part of what was called a "baby boom," put a space squeeze on schools and districts from coast to coast. A need to find a seat for all of the students expected to enroll, a circumstance situated in a time of public resistance to tax increases, prompted creative thinking. Overenrollment, limited seating capacity, and resistance to tax increases were a heady mix that brought forth the sustained use, over the next 3 decades, of multi-track year-round education to alleviate the overcrowding.

Multi-track achieved its purpose by putting portions of the student body on staggered schedules of class work and vacations. (See chapter 3 for an extensive look at multi-track schedules.) Multi-tracking was quickly found to be useful, practical, cost-effective, and academically sound.

From Becky-David Elementary's use of a four-cycle, 9/3 schedule (also known as four-track, 45/15), a number of derivatives ensued. Soon there were three-, four-, and five-track calendars, as well as the basic single-track model implemented for instructional, rather than overenrollment, reasons.

Over the next 4 years, multi-track traveled quickly first to Illinois, where Valley View, a suburban Chicago district, adopted essentially the same calendar plan as St. Charles. Multi-track then moved on to California, Florida, and beyond. All of these adoptions of a multi-track calendar in the early 1970s took place in fast-growing suburban communities, where the student population was largely white and middle class.

The first California multi-track schools began in 1971, simultaneously in the La Mesa–Spring Valley and Chula Vista City school districts, both in San Diego County and both experiencing exceptionally rapid growth. Originally just seven schools in the two districts, hundreds of other California schools followed their lead over the next 30 years in implementing a multi-track calendar to facilitate the safe housing of students. Combined with the implementation of single-track year-round schools solely to advance learning and curb forgetting, California became the leader in the number of year-round schools nationwide.

Other scheduling innovations abounded during the 1970s and early 1980s. Four-quarter, trimester, and multiple-access 45/15 plans, among others, were developed and sometimes initiated. While innovative scheduling was a phenomenon from East Coast to West Coast, a pattern was established in the early 1970s that is still extant today: the vast majority of schools that have modified and balanced their calendars have been west of the Mississippi River. While there have been and will continue to be significant increases in the number of modified-calendar schools east of the Mississippi, there has been to date greater receptivity to the schedules in the West.

The energy of calendar revision and adoption in the 1970s and 1980s continued into the 1990s and on into the new millennium. Unlike some of the pilot projects of the 1960s and 1970s, year-round education's early programs have continued to exist. Park Elementary, the first year-round school after World War II, continues today as a year-round school, though its original 50/15 schedule has been modified into a standard 45/15 calendar. Mission Viejo Elementary in Aurora, Colorado, one of the early multi-track schools, has continued as a multi-track school for over 3 decades. The early multi-track schools in California, initiated in 1971, continue today as year-round schools, though they have seen a leveling of enrollment to the point where multi-tracking, no longer needed, has given way to single-tracking.

YEAR-ROUND EDUCATION TODAY

As the modified-calendar movement matured, the National Association for Year-Round Education (NAYRE), and its predecessor organization, the National Council on Year-Round Education (NCYRE), served as the agent of professionalization and keeper of statistics demonstrating the movement's growth. During the 2004–2005 school year NAYRE located 3,206 schools in the United States that fell within NAYRE's guidelines to be included in its national directory. To be included, a school's vacation periods must be 8 or fewer weeks, including summer vacation, a stipulation that is true for both single-track and multiple-track schools. The 3,206 schools constituted about 3.5% of America's schools.

Modified-calendar schools are located in 46 of the 50 states, as well as the District of Columbia, and enroll over 2,284,000 students, which constitute about 4.9% of America's K–12 students. The schools encompass a wide variety of types and instructional patterns. Included in the total are elementary, middle, high, and K–12 schools; rural, suburban, and urban; very small (15 students) to very large (over 5,000); and magnet, charter, special education, Padeia, International Baccalaureate, Success for All, and similarly specified schools, both public and private. In addition modified calendars have been adopted in a number of Canadian schools, as well as several islands in the Pacific with strong ties to the United States. NAYRE has affirmed over 11,000 year-round students in Canada and nearly 16,000 in the Pacific Islands.

Not included in these totals are schools that serve students needing court-ordered protection or who are incarcerated because of illegal actions. Also not included are other movements that have a year-round aspect to them, but do not constitute the usual understanding of "school." For example, homeschooling, which in most instances operates year-round, is not included in the totals. If the numbers of students in year-round circumstances who are not in "school" were added to those gathered by NAYRE, the aggregate number of students involved in year-round programs is estimated to be at least triple the number documented. It is clear that continuous education is more widespread in the United States than heretofore recognized.

It is difficult to estimate the total number of individual students who have spent one or more of their years in schools listed in NAYRE's annual directory. However, taking into account the number of schools involved in the year-round movement and the number of students enrolled in those schools over the past 37 years, it would be reasonable to assert that more than 10,000,000 students in the United States have been a part of modified-calendar schools. The effect of these 10,000,000 year-round students becoming parents and teachers, or having already become teachers and parents, is an interesting projection that will be discussed in a later section of this chapter.

ORGANIZING THE YEAR-ROUND MOVEMENT

Prior to World War II, during which the first year-round schools appeared, and immediately after the war, in which the concept once again emerged, no entity existed to coordinate the accumulation of information about school calendar modification and to distribute pertinent information to interested individuals. Along with the launching of the first year-round school in the modern era in 1968, there also began the emergence of a national movement.

The first national seminar on year-round education was held in 1969 in Fayetteville, Arkansas, a result of a chance discussion. Fayetteville's superintendent, Dr. Wayne White, had proposed a new facilities program to the local board of education. President of the board Henry Shreve asked, "Why can't we operate schools year-round so that we can get maximum use of them and not have to construct more buildings?" That exchange prompted further exploration of the idea. Organized by Dr. Ann Grooms, president of Educational Services of Cincinnati, Ohio, the seminar included a presentation by Mr. George Jensen, president of the National School Calendar Study Committee, former president of the Minneapolis Board of Education, and a Minneapolis businessman. Indeed, one of the fascinating aspects of this first seminar was the strength of lay leadership in urging educators to consider innovations in the school calendar (Glines, 2002).

From this first seminar sprang a second, third, and fourth. It was at the Fourth Annual Seminar in 1972 that the NCYRE was formed, the first organization dedicated to the study of and reflection about modification of the common school calendar, now referred to as the traditional calendar by many, and unbalanced calendar by some. The NCYRE studiously tracked the progress of the calendar modification movement, organized annual conferences, and became the repository of the earliest studies about the effects on students and community of calendar modification.

In 1986 NCYRE's board of directors moved the organization from a largely voluntary, low-key status into a formal non-profit organization. The organization was renamed the NAYRE, which blossomed into a fully functioning organization with paid staff and a reach from coast to coast in the United States and Canada, and contacts in other parts of the world. NAYRE today collects statistics about the year-round movement, organizes conferences and seminars, and fosters research and publications about modification and balancing of the calendar.

YEAR-ROUND EDUCATION IN OTHER COUNTRIES

There are interesting schedules of schooling in other countries of the world, and a comparison of them shows variations in the length of the school year and (summer) vacations. Working from the NAYRE's definition of year-round education,[2] it is obvious that a large number of countries would qualify as having year-round education nationwide (and have qualified for many years). Some have a considerably longer school year, with up to 240 days of instruction (compared to 170 to 184 days in most U.S. states). Others have 180 to 190 student instructional days annually, interspersing them with holidays, making the year considerably longer by the wall calendar, but with relatively shorter vacations. Others have an additional 15 to 20 instructional days beyond that of the typical American school calendar, but nevertheless with a

9-week summer vacation, falling short of NAYRE's definition of year-round education. (See Tables 2.1 and 2.2.)

In their report, *Prisoners of Time* (1994), the commissioners of the National Education Commission on Time and Learning expressed serious concerns about the implications of additional time students have allotted to them to study core subjects in friendly countries that are nevertheless competitors educationally, politically, and economically. Commissioners worried that the additional time, both in length of day and length of year, would someday overwhelm the competitive edge of the United States. Interestingly, these same friendly, competitive countries are taking note of discussions in the United States relating to school year calendar realignment and are taking steps to remain competitive.

For example, a British document, *Review of the Evidence Relating to the Introduction of a Standard School Year* (Eames, Sharp, & Benefield, 2004) takes note of calendar change discussions in the United States and urges British educators to evaluate carefully the matter of length of summer vacation. Even though the British summer school vacation is shorter than it is in the United States (notwithstanding the British summer's less warm and fewer sunny days than in most of the United States), nevertheless a group of British educators have proposed that the common 6- or 7-week school summer vacation be shortened to 4 weeks to reduce summer learning loss and to stay competitive with other nations. From the *Review of Evidence* the authors of this book have gleaned general information about the school year that can be illustrated, as in Table 2.3.

After careful review of the three tables in this chapter, it is clear that there are differences of school calendars among the advanced countries of the world, and that there is not consensus among them as to what constitutes an optimum length of the school year.

THE FUTURE OF YEAR-ROUND EDUCATION

Since 1968 year-round education has grown steadily. In contrast to the rather isolated attempts at calendar modification in the first half of the

Table 2.1. Length of School Year/Vacation 2004–2005, Canada

Province	Length of the School Year (by Weeks or Days)	Length of the Summer Vacation (by Weeks or Days)	Notations
Alberta	36-46 Weeks /180-200 Days	3-6 Weeks (Year-Round) 8-9 Weeks (Traditional)	Year-round schools are both single-track and multi-track
British Columbia	37 Weeks /185 Days	4-8 Weeks (Year-Round) 9 Weeks (Traditional)	Year-round schools are single-track
Manitoba	39 Weeks /195 Days	9 Weeks	
New Brunswick	37 Weeks /185 Days	10 Weeks	
Newfoundland	36 Weeks /180 Days	10 Weeks	
NW Territories	38 Weeks /190 Days	9 Weeks	
Nova Scotia	39 Weeks /195 Days	9 Weeks	
Ontario	39 Weeks /194 Days	4-6 Weeks (Year-Round) 9 Weeks (Traditional)	Year-round schools are single-track
Prince Edward Island	39 Weeks /195 Days	9 Weeks	
Quebec	36-37 Weeks /180-185 Days	9 Weeks	
Saskatchewan	39.5 Weeks /197 Days	9 Weeks	School districts set schedules
Yukon	36-37 Weeks /180-190 Days	10 Weeks	School districts set individual schedules

Source: Internet—Home Pages for Provinces

Table 2.2. Length of School Year/Vacation 2004–2005, Countries Other Than the United States and Canada

Country	Length of the School Year (by Weeks or Days)	Length of the Summer Vacation (by Weeks or Days)	Notations
Australia	42 Weeks /210 Days	5-7 Weeks	School Year: Jan. 1 - Dec. 31
Denmark	40 Weeks /200 Days	7 Weeks	
France	37 Weeks /195 Days	8 Weeks	
Germany	38-39 Weeks /190-195 Days	6 Weeks	
Japan	42 Weeks /210 Instructional Days	6 Weeks	School Year: April 1 - March 31
Ireland	37 Weeks /195 Days	8 Weeks	
Netherlands	40 Weeks /200 Days	6 Weeks	
Norway	38 Weeks /190 Days	7-8 Weeks	
Sweden	180 Days	9 Weeks	
United Kingdom	39 Weeks /190 Days	5-7 Weeks	
Switzerland	38 Weeks /190 Days	7 Weeks	

Sources: Organization of School Time in Europe, Eurydice European Unit/Department of Education, Science and Training, Australian Government, STS Language Schools

Table 2.3. Comparison of School Calendars, USA, Canada, and Great Britain

Calendar Type	Country	Mesters/Periods Terms	Instructional Teaching Days	Summer Break	Notes
Traditional	**USA** - 50 States **Canada** - 9 Provinces	2 2	170 -184 Range from 180-200 (including teacher training days)	10-12 weeks: June, July, August, or mid-June to mid-September 8-12 weeks: July, August, partial September	September through the end of May or early June generally. **Semesters:** September to January, February to end of May or early June. September to late June generally
Single-Track YRE	**USA** - 50 States **Canada** - 9 Provinces	2 to 4	170-195	3-8 Weeks in May through September	July through June: August through July: September through July or August All students on the same track with staggered breaks throughout
Multi-Track YRE	**USA** - 50 States **Canada** - 9 Provinces	2 to 6	163-195	3-8 Weeks in May/ through September	Increases capacity of schools Tracks are staggered across year, with one track (group) on vacation while others are in school
Extended Year	**USA** - 50 States **Canada** - 9 Provinces	3 to 4 or Continuous	200 or More	3-6 Weeks in June through September	School open at least 10 to 12 months; more often, 11 of 12 months
Standard School Year	**Great Britain** Some LEA's as of Fall, 2004 Proposed by LGA for perhaps all LEA's as of Fall, 2004	Change from 3 to 6	195 (including teacher training days)	No less than 5 weeks, no more than 7 weeks Starts in July	First two-terms are no longer than 7 weeks, 3 days. Two-week break in October and a Christmas break no less than two weeks. Terms 3, 4, 5, 6 approximately 6 weeks in length. Spring Break is fixed and not scheduled because of Easter. Term 5 could be used as exam term Term 6 could be used for enrichment No multi-tracking or extended year calendars

Chart developed from Eames, Sharp, and Benefield, *Review of the Evidence*

Note: YRE = Year-Round Education; LEA = Local Education Authority (or Agency); EGA = Lccal Government Authority (or Agency)

20th century, implementation in the second half has taken root. There is a greater mass of interest in curbing learning loss and alleviating severe overcrowding that has allowed calendar modification to spread to 46 of the 50 states, the District of Columbia, three provinces in Canada, and some Pacific island nations with close ties to the United States.

There are educational, social, economic, and political forces that increasingly encourage calendar modification. A look at each of these four will illustrate more fully why balancing the school calendar is likely, over time, to transform the school year into one designed primarily for optimum student learning.

1. *Educational.* Within this subheading resides the push to alter the school year that comes from both classroom practitioners and educational researchers. Classroom teachers have long talked about summer learning loss, a factor recognized for more than 50 years. Students returning each autumn after a lengthy summer of fun exhibit characteristics of forgetfulness that prompt many teachers to question seriously whether anything was taught to the students in the preceding year.

Educational research over the past 20 years has confirmed the reality of summer loss and raised an awareness of this among those wishing to significantly boost the achievement level of American students. Practitioners and researchers alike are subscribing to the thesis that one likely way to reduce summer learning loss is to reduce the length of summer vacation. With practitioners and researchers in alignment on this issue, professional pressure grows, and will continue to grow, to change the American school calendar to fit more nearly the way students learn.

2. *Social.* An increasingly urban and technological America gives rise to the concern of whether or not America's young people are productively occupied during the summer months. The social concerns are highlighted by this thought-producing question: Of what value is it to society to have hundreds of thousands of America's youth largely unoccupied, unemployed, or unsupervised for up to 3 months each year?

There are homes where the single parent, or both parents, are gone, for good reason, for much of the time that students are out of school. Many children from these homes have little support or incentive to read a book, complete homework assignments, discuss and think about the important issues of the day over the family dinner table, or engage in learning activities generated by parental interests, hobbies, and everyday work. Because of this lack of parental support and supervision, coupled with the lengthy summer away from formal instruction, there are voices from community youth-serving agencies, academia, and law enforcement saying that it is time to rethink summer vacation.

Other critics of America's long summer vacation point out that many youth, particularly those living in the core city, not only lack strong parental support and supervision, but also live in communities with few youth-serving agencies available to offer productive summer activities, forcing many young people to find support and activity on the street, a not-so-positive prospect for them. Those who see social dynamite building in such circumstances are particularly eager to see diminution of the long summer vacation granted by most American schools (Austin, 1996).

3. *Economic.* Better usage of educational facilities is a matter of importance in growing communities unable to cope with the influx of school-age children. Currently, school buildings are generally used but 9.5 months of each year, 5 of each 7 days, and 10 to 12 hours of each 24-hour day. Some economists and business people argue that unused capacity is costly to an enterprise and optimum use of facilities all 12 months makes economic sense.

When overenrollment occurs and discussion in a community turns to the possible need for new classrooms, some ask whether full utilization is being made of current facilities. Multi-track year-round education is one solution to overcrowding that makes greater use of existing facilities by utilizing school buildings all 12 months of the year. With resistance to new taxes a political reality in many communities, economic pressure grows to utilize fully what school districts already have—another force prompting further consideration of multi-track year-round education.

4. *Political.* Elected officials generally respond to community forces that promote a given solution to an identified problem. Sometimes elected officials, previously opposed to an idea because of community opposition, lessen their opposition as communities also lessen their concerns, and accept the previously frowned-upon idea as "an idea

whose time has come." To a large degree, calendar modification is entering that stage of "an idea whose time has come." Earlier in this chapter there was a notation that perhaps 10,000,000 or more students had participated in year-round education to date. There is a strong likelihood that these students, upon becoming parents, will readily understand the purpose of reducing the traditional summer vacation to reduce forgetting and will lobby for calendar modification for their children. With the emergence of educational, social, economic, and political forces leading to calendar change, it becomes easier for elected officials to advocate also for a lessening of summer learning loss. Thus, today one can see greater verbal support for calendar modification from elected officials in conjunction with the other forces promoting balancing of the school calendar.

SUMMARY

From scattered attempts at altering the school calendar during the first half of the 20th century to a significant amount of calendar modification in the second half, year-round education has increased its presence on the American educational landscape. Bolstered by stronger organization of the year-round calendar movement, year-round schools are now found coast to coast in most American states, in Canada, and in Pacific islands with close ties to the United States.

Comparison of the American school year with that of other nations reveals extensive year-round education in several developed countries, but there is not yet a clear consensus on the optimum length of the school year.

NOTES

1. For a fuller perspective on school calendar development, see Glines (1994), Glines (2002), and Gold (2002).

2. NAYRE defines year-round education as any school or program that has 8 or fewer weeks of vacation at any time of the year, including summer vacation.

CHAPTER 3

Rethinking the School Year: Flexibility in the Annual Calendar

A common school year calendar, long established in North America and judged by the National Education Commission on Time and Learning to be an unacknowledged design flaw in American education, impacts everyday life in many communities. Beginning around September 1 and ending around June 1, it is seemingly unyielding.

Yet the school year can be more flexible than usually realized. That flexibility, once understood, will help educational leaders to convey to parents, students, and the larger community that there can be a better calendar design for optimum student learning. Since the traditional school calendar has not been and is not now designed for student learning, having been aligned instead with the economic and social circumstances of an earlier America, it is imperative that there be a clear illustration of what can be in the way of calendar reform. Figure 3.1 begins to offer an insight into how much flexibility there is in a year.

As demonstrated in Figure 3.1, after acknowledging and deleting all of the legal and societal considerations—such as mandated annual days of instruction, weekends, and holidays—there remain 60 days (equiva-

365 Days per calendar year
-180 Days of legislatively mandated instruction annually
-104 Weekend days (Saturday and Sunday)
-10 Winter holidays (Christmas, New Year's)
-11 Other legal holidays

60 Remaining optional/flexible days

Figure 3.1. *School Year Flexibility*

lent to 12 weeks of Monday–Friday days) with which to design a learning-friendly school calendar that takes into account learning patterns, learning loss, and both parental and staff concerns.

Reducing the learning loss that occurs during the long summer vacation of the traditional calendar is an important goal of calendar modification and is an issue that rightfully should have been addressed long ago. Teachers have known for decades about the summer loss. That is why they have typically spent 4 to 8 weeks (20 to 40 school days) each autumn reviewing material presumably covered in the previous grade/course level. Fewer days of review at the beginning of each year would allow more days for new instruction.

Parents have also recognized, and tried to minimize, the learning loss by enrolling their children in structured learning experiences such as summer school or summer camp. Far too often, unfortunately, parents of children who most need the continuity of learning that structured summer experiences provide are the ones who do not, for a variety of reasons, enroll their children in productive learning experiences.

By comparing the circle graphs immediately below (see Figure 3.2), one can see immediately the imbalance of the traditional calendar, as compared with a year-round calendar, and begin to understand why those educators calling for calendar modification are so motivated.

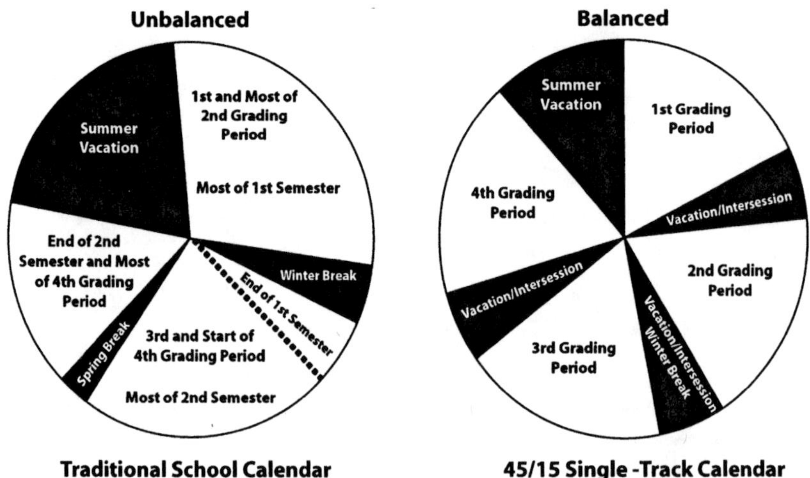

Figure 3.2. *The Unbalanced Versus the Balanced Calendar*

By balancing the school calendar to have rhythmic patterns of learning and vacation, year-round education (YRE) restructures the "traditional" school year to shorten its long summer to reduce learning loss. Working within the guidelines of an acceptable length of vacation time set by the National Association for Year-Round Education (NAYRE)—NAYRE recommends that vacation periods be no longer than 6 weeks, though it will accept up to 8 weeks for inclusion in its national directory of year-round schools—current modified calendar schools generally schedule vacations from 1 to 8 weeks in length, up to five times a year.

Year-round calendars offer, at a minimum, the same number of legislatively-required instructional days (or their equivalent hours or minutes) as the traditional calendar. Some states list their minimum requirement of annual instructional time as a number of days; some, as hours of instruction; some, as an equivalency choice of days, hours, or minutes.[1] California, for example, is one of the states that allows a time flexibility in law.[2] Thus, if a state legislature requires 180 instructional days annually (not all do), a year-round calendar will also offer 180 instructional days. If a state requires 900 hours of instruction, year-round calendars will have a minimum of 900 hours of instruction.

While a majority of states (31)[3] now require 180 days of instruction annually (or the equivalent hours or minutes), eight require 175 days. Six have varying amounts from 174 upward, while four require a minimum of hours fluctuating with grade level. One, Minnesota, has no defined minimum days of instruction annually,[4] leaving the number of annual instructional days to the discretion of local boards of education.

A few state legislatures, responding to the pocketbook pleas of some components of the summer recreation industry, have mandated school opening dates to be after Labor Day. The intent of this legislation is to help recreation businesses obtain maximum revenue and profits. The legislation ignores the problem of summer learning loss.

With few exceptions, however, legislatures of these states have also granted a waiver process, whereby schools/school districts may petition for relief from particulars of this restrictive legislation. School leaders interested in calendar modification should be assured that rarely are such waiver requests denied. School leaders should also recognize and work with the calendar flexibility described in this chapter. Year-round education is the embodiment of flexibility.

Modification of the school calendar, then, is clearly compatible with legislative requirements and responds to the flexibility required in local circumstances to meet the learning needs of students and the community.

THE THREE STRANDS OF YEAR-ROUND EDUCATION

There are three strands, or types, of modified school calendars: *single-track*, *multiple-track*, and *extended year*. An extended review of each, along with sample calendar models, will provide further insight into the considerable flexibility of the school year.

SINGLE-TRACK

A *single-track* year-round calendar is one in which a school, or a school district, and all of its students, teachers, and ancillary school staff, follow a schedule that has no vacation exceeding 8 weeks. Track refers to the administrative calendar arrangement of in-school and out-of-school time. It does not refer to curriculum sequencing or to student academic placement. Single-track calendars are adopted to provide a more balanced schedule of delivering the instructional program (hence, the term *balanced calendar*); to reduce the amount of forgetting over the long summer vacation of the traditional calendar (thus, the term *instructional calendar*); to accommodate parental or business needs of a particular community (thus, a *community*, or a *custom*, calendar); to parallel student learning patterns (thus a *personalized* calendar); or variations of these four.

Single-track, balanced calendars are introduced almost solely to conform more nearly with the natural learning patterns of students. They are not introduced to provide additional space or promote additional efficiency of resources, nor to solve administrative or logistical problems. The NAYRE listed 1,944 single-track schools in the United States for the 2004–2005 school year.[5]

Common Single-Track Calendar Plans

Choosing a calendar plan for optimum learning, while acknowledging the need for occasional vacations, is a process of giving thought to how students learn, how vacations add to the quality of life, and how the wants and requirements of adults come to bear upon the community's school calendar. Among the questions to be asked and answered while calendar consideration is in progress are the following:

1. How long, generally, does a vacation need to be? For example, is a 3-week vacation better than a 6-week vacation in terms of student learning or forgetting? Is a 6-week vacation better than a 12-week vacation?
2. Is the student population composed of groups that are especially vulnerable to learning loss? How can the calendar be designed to help those most in need of support to learn?
3. Should the instructional program be thought of as continuous, sequential, or organized as quarters, trimesters, or semesters?
4. What does educational research say about summer learning loss?
5. Do teachers need time, after completing an instructional unit, to complete tasks such as grading papers and tests, recording grades, and rethinking the curriculum outline for the upcoming period of instruction? To complete these tasks and also have some time for personal recuperation, should a teacher's vacation be 3, 4, 5, or 6 weeks? Or should it be as needed, in those calendar arrangements that are the most flexible and personalized?

Answering these questions will help to select a calendar from among the many single-track calendars available. Examples of single-track calendars follow.

45/15 Plan

The 45/15 plan (45 class days, followed by 15 vacation days, Monday–Friday) is a common calendar at both the elementary and secondary levels. This calendar (sometimes also called the 9/3 plan) is divided into four 9-week instructional quarters, each separated by a 3-week vacation called *intersession* in many communities.[6] Thus, in the 45/15 schedule, students, teachers, and classified staff members accumulate a total of 180 instructional days annually in school. Keeping in mind the flexibility of days illustrated in Figure 3.1, the basic 45/15 (or 9/3) plan can be shown as in Figure 3.3.

Forty-five (45) days of instruction X 4 quarters = 180 days of instruction annually. By translating Figure 3.3 into a realistic school calendar, Figure 3.4 shows how balanced a 45/15 calendar can be, with its alternating periods of learning and vacation (intersession).

A 45/15 calendar can itself be flexible in other ways. Some schools have modified the pattern to include 40/15, 45/5, and 45/10 arrangements.

Some schools offer a choice of a 45/15 track or a traditional calendar track, within the same school, whereby parents have schedule options available to coincide with family requirements. This offering of two calendars within one school—very similar to a school-within-a-school (SWAS) arrangement—is called a *dual calendar plan* and can be illustrated as shown in Figure 3.5.

45 Classroom Days	15 School Days Off	45 Classroom Days	15 School Days Off	45 Classroom Days	15 School Days Off	45 Classroom Days	15 School Days Off

Figure 3.3. *45/15 Single-Track Model*

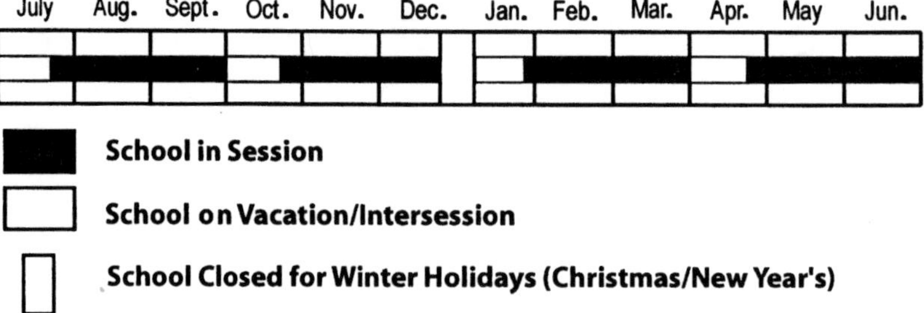

Figure 3.4. *45/15 Single-Track Calendar*

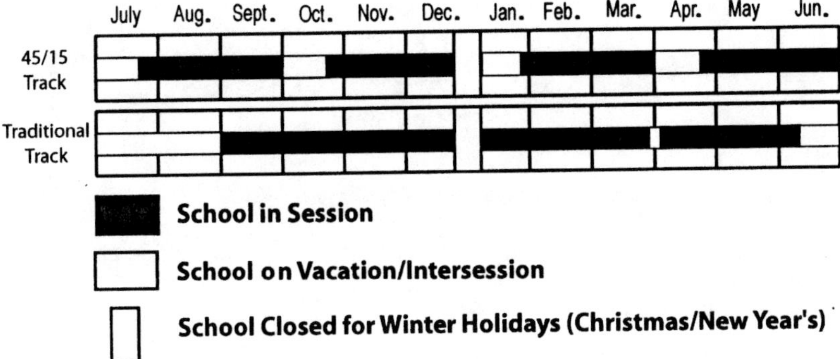

Figure 3.5. Dual Calendar Plan—45/15 and Traditional

60/20 Plan

The 60/20 Plan is similar to the rhythm of the 45/15, but it divides the year into three 60-day trimester sessions, interspersed with three 20-day vacation periods. Student schedules rotate 60-day instructional periods with 20 weekdays away from school. The 60/20 model looks like this, as shown in Figure 3.6.

Sixty (60) days of instruction × 3 semesters annually = 180 days of instruction. The model of Figure 3.6 can be translated into a 60/20 calendar as shown in Figure 3.7.

Some schools have developed variations of the 60/20 plan into calendars such as 55/18, 60/10, and 65/20.

60/15 Plan—A Hybrid of 45/15 and 60/20

Some schools have developed a hybrid calendar utilizing aspects of both the 60/20 and 45/15 plans. The 60/15 features the three 60-day learning blocks of the 60/20 calendar and three 15-day vacation periods

Figure 3.6. 60/20 Single-Track Model

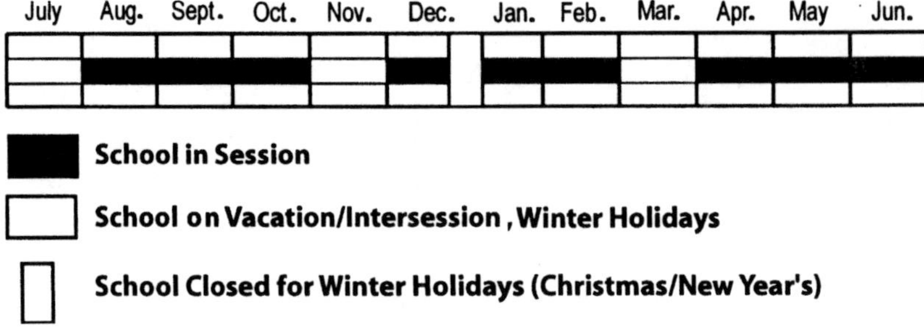

Figure 3.7. *60/20 Single-Track Calendar*

from the 45/15. By rearranging learning and vacation days this way, an additional 15-day vacation period is formed, and when added to a second 15-day period, provides a 6-week vacation for students and teachers during the summer, the winter, or whichever month best suits the climate, lifestyles, and employment cycles of the parents in the community, as well as in keeping with any related state laws. A 60/15 model, placing the 6-week vacation in the summer, is shown in Figure 3.8.

Sixty (60) days of instruction × 3 semesters annually = 180 days of instruction. Translated from the model to an actual calendar arrangement, the calendar would look like Figure 3.9.

90/30 Plan

Similar patterns of learning and vacation time apply to the 90/30 calendar. The major difference from other calendars is that students attend school for 90 days, vacation for 30 weekdays, attend for 90 more, and then vacation for another 30, following closely the semester concept. Some secondary schools prefer the two longer teaching and vacation blocks, because retention of the semester syllabus eliminates the need

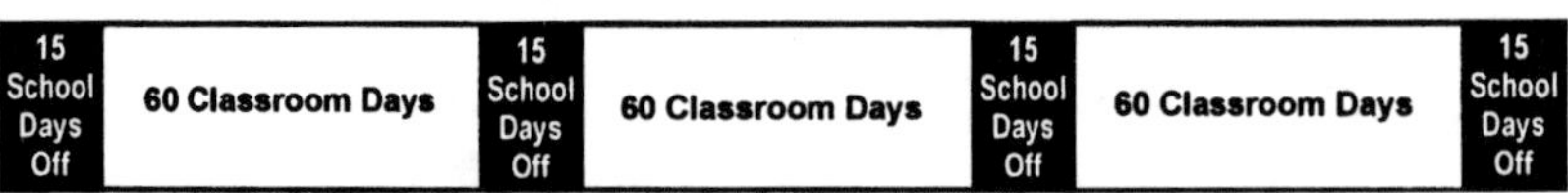

Figure 3.8. *60/15 Single-Track Model*

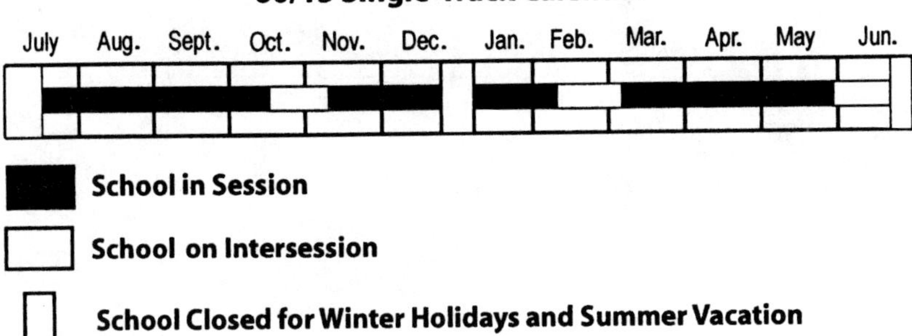

Figure 3.9. *60/15 Single-Track Calendar*

to revise the curriculum into other patterns of delivery. The model looks like Figure 3.10.

Ninety (90) days of instruction × 2 semesters = 180 days of instruction. Translated from the model to a calendar arrangement, the calendar would look like Figure 3.11.

Flexible All-Year and Personalized Continuous Calendars

For those seeking cutting-edge calendars to fit school-year models to individual student needs, flexible all-year and personalized continuous plans are available for consideration. Both require a willingness to be flexible on the part of the school administration, the instructor, the parent, and the student. These two models clearly forestall the usual schedule concept of one size fits all.

The flexible all-year approach operates continuously, thereby allowing the student or teacher to vacation at any point in the year for whatever length of time is desired—1 day, 1 week, 2 months—without loss of continuity, so long as minimum time legislative requirements are met. The plan is based on the premise that education can and should

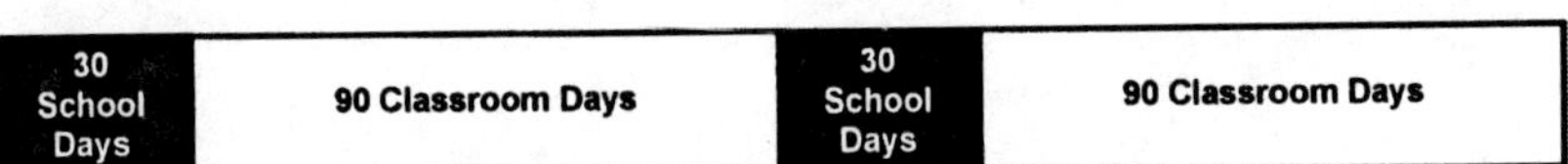

Figure 3.10. *90/30 Single-Track Model*

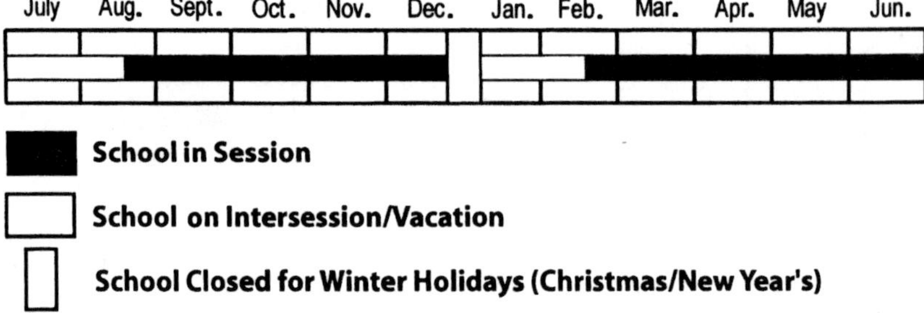

Figure 3.11. 90/30 Single-Track Calendar

be totally individualized, both in time and methods. Curricula can be constructed in 3-week, self-contained instructional packets that can be used individually or in small groups. Such an arrangement or one similar allows the student flexibility to vacation at several intervals. Upon return, the pupil begins wherever he or she left the activity. Instructional packets of lessons can even be taken on vacations for independent study and credit purposes. The concept was first pioneered at the Clarion University of Pennsylvania Research-Learning Center. The calendar model is found in Figure 3.12.

The personalized continuous plan, like the flexible all-year plan, theoretically is in operation continuously. While all days are potentially available, both actually operate only 230 to 250 days, unless students (and their parents) are willingly involved in weekend learning projects, earning credit in independent study activities (even on a holiday), or studying, for example, the Civil War engagement at Gettysburg while on vacation. Unlike other modified calendars, this plan has no blocks of instructional time or curriculum packages. Learning is entirely personalized and individualized. Students must attend the minimum time annually required by legislative action. Students may come and go throughout the year as agreed, as long as they are making progress

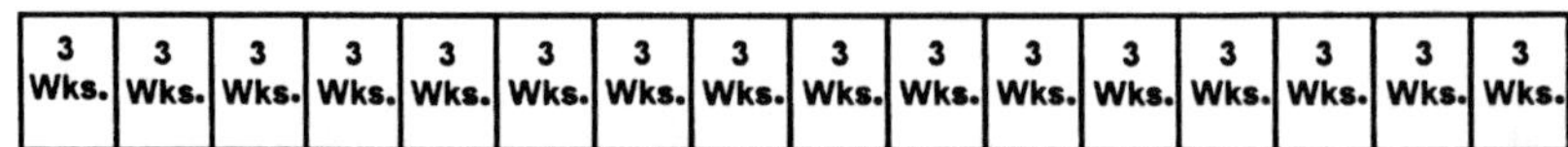

Figure 3.12. Flexible All-Year Model Single Track

toward the required number of days. Group learning does occur, because most students are together at school the majority of the year. Students can schedule vacations around planned group activities, including sports, music, special science projects, cultural exchange programs, or other exciting learning activities. Students who participate in professional sporting or artistic endeavors may also find this calendar arrangement suitable for their schedules, while also providing some group learning experiences.

This sophisticated calendar was in place for 9 years at the Wilson Campus School, a highly successful pre-K to grade 12 laboratory program at Mankato State University, Minnesota, from 1968 to 1977 (Glines, 1994). The calendar model for the personalized continuous year looks like Figure 3.13.

Other Single-Track Plans

There are other single-track calendar arrangements besides the basic plans already described. Calendar theorists and practitioners such as Glines (1994) have formulated schedules such as 25/10, 25/5, 30/10, 30/5, Trimester, Quarter, Quinmester, Concept 6, Modified Concept 6, Concept 8, Concept 9, Concept 12, Concept 16, YRE-Without-Walls Plan, Octamester Plan, Variable Term Plan, Experimental City Plan, Modified Calendar Plan, and Mountain Calendar Plan. Glines has suggested that there is a potential for 14,000 calendar plans, one designed for each school district.

Suffice it to say here that there are many calendar plans that rearrange instructional time. School time is flexible enough that student learning can be enhanced and parental and community needs can be met.

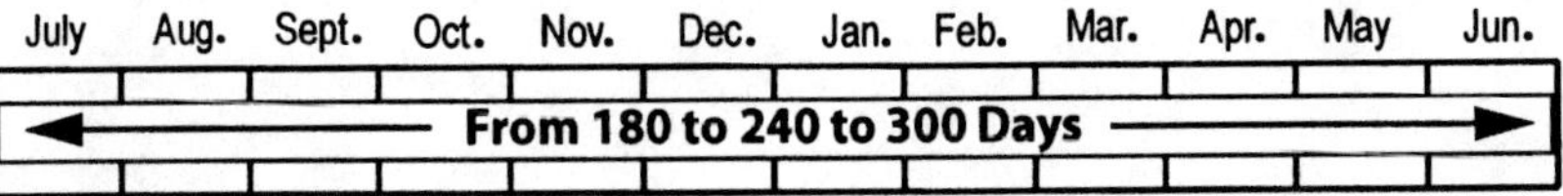

Figure 3.13. *Personalized Continuous Calendar-Single Track*

Summary of Single-Track Plans

Single-track modified calendar plans are designed to conform closely to the natural learning patterns of students. All vacations, irrespective of the calendar, are 8 weeks or less. By avoiding the long summer vacation of the traditional calendar, single-track schools balance the calendar to lessen summer learning loss.

The single-track plans presented in this chapter have curricular time frames. The 45/15 single-track plan is essentially a quarter arrangement, the 60/20 and 60/15 calendars are trimester arrangements, and the 90/30 is a semester model.

MULTIPLE-TRACK (MULTI-TRACK)

Multiple-track (usually shortened to multi-track) year-round education is implemented to provide additional capacity within already-existing space to accommodate an overenrollment of students, maximize the efficient use of current resources, solve one or more administrative or logistical problems, or a variation of these three. Multi-track calendars, like single-track calendars, have shortened vacation periods, thus fostering reduced learning loss. The implementation of multi-track can enhance school reform efforts, even while alleviating a prior problem, such as overenrollment. The NAYRE listed 934 multi-track schools in the United States for the 2004–2005 school year.

When choosing a multiple-track (multi-track) calendar, the school district and community need first to ask and answer the five questions that were asked in the discussion of introducing single-track calendars:

1. How long, generally, does a vacation need to be? For example, is a 3-week vacation better than a 6-week vacation in terms of student learning or forgetting? Is a 6-week vacation better than a 12-week vacation?
2. Is the student population composed of groups that are especially vulnerable to learning loss? How can the calendar be designed to help those most in need of support to learn?

3. Should the instructional program be thought of as continuous, sequential, or organized as quarters, trimesters, or semesters?
4. What does educational research say about summer learning loss?
5. Do teachers need time, completing an instructional unit, to complete tasks such as grading papers and tests, recording grades, and rethinking the curriculum outline for the upcoming period of instruction? To complete these tasks and also have some time for personal recuperation, should a teacher's vacation be 3, 4, 5, or 6 weeks? Or should it be as needed, in those calendar arrangements that are the most flexible and personalized?

In addition to the above five, schools and their committees need to answer the following three questions as well when considering the implementation of multi-track:

1. What is the degree of overcrowding now and in the future at the targeted school, neighborhood schools, and eventually the entire school district: 10%, 15%, 25%, 40%, 50%?
2. What are the options available to the school (district) for resolving overenrollment? Which is most efficient and equitable? Which is most cost-effective?
3. If multi-track is deemed necessary, and is the best of the options to alleviate overenrollment, which of the available multi-track calendars best fits the school's curriculum program, most reduces the degree of overcrowding, and is most compatible with the school and community culture?

Common Multiple-Track Calendar Plans

Consideration of multi-track calendar plans first requires an understanding of the *problem* forcing a review of possible *solutions*, as well as the technical considerations of choosing among the multi-track calendars. The *problem* to be solved is *overcrowding*.

There are generally 10 *solutions* identified to alleviating the *problem* of overcrowding. They are: 1) construction of new buildings; 2) using relocatable (portable) classrooms; 3) redrawing district boundary lines; 4) double sessions; 5) extended day; 6) busing students to nearby underutilized schools; 7) use of other community spaces; 8) increased class size; 9) redesignating special-purpose classrooms as ordinary classrooms; and 10) multi-track year-round education.[7] Not all of these solutions are available or viable in all communities, however. For example, voters in some communities may reject a school district's request for a bond measure to provide money to construct new schools.

All of these solutions have advantages and disadvantages. The only one to have an educational component within it is multi-tracking, which like single-tracking reduces the long summer of the traditional calendar to reduce summer learning loss.

A significant *solution* to overenrollment is the implementation of multi-tracking. It is the *degree* of overenrollment in a district or school that dictates which of the multi-track calendars can best serve local needs. The space gained by the choice relates specifically to the number of tracks utilized in the calendar.

In a study comparing the costs of using relocatable (portable) classrooms or implementing multi-track year-round education to alleviate overcrowding, Coleman and Freebern (1993) indicated that the option of multi-tracking became cost-effective when enrollment was about 16% to 20% over the rated capacity of the school. From 1% to 16% above capacity, relocatables were more cost-effective.

Thus, if a school with a rated capacity of 600 climbed in enrollment to 665, or about 11.5% above rated capacity, the district might well choose to add portable classrooms to the site to provide less crowded learning conditions. However, once the enrollment climbs to 700 or higher, over 16% above rated capacity, it is more cost-effective to implement multi-track year-round education. Some degree of foresight among decision makers will forestall the possibility of advancing money to initiate the use of relocatables, only to have that option overtaken in a short period of time by the need for multi-tracking.

After the decision to implement multi-track, the next step is to consider which of the multi-track calendars will serve best to alleviate the overcrowding, since there is a variety of multi-track calendars with different loading capacities. Making the right choice of calendars will play an important role in the community's acceptance of multi-tracking.

If the degree of overenrollment is less than 25% above rated capacity of the school facility, a local district has the option to implement either a four-track or five-track calendar. If the overenrollment is 25% to 40% above rated capacity, the five-track calendar can no longer be an option; rather, only four-track or three-track calendars can be considered. Since a four-track calendar serves this degree (25% to 40%) of overenrollment efficiently, it is the most commonly-selected option. Once enrollment is 40% or more over stated capacity, only a three-track calendar will serve well its purpose: to bring attendance on a given day within the capabilities of the school to have a seat for each attending student.

Clarifying with actual numbers will show the logic of adopting one or another of the multi-track calendars. Suppose a middle school was originally built to house 600 students. Once the number of students enrolled begins to hover around 600, astute school administrators should have already been thinking of the possibility that the number of students attending might go well beyond 600. If the following year the enrollment is expected to increase to around 640 to 650, that is enough growth to warrant a discussion of the best options to handle overenrollment. One possible option might be the use of two relocatables to house the additional 40 to 50 students. By adding the two relocatables, the district experiences, in addition to the salary and benefit costs of additional teachers, the costs attendant to purchasing/leasing of the relocatables, transporting them, preparation of the site, moving supplies from one facility to another, utilities, maintenance and upkeep.

However, if in the succeeding year there is expected to be additional enrollment, bringing the total to about 690 or more students, the school board and administration have an important administrative and budgetary decision to make: Will additional portables/relocatables continue to be a better choice, or is it the right time to move toward a multi-track schedule? From 700 students upward—assuming there is little likelihood of a new campus or new buildings built soon enough to handle the growth—then the district usually moves toward establishing a multi-track calendar.

Continuing with the numbers given above (still using the original school capacity of 600 students), enrollment growth of up to 720 would allow use of either four-track or five-track calendars. Enrollment at 800 and above would allow the usage of only four- or three-track calendars since five-track calendars are no longer feasible. Once the enrollment climbs to 900, a four-track calendar is no longer an option. Only three-track calendars can comfortably house 900 students in a school built for 600 students.

What has been reflected in previous paragraphs is that multi-track arrangements can handle larger numbers of students comfortably in existing space. What will be demonstrated now is that a five-track calendar can house an additional 25% of students beyond stated capacity, a four-track calendar can house an additional 33%, and a three-track calendar can house an additional 50%. To show how these percentages are obtained, a review of multi-track calendars follows. The first examined is a 60/15, 5-track calendar, shown in Figure 3.14.

In a five-track calendar school, one track is always on vacation, while four tracks are in school (see Figure 3.14). Thus, 20% of students are on vacation (1 of 5 tracks = 20%) at any time, while 80% (4 of 5 tracks) are in school. However, the increase in capacity is calculated a different way: One of the five groups is out of school, while the other four groups are in school. The equation becomes one over four (1/4), or a 25% increase in capacity. There is another way to illustrate how a school built for 600 can enroll 750 students comfortably. By using a

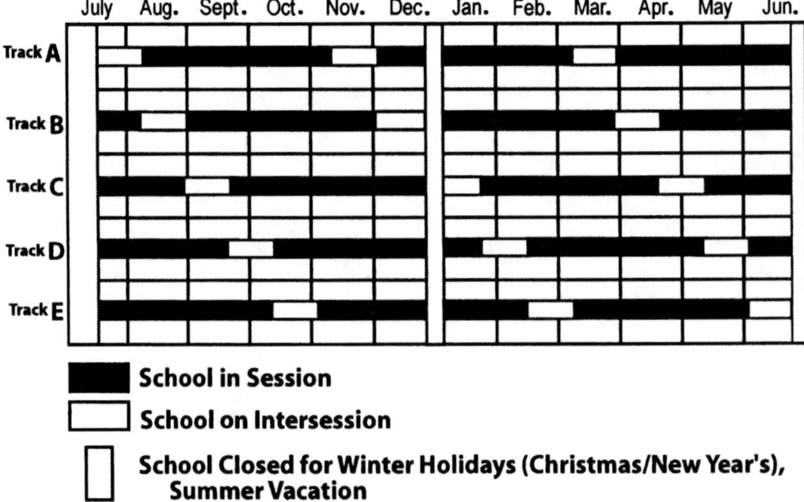

Figure 3.14. 60/15 Five-Track Calendar

five-track calendar, and dividing the student body equally among the tracks, one can see that while 150 students are on vacation, 600 are in school, exactly the originally-rated capacity of the school. The increased capacity shown is a 150-student increase over the original 600 capacity. Thus, the equation becomes 150/600 = 1/4, or 25% growth in capacity by using a five-track calendar.

A creative innovation has developed within the realm of a five-track calendar. In most multi-track situations, students and teachers move together in and out of school during the designated times of the calendar. Classroom teachers follow the same schedule as their students. An exception to this general rule is an arrangement called the Orchard Plan.

Using the 60/15, five-track plan, each Orchard teacher is assigned a given number of enrolled students. The students in that classroom are assigned equally to tracks A through E. Students rotate in and out of the classroom as determined by the 60/15, five-track schedule. Each teacher stays in a classroom for the year and teaches 11 of the 12 months.

To illustrate how the Orchard Plan works, an example with numbers may explain. A teacher has an enrollment of 35 students. Seven of the 35 are assigned to track A, seven to Track B, and so on. Five tracks of seven students is the full complement of 35 students in the classroom. Staying true to the 60/15, five-track schedule, one group of students (track A) from the classroom are on vacation at any one time, while the other four groups are in school. When track A's seven students return from vacation, track B's seven students leave for vacation. The rotation continues throughout the year.

Of course, delivery of the Orchard instructional program is dictated by the calendar arrangement. Accordingly, the Orchard plan clearly requires a commitment to 3-week units of study. At any one time 27 of the 35 assigned students are receiving instruction in a unit of work; seven students are not. When the seven on vacation return to school, they must receive the unit of study given in their absence. Without dedication to the unit concept of 3-week instructional periods, the Orchard Plan becomes unnecessarily difficult administratively.

Orchard Plan teachers who believe in the unit method of teaching have given this arrangement positive comments. The Orchard Plan was first initiated at Orchard School, Orem, Utah.

The figures for four-track calendars can be illustrated similarly to those of five-track. Continuing the illustration with the original rated capacity of 600, one can see that this school can comfortably enroll 800 students. In a four-track school (see Figures 3.15, 3.16, 3.17), one group is on vacation, while the other three groups are in school.

Thus 25% of the students are on vacation, while 75% of the students are in school. However, the capacity gained by using a four-track calendar is actually 33%. The equation becomes one group on vacation over three groups in school. One over three (1/3) is the equivalent of 33%. Using actual numbers, one can see that the original school built for 600 students can comfortably enroll 800 students. While 200 students are on vacation, 600 students are in school. The equation becomes 200 over 600 (200/600) which becomes 1/3, or 33% in capacity growth.

Finally, it becomes apparent what a three-track calendar can do for exceptionally large overenrollment. Using the calendar model of Figures 3.18 and 3.19 (see page 66) one can see that a school built for 600 students can comfortably enroll 900 students. While one track of students is on vacation, two tracks are in school. Thus, one third of the students are on vacation (33%) while two thirds are in school (66%).

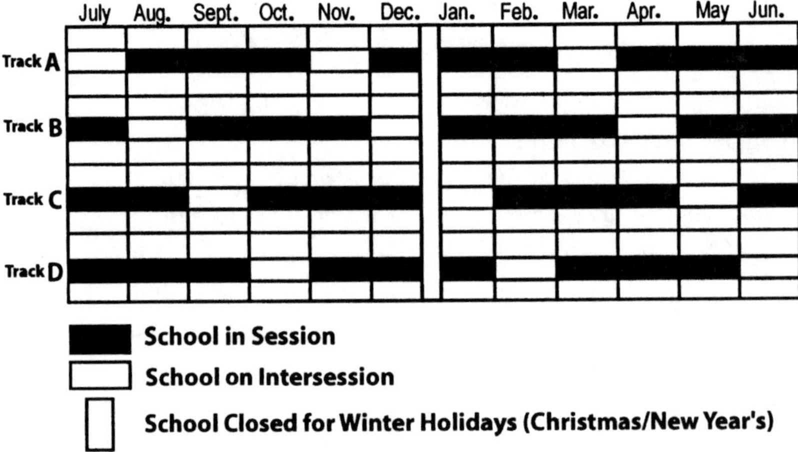

Figure 3.15. *60/20 Four-Track Calendar*

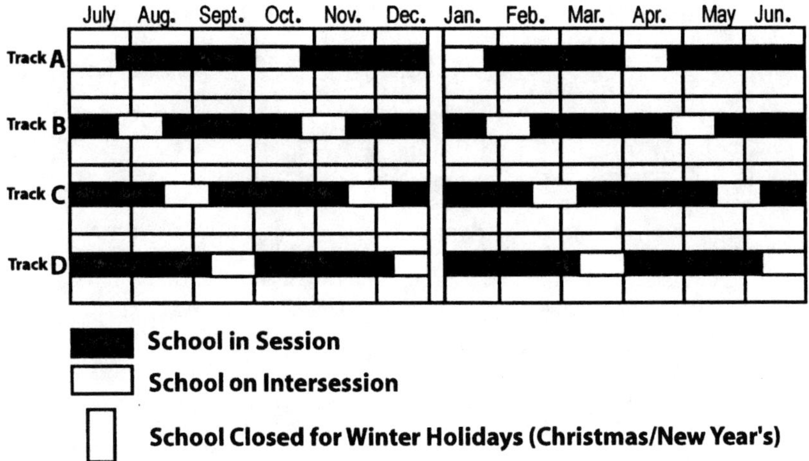

Figure 3.16. *45/15 Four-Track Calendar*

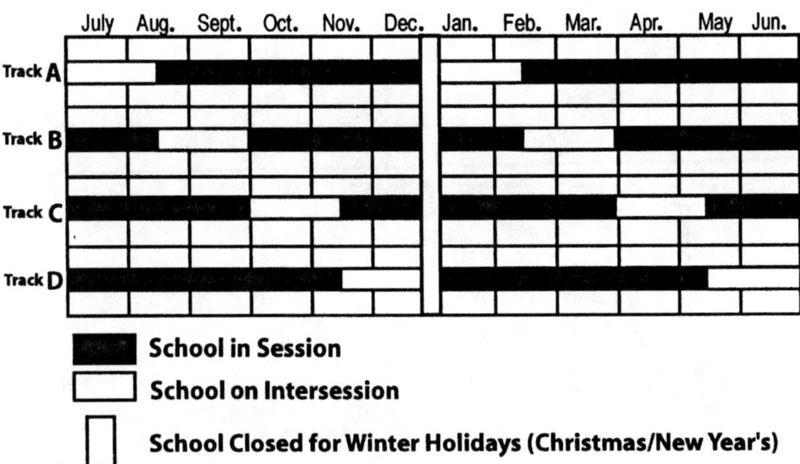

Figure 3.17. *90/30 Four-Track Calendar*

However, while 33% of students are on vacation, the capacity increase is 50%. The equation is that one group is on vacation, while two groups are in school (1/2, or 50%). Using actual numbers, one can see that a school built for 600 can comfortably enroll 900 students. When one group of 300 is on vacation, while another 600 students are in school, one can see a capacity increase of 300/600, or 1/2, or 50%.

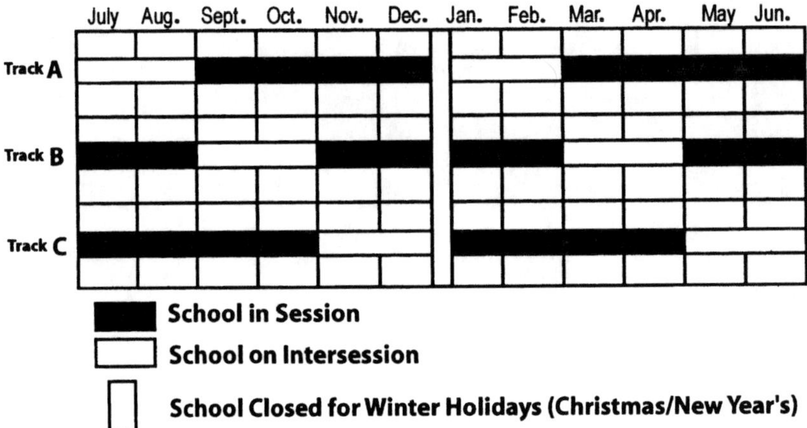

Figure 3.18. *Concept 6 Three-Track Calendar*

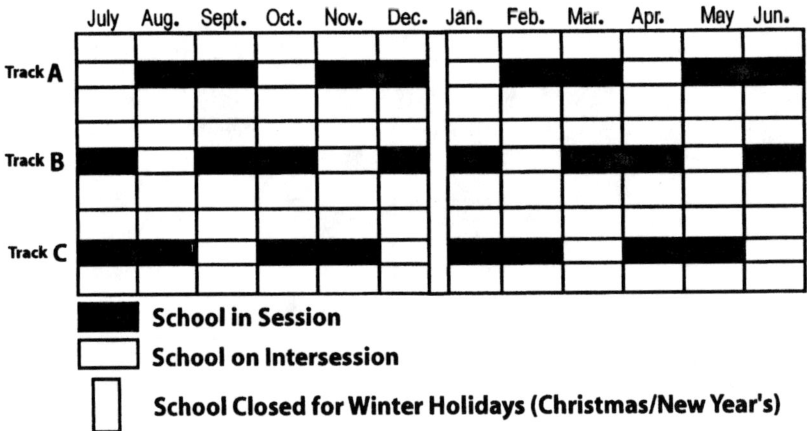

Figure 3.19. *Modified Concept 6 Three-Track Calendar*

Summary of Multi-Tracking

For school boards and administrators facing the task of safely accommodating enrolled students far beyond current seat capacity, multi-track year-round calendars are a reasonable, tested solution. In addition, multi-tracking has one component that all other solutions to overenrollment do not have: an educational component. By reducing the long vacation of the traditional calendar, there is the likelihood of reduced forgetting, with more time available for new teaching and learning. Thus, multi-tracking has an educational advantage over other possible ways to handle overenrollment. Multi-tracking also reduces the number of students in a school's common areas such as the lunchroom, the library, the gymnasium, and the hallways, resulting in a less cramped, less tense school environment. Since school boards and school administrators are in the business of fostering quality education, is it any wonder, then, that multi-tracking is favored by many as the preferred solution to overenrollment?

EXTENDED YEAR

Extended-year education is a plan whereby the school year is lengthened significantly beyond the minimum days of annual instruction required by most state legislatures. For most extended-year schools this means 200 or more instructional days each year. Extended-year calendars can be either single-track or multi-track, though in practice all or almost all operate on single-track schedules. The NAYRE listed 329 extended-year schools in the United States for the 2004–2005 school year.

There are various ways to achieve an extended school year. Some public schools are able, through a combined pool of financial resources, to offer students up to 220 days of instruction. This pool may be a combination of basic financial support, categorical funding, foundation funding, and summer school fees, as federal and state laws allow. Private schools can extend the school year to the degree to which patrons are willing to pay for the service.

Some extended-year schools offer a basic year of 200 instructional days. Enrollees in these schools are voluntary and usually are allowed to transfer to a 180-day school, if a parent so chooses. Other extended-year schools offer the state-mandated minimum of 175 to 180 instructional days, plus 20 to 30 days of full-day summer programming. The emphasis here is on full-day programming, to distinguish these days from the more common American summer school days that are quite short (for example, 2 hours), ill-conceived (little relationship to the school's curriculum), and underfunded. Schools offering full-day summer classes are often located in states that allow fee-based programming, that is, where parents pay a fee for enrolling the child in a full-day summer program.

There are voices in the political, economic, and educational worlds that regularly call for an extension of the school year to provide a well-educated pool of talented workers to vie with what they see as economic competition from countries around the world that require their students to be in school many more days than the number required of American students. While these calls for a longer school year have both purpose and long-term urgency, it may be some time before the extended year becomes a reality in large numbers. There is significant cost to a school day, and the cost of additional days is hard to justify when support for the current length of the school year wanes in economically-difficult times.

Visualization of the extended school year could look like these examples in Figures 3.20, 3.21, and 3.22.

INTERSESSIONS

A common, but significant, feature of year-round, modified calendar schools is *intersession*. Intersession is the term applied to the time students are on scheduled vacations from school. Intersession means, literally, between sessions, which has been expanded to mean scheduled learning between sessions or learning blocks of time. During intersession, schools can offer remedial and/or enrichment classes, if space and financing are available, as a way of improving overall student achievement. Intersessions can occur in both single-track and multi-track schools, albeit with more difficulty in multi-track arrangements, and can be offered by extended-year schools with careful scheduling. Since these classes are available during out-of-school (i.e., vacation) time, they can be thought of as summer school rescheduled and ordinarily

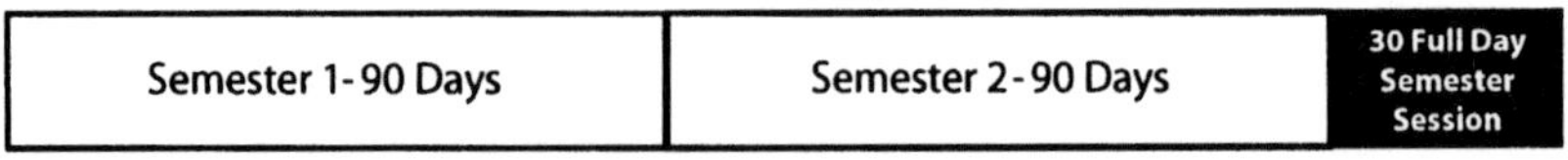

Semester 1-90 Days	Semester 2-90 Days	30 Full Day Semester Session

Figure 3.20. *Extended Year Model*

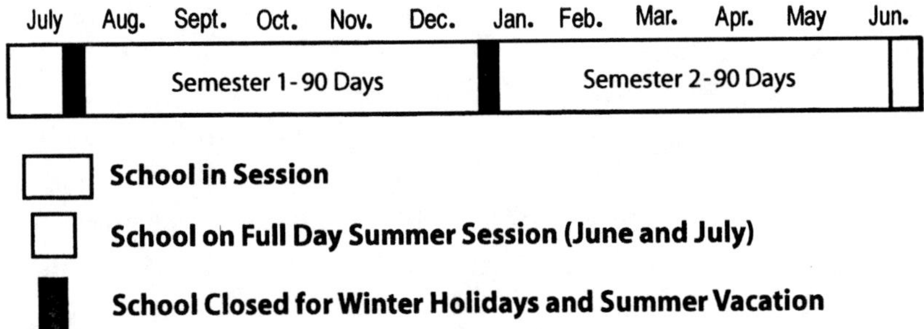

Figure 3.21. *Extended-Year Calendar*
2 Semesters, Plus a 30 Full-Day Summer Session 2 Semesters, Plus a 30 Full-Day Summer Session

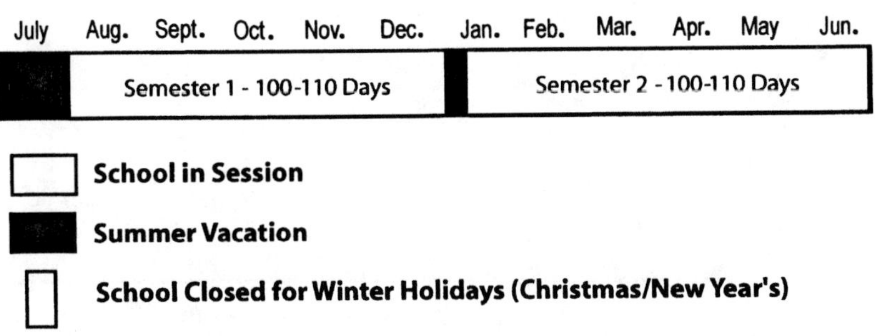

Figure 3.22. *Extended Year Calendar 2 Lengthened Semesters*

are optional in attendance. Likewise, they are financed in the same manner as summer schools.

There is a good reason for the oft-heard comment that intersession may be the most attractive element of calendar modification. A look of comparison between the traditional calendar and a balanced calendar demonstrates why the evaluation is regularly made.

If a student experiences difficulty with a particular subject or level of competence early in the first semester of the traditional calendar, it may well be that intervention will not be readily available, causing frustration and failure. Remediation indeed may not be available until the summer, significantly too late to be of help to the troubled, discouraged student.

In contrast, a student experiencing difficulty may have a chance for significant intervention during the scheduled intersessions of the year-round calendar. If a school plans intersession classes to fit the needs of students, intervention may well be available within a week or two of the observed learning blockage. Quicker intervention should lead eventually to higher achievement levels on the part of students.

Intersessions can also be a dedicated time to prepare for academic competition (such as academic decathlons) or for specific tests (such as preparation for PSAT, SAT, or ACT testing). An intersession of 3 or 4 weeks in late winter or early spring may be highly desirable for a student wanting to do well on such tests.

While intersessions, like summer school, can offer standard courses in mathematics, English language, science, history, and the arts, there can also be extraordinarily-useful intersession programs that can add to student informational background in preparation for an ensuing unit of learning. Examples are listed in Table 3.1.

SYNCHRONIZING CURRICULUM OFFERINGS WITH CALENDAR CHOICE

A review of the various calendars for one best suited to local needs and circumstances should include another step to synchronize curriculum

Table 3.1. A Short List of Common Intersession Classes

Elementary	
Remedial Classes	*Enrichment Classes*
Reading Grade 3	Discovering Dinosaurs
Language Arts Grade 4	Learning About the Ocean
Mathematics Grade 5	Young Poets
Language Arts Grade 5	Science in the Laboratory
Science Grade 6	Exploring the Nation's Capital
High School	
Remedial Classes	*Enrichment Classes*
English 9	Astronomy
English 10	Music Appreciation
Second Language Learners	Psychology
Algebra I	History of Art
Algebra II	Science Fair
American History	Geology

offerings with the instructional patterns dictated by calendar choice. Table 3.2 illustrates the association between the common calendars utilized in schools and the various elements of the instructional program provided to students. For example, if a 45/15 schedule (sometimes called the 9/3 plan) is adopted, it follows that the school year is essentially partitioned into four instructional blocks of 9 weeks each. Four such periods in 1 year would lead to a quarterly organization of instructional material. There would likely be a report of achievement, or grade, in each of the four quarters. Units of work could be organized as a unit of study 9 weeks in length, or there could be three 3-week units during the 9 weeks of the quarter. Other common calendars would follow similar patterns (Ballinger, 1988).

Personalized calendars, which Glines calls the "most sophisticated of calendars" (1994), also govern delivery of instruction, but in a considerably different way. Instruction is available throughout the year, but its delivery is negotiated by the student and parent in cooperation with school personnel. Instruction may come in 3-, 4-, 9-, or 12-week units of work shared with other students, or it may occur in individual packages and schedules suitable to a particular family's circumstances.

Table 3.2 is not meant to be a static, conclusive document. Rather, it is a guide and may easily be modified to fit other calendars and local circumstances.

SUMMARY

The school calendar, often perceived as static and inflexible, is actually quite open to modification. Balancing the calendar to improve delivery of instruction and to reduce learning loss is an important goal for educational leaders to attain. Modifying the calendar to alleviate overcrowding can be accomplished with selection of the appropriate multitrack schedule.

Intersessions provide a means to intervene throughout the school year when a need for remediation arises. Intersessions also offer the opportunity to enlarge a student's experiences in preparation for ensuing higher level work.

Table 3.2. Instructional Considerations of Common Year-Round Calendars

Name of Calendar	Calendar Sequence	Weeks Used	Days of Instruction Per Year	Curriculum Format	Teaching Format	Number of Grading Periods	Intersession (Vacation) Instructional Possibilities	Number of Tracks Usually Used in Plan
45-15	45 School Days (9 Wks) 15 M-F Days Vacation (3 Weeks)	36 Weeks in School 12 Weeks Out 4 Holiday Weeks	180 Days	4 Periods (Quarters) of Work	One 9-Week Study Unit Three 3-Week Units One Quarter Study Unit	4 (1 Each Quarter)	Yes	One or Four (a Traditional Track Can Also Be Offered)
60-20	60 School Days (12 Wks) 20 M-F Days Vacation (4 Weeks)	36 Weeks in School 12 Weeks Out 4 Holiday Weeks	180 Days	3 Periods (Mesters) of Work	1 Mester (12-Week) Study Unit Four 3-Wk Study Units Two 6-Wk Study Units	3 (1 Each Mester) or 6 (2 Each Mester)	Yes	One or Four (a Traditional Track Can Also Be Offered)
60-15	60 School Days (12 Wks) 15 M-F Days Vacation (3 Weeks)	36 Weeks in School 12 Weeks Out 4 Holiday Weeks	180 Days	3 Periods (Mesters) of Work	Same as 60/20 Calendar Above	3 (1 Each Mester) or 6 (2 Each Mester)	Yes	One or Five

Continued on Next Page

Table 3.2. *(Continued)*

Name of Calendar	Calendar Sequence	Weeks Used	Days of Instruction Per Year	Curriculum Format	Teaching Format	Number of Grading Periods	Intersession (Vacation) Instructional Possibilities	Number of Tracks Usually Used in Plan
90-30	90 School Days (18 Wks) 30 M-F Days Vacation (6 Weeks)	36 Weeks in School 12 Weeks Out 4 Holiday Weeks	180 Days	2 Periods (Semesters) of Work	One Semester Unit of Varying Lengths	2 (1 each Semester) or 4 (2 Each Semester) or 6 (3 Each Semester)	Yes	One or Four
Concept 6	82 School Days 41 M-F Days Vacation	32 Weeks in School 16 Weeks Out 4 Holiday Weeks	164 Days (Days Are Lengthened to Equal Instruction in a 180-Day year)	2 Quarters, Back-to-Back 41 Days Each Quarter	Quarter Units of Work	4 (1 Each Period) or 8 (2 Each Period)	Yes	Three
Personal	In/Out of School Organized by Parent or Student Request	34-48 (Must Meet State Minimum)	All Days Are Potentially Available	Individual Time Periods	Individualized Units of Varying Time Requirements	Negotiated Individually	Yes, but Organized Irregularly	Individualized, No tracks

Notes

1. Data for this discussion of days, hours, and minutes come from the website of the Education Commission of the States, specifically the section entitled Scheduling/School Calendar (www.ecs.org/scheduling/school/calendar).

2. California Education Code Section 37670. Information located at www.leginfo.ca.gov.

3. Data was provided from the website of the Education Commission of the States (www.ecs.org/scheduling/school/calendar).

4. Information was provided from Minnesota Statutes 120A.40, 120A.41, 120A.415. Source: Office of Revisor of Statutes, State of Minnesota, 2004. Website: www.revisor.leg.state.mn.us/stats.

5. Data for the number of year-round schools come from the Year-Round Education Reference Directory (2005), 2004–2005 School Year, a publication of the National Association for Year-Round Education.

6. A fuller discussion of calendars can be found in Glines, 1994, *Year-Round Calendar and Enrollment Plans*, and Brekke, 1993, *Year-Round Education Calendars*.

7. A fuller discussion of these 10 options can be found in chapter 1.

CHAPTER 4

Frequently Asked Questions About Calendar Modification and Year-Round Education

Questions arise frequently when institutional change is proposed. School calendar revision is no exception. The questions come from all of the stakeholder groups: teachers, administrators, central office staff, school board members, parents, students, youth-serving agencies, and community businesses.

Sometimes questions are asked simply for information. At other times, proponents and opponents of change seek widely divergent answers, often with the hope that the answers will bolster already-held opinions. All stakeholders assess the proposed change in the light of their own experiences, philosophy of education, and individual circumstances.

The questions that follow are real inquiries that have been posed to the authors, to staff at the National Association for Year-Round Education (NAYRE), and to school leaders who have initiated calendar change in their districts. The questions have been grouped together by category, and fall under one of the following headings: calendars; implementation and process; community concerns; program issues; savings/costs; and research/history/rationale.

CALENDARS

Question

1. What is the difference between year-round education (YRE), modified school calendar, and balanced calendar?

Answer

Essentially, all three terms describe the same entity. All three are applied to a reorganization of the school year during which no vacation is longer than 8 weeks in length.

Some educators and community leaders feel that *year-round education* is a misnomer in that it suggests that students are in class every day of the year. Consequently, they choose another name for calendar change. For some, *modified school calendar* is an apt term in that the traditional school calendar is tweaked slightly, or modified, so that vacations, including summers, are no longer than the 8 weeks mentioned previously.

Still others prefer the term *balanced calendar* because the proposed restructuring carefully balances learning and vacation periods. This arrangement provides a stark contrast to the traditional calendar, with its wild swings between a semester broken up repeatedly by holidays, followed by a semester with little time for breaks, followed by a summer vacation of up to 13 weeks.

There are other terms utilized in some communities to describe the calendars in operation or proposed. They include *four quarter plan, continuous all year plan, four vacation plan, alternative calendar plan, mountain calendar plan, personalized calendar plan, community calendar*, and *custom calendar.*

Question

2. The term *track* is often used in discussions of calendar change as in single-track, multi-track, dual-track. What is a track? Is this tracking the same as honors track, for example?

Answer

The term *track* describes the movement of people along a calendar design. Sometimes a school district will substitute the terms *cycle* or *group*, for the term track.

A single-track schedule (single-cycle) is one in which all students and staff follow a year-round, or modified, calendar. All are in school on the same days; all are on vacation at the same time.

A multiple-track (multi-track, multi-cycle, multi-group) calendar is one that is organized so that a portion of the student body and staff are on vacation during a given period of time, while the remainder are in school. This arrangement is implemented to ease overcrowding or to gain space to allow designation of some classrooms as special-purpose rooms. Multi-track calendars may have three, four, or five tracks, or groups, with each group on scheduled vacations throughout the year. To accommodate overenrollment, multi-track schools are open all year, except for weekends and legal holidays.

A *dual-track* calendar is one in which parents are given the option of choosing between the traditional calendar year and a single-track year-round schedule. A fuller explanation of these calendar designs is available in chapter 3 of this book.

Calendar tracking is different from curriculum tracking in that the former is an arrangement for equalizing attendance loading or instructional pacing. Curriculum tracking offers differentiated instructional programs to different classes of students, depending on student grade levels, achievement results, and the like.

Question

3. How many modified calendars are known to exist?

Answer

The latest edition of *Directory of School Districts on Non-Traditional Calendars*, published annually by the NAYRE, lists 22 calendar variations in use.

There are another 15 calendar plans that have been implemented in previous years but are not currently in use, or are on the drawing board waiting to be implemented.

One author has written that there are 14,000 potential year-round education calendar plans: that is, one designed specifically for each of the school districts in the nation (Glines, 1994).

Question

4. What is the most popular year-round calendar?

Answer

The quick answer, of course, is that the calendar chosen by a local community is the most popular one. School districts select a calendar to fit local circumstances, as they should. Currently 60/20 has a slight lead over 45/15 in total numbers of schools involved. However, if each of the 45-day variants (45/15, 45/10, 45/5) are totaled together, the combined number is slightly ahead of the combined total of the 60-day variants (60/20, 60/15, 60/10), though each of the two basic calendar plans has over 1,000 schools involved. Looking at the numbers another way, 60/20 has a long lead in the multi-track arrangement, while 45/15 has a long lead in the single-track mode.

The annual directory of the NAYRE keeps track of the calendars adopted in the United States, Canada, and the Pacific Islands. Calendars currently in use: 30/5, 30/10, 35/10, 40/5, 40/15, 45/5, 45/10, 45/15, 50/10, 50/15, 55/18, 60/10, 60/15, 60/20, 90/30, concept 6, modified concept 6, continuous, flexible, personalized, custom, extended year. That's a rich variety of time sequences.

Question

5. In some districts the elementary schools are on a modified calendar while secondary schools have remained on a traditional schedule. Can parents adjust to having their children on two calendars?

Answer

Yes. While it is true that some parents object to having their children on different schedules, others don't. There are modified-calendar districts in the United States that have had their elementary schools on year-round schedules for over 30 years, while the feeder high schools have remained traditional. So it is clear that many parents have worked around and adjusted to the schools' schedules.

There are ways that districts can reconcile two distinct calendar plans. Sometimes districts have adjusted the two calendars to shorten the traditional school's summer vacation, while lengthening slightly the modified calendar's summer vacation to offer parents and students a "common" vacation of up to 8 weeks. Sometimes districts have simply scheduled summer vacations on a single-track calendar for 6 weeks, pointing out to parents that 6 weeks offer plenty of time for family vacations and that those 6 weeks overlap with siblings' traditional summer vacations.

Question

6. Do most other advanced, industrialized nations follow a calendar similar to that of the United States?

Answer

No. Most western industrialized nations have a longer year with more instructional days than that of the United States. Sweden, which has 180 days of schooling, as do most of the U.S. states, organizes the in-school days in such a way that the Swedish summer vacation is shorter than that of the United States'. Most industrialized nations have 7 or fewer weeks of vacation at one time. It is the long summer vacation of the U.S. school calendar, wherein students are away from formal instruction for up to 13 weeks, that causes so much documented summer learning loss.

Question

7. What alternative or modified calendars can be suggested for a small school district with overcrowding to increase learning and utilize existing facilities more efficiently?

Answer

Multi-track can be implemented in smaller schools as well as larger. However, the smaller the school, the more necessary it is to rethink delivery of instruction and the organization of the school. Multi-track has been implemented in schools as small as 300 students.

There are several calendars—they go by the names of 45/15, 60/20, 60/15, 90/30, among others—that can help to reduce overcrowding, to provide additional space allowing smaller class size, and to utilize existing facilities more efficiently. All provide the learning benefits of year-round education. All of the enumerated calendars must be in the multi-track mode to achieve maximum utilization of existing facilities.

Question

8. Do multi-tracked schools have "balanced" tracks?

Answer

Yes, most year-round education multi-track schools try to keep "balanced" tracks, in which the numbers on each track are similar, if not precisely the same size. Multi-track schools are administered most smoothly when track enrollment is balanced in numbers.

Question

9. What is the Orchard Plan?

Answer

The Orchard Plan uses a 60/15, five-track calendar, a trimester arrangement in which students attend 60 school days followed by 15 school days of vacation. The distinctive aspect of the Orchard Plan is that instead of rotating several classrooms at once, the five tracks are created within self-contained classrooms. To complete this arrangement, teachers teach approximately 225 days on an 11-month contract.

If the enrollment within the classroom is 35 students, with five tracks (or groups) within the classroom, each of the tracks will have seven students. Four of the five groups will be in school; the fifth group will be on its vacation of 15 school days (3 weeks).

The delivery of curriculum in this arrangement is by learning modules, or units. When 80% of the class (four tracks) is learning about dinosaurs, 20% of the class (one track) is on vacation. When the track on vacation returns, it is ready for the unit on dinosaurs, while another 60% is ready to move on to a new unit of study. Of those originally studying dinosaurs, 20% have departed for their 15 days (3 weeks) of vacation. This curriculum arrangement demands consideration of unit study and team teaching. The Orchard Plan originated at Orchard School, Orem, Utah.

IMPLEMENTATION AND PROCESS

Question

1. If a district is thinking about modifying the school's calendar, how much time is required for successful implementation?

Answer

Seasoned observers of the calendar change process would recommend 1 to 2 years for successful implementation. There are instances where a lesser or greater time period may be required, but 1 to 2 years has been the standard recommendation.

Question

2. What are some potential barriers to the implementation of modified calendars and how can each of these barriers be addressed?

Answer

Three significant barriers to reformulating the school calendar include:

1. *Tradition.* The force of "doing it the way we've always done it" is very strong. To counteract this force, frequent communication with parents and community members is needed about how a

year-round, balanced, modified calendar can help students. Adequate time to explain thoroughly to parents the rationale for change is required. There is rarely a situation in which too much information has been given to parents about the reasons for calendar modification.

2. *Misinformation.* Opponents of change frequently misunderstand year-round and its educational possibilities for students. They sometimes have trouble understanding calendar modification because there are so many varieties and formats. Thus, negative information about one type of year-round education is thought to describe also another, which in reality may not apply at all. Sometimes opponents to calendar modification deliberately spread emotional falsehoods to stop the proposed change. Unfortunately, both truths and false information become a part of the community discussion. Full, accurate information about year-round education will eventually prevail, fortunately, if the process of change is given enough time.
3. *Haste.* The NAYRE recommends an educational process within which the change can occur equitably, efficiently, and fairly. The timeline for the process should ordinarily be from 1 to 2 years. Examples abound of the change occurring in as little as 2 months and as long as 7 years. Both ends of this time spectrum are possible, but not recommended.

Question

3. What about surveying parents and students to determine their concerns about, and level of acceptance of, calendar modification?

Answer

Surveys given too early in the study of a new concept or program, before respondents are knowledgeable about the subject, result in a greater negative response. That is true of any survey on any subject. People tend to vote no on issues which they do not understand. Surveys inquiring about acceptance of an idea, then, are most informative and productive after people are knowledgeable about the subject.

If the surveys are to determine concerns, however, the questions should be open-ended, in a way that gathers information. An example of such a survey follows.

Survey background: Hundreds of schools across the nation have modified their schedules to aid student learning and to reduce vacation learning loss. The intent of the survey is to gather information that will be useful in the process of studying calendar modification.

Questions:

- Can you see how modifying the school year calendar could result in improved learning and less forgetting?
- If you say no, why not?
- What is your greatest concern about changing the school calendar?
- Are you and your family interested in learning more about the many ways, schedules, and formats other communities have used to modify the calendar for better learning?
- What kind of additional information about calendar modification would be most helpful to you?
- What is the best way to communicate with you? By newsletter? By e-mail? In person? If by newsletter or e-mail, please provide the respective addresses.

Answers to these questions will give a sense of what information is needed to provide a balanced picture of the topic and to respond to obvious concerns of the public.

If a survey is needed to gauge responses after implementation, the surveys should use a combination of checked responses and open-ended questions. The checked responses may attempt to elicit a grading of reactions from very positive to very negative, with variations in between.

All surveys should *always* be tested with several respondents to discover flaws or unclear meanings before general distribution to a larger audience, including open-ended questions similar to those above.

Question

4. What questions should be asked of teachers regarding their opinions of implementing modified, balanced school calendars?

Answer

There is a difference—significant difference—in surveying teachers who are experienced with year-round education and those who are not. Consequently, the questions to be asked in a teacher survey are substantially different.

Questions to the novice group would center around 1) how much they know about summer learning loss and research about the loss; 2) how much they know about year-round education (or balanced, modified calendars) in general, the numbers of districts, schools, and students involved in year-round education, and the different formats and calendars; and 3) feelings and reactions about change, the change process, year-round education rationale, and whether or not the interests of students or adults should prevail when decisions about modifying the school year calendar are being made.

Questions to the experienced group would focus on such items as 1) personal reaction to the established change; 2) how delivery of the instructional program has changed with the calendar; 3) student results on various standardized tests; 4) results in other categories such as attendance, discipline, referrals, and dropout rates; and 5) flexibility in the program for achieving results.

Question

5. Do teacher unions support year-round education?

Answer

Most teachers, as well as other educational professionals, are aware of the research that confirms serious summer learning loss. Consequently, most educational organizations are generally supportive of school calendar modification, though some are hesitant about the means, processes, and methodologies used to adopt calendar change at the local level. Specific to the question, the answer is that teacher unions have remained officially neutral, saying that implementation of calendar change requires teacher involvement and negotiation before its final adoption.

Question

6. Is it necessary to install air-conditioning at balanced/modified-calendar schools? What of the concerns about being too hot or too cold for learning?

Answer

There are a number of variables that come into play on this matter: degrees of temperature, humidity, air movement, and the like. For example, in many situations 78° F may feel worse than 85° F. There is no specific answer to the question.

If the assumption is made that learning cannot take place when it is "too warm," then real questions are raised as to whether school can be conducted in "hot" May or September days, or even summer school. If children cannot learn when it is "hot," then in any given year there may be 20 to 40 wasted "hot" days, days in which taxpayers are not getting their money's worth. On the other hand, if children can learn during summer school, for example, then they can also learn during summer days of a year-round program.

It is noteworthy that the nation's leading advocate of modifying the school calendar, the NAYRE, favors air-conditioning. If adults are more productive in air-conditioning, then so would be children and young adults.

If a school district is considering implementing climate control as a result of year-round education, it is important to remember that it may not be necessary for the district to implement air-conditioning in every district school at the same moment. A phase-in schedule will help to reduce up-front costs, will allow longer-term amortization, and will allow the beginning of fiscally-sound development of school facilities.

There can be "cold" days in the school year, as well. If school is suddenly cancelled for weather- or climate-related circumstances, the days can be made up during intersessions, Saturday school, or independent study, depending upon state law and community choices.

Question

7. In a community's discussion about whether or not to change the school year calendar, how can leaders of the discussion present a fair, balanced picture of the options?

Answer

There is a built-in dilemma in any discussion of change, and a sense of fairness is created by encouraging an open and vigorous discussion of the possibilities of the options. The dilemma is that almost all parents and school staff have experienced a traditional calendar, so there is familiarity with the status quo, while few have experienced a year-round calendar.

A full discussion of the many ways to modify and balance the school calendar requires time. Presenting many details, at length, may create the appearance of "pushing" an agenda. Yet, simply presenting an equal listing of debate points on both sides of whether to change or maintain the current school calendar may only serve to reinforce the status quo, the familiar.

Leaders of calendar change discussion must acknowledge up-front familiarity of the study group with what has been, offer the intent to compare the known (the traditional calendar) with the possibilities (the modified calendar), and confirm the openness of the ensuing discussion. Discussion leaders also need to accept the fact that a portion of any community will be opposed to any change, no matter how convincing the argument for change may be, a portion will be ready for change, no matter how weak the argument for change will be, and a middle portion will be willing to think about change, given enough time to assimilate the possibilities of what might be, or could be.

Question

8. To what degree should there be parental/community support of a change, such as school calendar modification, to ensure the adoption and continuation of the change?

Answer

Some school boards have required a simple majority to enact calendar change; others have required an 80% approval rate by parents. A reasonable answer is a favorable support rate of about 60%.

Calendar modification, powerful though the instructional possibilities may be, is not welcomed by all parents and community members. Thus, the discussion of degree of support needs to focus on what is needed to ensure the implementation of successful change.

A simple, or slight, majority may not be quite enough to ensure effective implementation. Just as national politics are riled when there is not a clear majority, so too, will local community politics be riled. On the other hand, an approval rate of 80% is extreme and unwarranted. It is near impossible to get any large group to agree on a major undertaking at 80%. In comparison, a national president is thought to have a sweeping mandate from the voters if 55% to 59% of the voters support a particular candidate. Thus, an approval rate of 60% from parents and community members seems reasonable, doable, and most likely effective.

Question

9. How does a year-round or modified calendar affect the school office staff?

Answer

If the calendar is single-track, then the effect will be minimal after implementation. Single-track, with its built-in intersession periods, allows office staff to regroup and "catch up."

Multi-track schools require more staff time because of the beginnings, endings, and cross-tracking associated with the multi-track system. Since many more students are being accommodated at one school site, obviously additional staff and staff time are required.

If current office staff are called upon to work extra hours or days to meet the deadlines and increased workload that a multi-track system may require, it is important to 1) negotiate in advance with union representatives conditions of service and rate of pay; 2) hire additional support staff during the changeover to multi-track, if required; and 3) give office staff the opportunity to learn in advance how to implement multi-track year-round, which they can attain by attending professional conferences and seminars conducted by organizations such as the NAYRE.

Question

10. Many schools do their annual maintenance in the summer. Won't multi-track year-round schools be dirtier than traditional schools? Won't year-round education lead to building burnout?

Answer

No, to both questions. Long ago districts using multi-track year-round education abandoned the thinking that cleaning and refurbishing could only happen in the summer. Hospital, hotel, and department store administrators know how to clean and refurbish throughout the year; cannot school administrators and custodians do the same? Fortunately, many districts have moved beyond that old—and at one time only—way of doing school refurbishing. Now, an outside contractor can paint the interior of an elementary school in one weekend, which has been done. Routine deep cleaning occurs one room at a time, continually and regularly. There is no need to wait until summer to do these things.

Building burnout? Is there building burnout in hospitals, hotels, or department stores, which are in use all year? Or is usage what they were built for in the first place? The question is not unlike that of a librarian who complains that books are being worn out because they are being read.

Of course, a 33% factor of additional usage (usually about 60 days) in a multi-track school will wear out carpets and similar consumables at a faster pace than single-track and traditional-calendar schools. However, the structural part of the building should not be damaged at all. Even if the consumables wear out a little faster in a multi-track school, those costs have to be compared to the costs of building new buildings to handle overcrowding, buildings which will be used 180 days or more each year with the resultant wearing out of the carpets and similar consumables. Sixty additional days in an existing school are certainly cheaper than 180 days in a new school. Multi-track year-round education is clearly a savings to the taxpayer, when compared to the other options for dealing with overcrowding.

Question

11. Have year-round education programs created significant obstacles to the provision of federal school lunch programs?

Answer

No. Over 2,000,000 American students attend year-round schools and to date there have been no problems with federal school lunch programs in either single-track or multi-track schools. There have been year-round schools in the United States since 1968; no problems have been cited because of the calendar.

Some critics of calendar modification have raised their concern about students not being fed nutritionally for the 3 or 4 *weeks* of vacation. Why would these same people not be more concerned about the 10 to 12 weeks without food services for students in a traditional calendar school?

Question

12. Are there school districts which have all of the schools in the district on a year-round schedule?

Answer

Yes. There are K–12 and K–8 districts on a single-track, or multi-track, common calendar; there are also K–12 districts utilizing both single-track and multi-track schedules in the same district. There are several instances of a countywide system on a modified, or year-round, calendar. With around 600 school districts and 3,000 schools involved, there is at least one example of almost any kind of school arrangement or program connected to a restructuring of instructional time.

Question

13. What means are available to school administrators to relieve overcrowding? How does multi-tracking compare with other options?

Answer

Experts in the field of educational administration usually offer 10 ways to relieve overcrowding. They are:

- Passage of bond measures to construct facilities
- Use of relocatable (portable) classrooms
- Redrawing of district boundary lines
- Double sessions
- Extended day
- Busing students to nearby underutilized schools
- Use of other community spaces
- Increased class size
- Redesignating special-purpose rooms as classrooms
- Multi-track year-round education

While all 10 can alleviate the nuisance of overcrowding, multi-tracking is the only one of the 10 with a specific educational component tucked into it: the shortening of summer vacation to reduce learning loss.

Question

14. On a multi-track calendar, do teachers have to share rooms? Are experienced teachers who have collected and stored reams of materials expected to pack up and move every few weeks? How is this done?

Answer

On a five-track schedule, five teachers share four rooms. On a four-track schedule, four teachers share three rooms. On a three-track schedule, three teachers share two rooms. Clearly, teachers share rooms and there is in and out movement in the process.

There are two arrangements for sharing rooms commonly used at multi-tracked schools. One is the "roving" plan, in which one of the teachers sharing rooms volunteers to be the one annually who moves with each track change; others of this group maintain "their" rooms throughout the year, whether in school or on vacation, but allow the roving teacher to use the room while their groups are on vacation. The "rotation" plan, in which a teacher leaving for vacation rotates completely out of a room at the end of the instructional period, to be filled immediately by the incoming teacher, is favored in some schools.

Schools provide large, movable storage cabinets for teacher and student supplies, which custodial staffs move at room change time. Students and teachers move together, ordinarily, and although this arrangement may require better organization and cooperation in many respects, staff soon accommodate to room sharing. The teacher-student relationship remains throughout the year and is not changed by either the rotation or roving method.

Question

15. If multi-track is used to solve an overcrowding problem, can it be used for any reason other than overcrowding?

Answer

Multi-track is used ordinarily to relieve overcrowding. However, a few schools, though technically not overcrowded, have utilized multi-tracking to gain space for other purposes, such as providing rooms for laboratories or special-needs students.

Question

16. From an administrative standpoint, aren't year-round schools more difficult to run, especially multi-track? Do administrators of year-round schools receive pay raises?

Answer

Multi-track year-round schools are more complicated than traditional or single-track and therefore require stronger administrative skills. Many administrators enjoy the challenge. Usually there is a higher rate of pay because multi-track year-round principals and their administrative staff work a longer year and have more responsibility. Some multi-track principals maintain that their schools are easier to administer because one third or one quarter of the enrolled students and staff are off campus at any one time, making campus management easier than it would be with a school overcrowded. Many multi-track schools report better attendance, higher grades, and fewer discipline problems after implementing multi-track, making the day-to-day operations easier and more pleasant, when compared to an overcrowded school.

Single-track administrators have a workload comparable to traditional calendar principals and ordinarily are on a similar pay scale to their traditional colleagues.

Question

17. A school district, located approximately 35 miles from one of the nation's largest cities, covering 118 square miles and several municipalities, serving 15,000 students grades K–12, is considering calendar modification. The district is growing by approximately 600 students per year and is projected to reach over 17,000 students within 3 years. The communities served by the school district have defeated a bond referendum for new school construction for a second time.

A districtwide summit for the purpose of informing residents about implementation of multi-track year-round education has been called. The district administration actually has studied multi-tracking for 5 years and has sent representatives to year-round/modified-calendar conferences during that time. Any suggestions or advice for this summit?

Answer

The district has real problems of growth and voter dissatisfaction with which to deal. To change a school calendar successfully, a good job of communicating with parents and the public is crucial. However, the task of communication need not, should not, open with a large community meeting, sage advice which is routinely ignored and later regretted by school districts across the nation. Such a meeting is often an open invitation for grandstanding by opponents of change and chronic complainers, while others may use the meeting as a pretext for anti–school board or anti-administration rhetoric. If a large community meeting is warranted, it can be scheduled toward the end of the communication process.

Since the school district has studied balancing of the school calendar for several years, the administration should have already formulated a plan for communicating possible calendar change with the larger public. If parents and community members have not yet been involved in the process, then the district needs to schedule many small meetings throughout the neighborhoods at various times of the day and different days of the week. Each meeting should be informative, positive, and interactive, so that attendees may ask questions. Sometimes a district will first meet with 10 to 20 opinion leaders from several school/community organizations, then expand the contacts to other community representatives and parents in many quite small meetings (5 to 15 people) before scheduling a communitywide meeting.

If the district has already announced a big public meeting, however, then the district must honor its commitment. Otherwise, it is subject to criticism that it has something to hide.

During bond campaigns, it is important that the district not in any way threaten imposition of multi-track year-round education as a punishment if voters fail to pass a bond referendum. If the district does so, there will likely be a lingering political issue, since some residents will see the eventual implementation of multi-track to handle overcrowding as less of a solution, which it surely is, than as district retribution for an unfavorable vote.

Question

18. Some states have a mixture of traditional and modified-calendar schools. Should one calendar, traditional or year-round, be implemented statewide?

Answer

No. Mandated uniformity is part of the current situation prompting calls for calendar reform. Different communities, different school districts, different schools have different needs, interests, and priorities. No one curriculum, no one text series, and no one calendar can be best for all circumstances. In a phrase, one size does not fit all.

Yet uniformity and conformity are the guideposts of states and school districts that do not offer, nor allow, alternative calendars. Legislation in some states to force all districts to open the school year after Labor Day and end the year around Memorial Day is another example of one-size-fits-all philosophy.

COMMUNITY CONCERNS

Question

1. In how many countries of the world do children get a summer vacation similar to that of children in the United States? Is year-round education the norm in most countries?

Answer

Few advanced countries of the world offer their students a long summer vacation similar to that of the United States. These countries already have a school calendar that fits the common definition of year-round education. Countries such as the United Kingdom, Germany, France, Russia, Australia, Japan, and Korea all have longer instructional years and shorter summer vacations.

Those in the modified-calendar movement do not oppose summer vacation. It is the *length* of the summer vacation that is the issue. How long, really, does summer vacation need to be, keeping in mind the forgetting that occurs the longer a vacation lasts?

Question

2. What about the valuable lessons students learn by going to summer camps or traveling with their families in the summer?

Answer

Modified-calendar students go to camps and travel with their parents just as traditional calendar students do. However, year-round families choose to travel and camp in the fall, winter, and spring, as well as summer. Why would a family want to travel only when everybody else is traveling and recreation areas are packed and overflowing with people?

It is important to remember that most families in the United States do not send their children to summer camp and most do not take extended vacations for several weeks. Indeed, only about 15% of the nation's children go to camp. Year-round education is flexible enough that those who choose to go to camp and travel can still do so, in all seasons of the year.

Question

3. How are extracurricular activities—such as music lessons, summer camp, and semester-abroad programs—affected by modification of the school calendar?

Answer

The activities you mention—music lessons, summer camp, living in other countries—are available to students on modified calendars. All year-round schools have 3-, 4-, or 6-week summer vacation periods called intersessions, which allow for any or all of these kinds of activities to occur in all seasons of the year.

Semester-abroad programs can occur throughout the year. They fit naturally with year-round education. April in Paris is a better time for a high school student to learn about Parisian life than August in Paris, when Parisians leave the city in large numbers.

Musical performance clearly requires all-year practice, as any professional musician will affirm. Musical skill builds with continuous practice. Aspiring musicians need the support and help of the music instructor throughout the year, including summer.

Realistically, most students do not have the opportunity to attend summer-long camps, because of the costs involved. The vast majority of students who do go to camp go there for 1 week, or join their parents for a 1- or 2-week trip. However, for those few who have the opportunity for extended camping/travel, every effort should be made to encourage and support the student, but within the context and flexibility of a year-round education environment. It is not necessary to have 10 to 12 weeks of vacation time to engage in these activities.

Question

4. Is a long summer vacation necessary to strengthen a family's bonding?

Answer

No. Those unwilling to shorten summer vacation are advancing the idea that fun and relaxation have higher priority than reducing summer learning loss. However, fun and relaxation can be had in short, as well as long, vacations. Thanksgiving weekend is usually a wonderful family bonding experience. It is 4 days. The winter (Christmas/New Year's) holiday is also a magical time for many children and their families. It is 2 weeks. The idea that it is necessary to have 10 to 12 weeks of vacation each summer, for 12 years, to gain family cohesion, doesn't survive reasoned examination.

Question

5. How can students attend school in the summer without air-conditioning?

Answer

Do students learn in summer school without air-conditioning? If they don't, why has summer school continued all these years? If they do, why wouldn't students in year-round programs learn as well? Having posed these rhetorical questions, it is nevertheless important to remember that most adults who work at a desk now work in climate control of some kind, on the presumption that a comfortable person is a more productive person. That reasoning seems logical in a school setting as well, particularly for adults and older children.

Younger children are more impervious to temperature changes, though not entirely. They like to play outdoors, no matter how hot or cold it gets. Adults notice temperature changes more readily. Air-conditioning, then, can be a positive for optimal learning. Required? No, but certainly most welcome.

Question

6. What about children who attend Bible study during the summer? Can they still be in both Bible school and a school with a balanced, modified calendar?

Answer

Yes. Why not? A single-track year-round schedule should have ample time during the summer vacation for a student to attend a vacation Bible school. Usually religious study programs run for a week or two; single-track schedules usually have from 4 to 7 weeks of summer vacation.

Students in multi-track schedules may find it a little more difficult to meet a particular week's Bible program. Churches in communities with multi-track schedules, however, have become more flexible, and understand that because students and families go on vacations at different times of the year, Bible study may have to be scheduled more than once in the summer.

Some ways churches have become flexible: one church scheduled Bible study in each season of the year, so that students would be able to attend one or all four of the sessions. Another church had an all-day Bible study for students each Thursday of the summer, thus enrolling all students electing to attend, from any track. A third church scheduled its vacation Bible school for summer evenings, encouraging parents to study the Bible right along with their children (though not in the same classrooms).

Question

7. What percentage of schools and students in the United States are on a modified school calendar of some kind?

Answer

About 3.5% of America's schools are on a year-round schedule, incorporating a little over 4.9% of the nation's students. That represents over 2,000,000 students. For a perspective on these percentages, compare year-round education to other reform efforts. Year-round education is larger in numbers than charter schools, similar in numbers to magnet schools, and larger than most other reforms. The growth in modified-calendar numbers over the past 3 decades has been steady.

Question

8. Does year-round education change the culture of the school?

Answer

Yes, there is some minor change in the culture of the school when a single-track schedule is implemented, and a greater change when a multi-track calendar is required.

Single-track calendars enhance the culture of the school in that students and teachers have periodic breaks (intersessions) of 2 to 8 weeks. The breaks allow both students and teachers to refresh or relax, or to attend classes of enrichment or remediation between learning blocks of time.

In a multi-track schedule, each student follows a single-track schedule, maintaining the periodic breaks that allow for refreshment, relaxation, remediation, or enrichment. However, the multi-track school's routine is altered, in general, in that one group of students is always on vacation. Each track has its own representatives to student council and its own officers. All-school functions such as ball games, prom night, graduation ceremonies, plays, and music concerts remain scheduled as they were in a traditional calendar setting.

Question

9. When schools change their calendar, the following issues are potential concerns for parents and students: child care during the 15-day vacation and summer programs administered by parks and recreation departments. How do schools respond to these concerns?

Answer

While these issues are important to consider, it must be acknowledged that they are primarily non-instructional concerns and secondary to the main mission of schools, which is to help students to retain what they have learned and to achieve at the highest levels possible.

Child care providers respond both to the school schedule and the law of supply and demand. If child-care centers don't respond to the needs of parents, they quickly go out of business. Consequently, child care availability responds to a situation and has not been a problem in a community that has moved toward a balanced calendar. Where child care is handled among family members, often without commercial backup, there would obviously be a change of schedule involved.

Parks and recreation departments usually respond to the changing school calendar as well, acknowledging the law of supply and demand. If parents want and need recreational activities throughout the year, parks and recreation respond to that need or suffer criticism for being unresponsive. Now that modified school calendars are in place at so many communities, scores of city park and recreation departments have developed all-year programs.

Question

10. What about year-round education and its effect on students' jobs?

Answer

Students in year-round high schools actually have more job opportunities than before! Why? 1) They are not competing in the summer with all other students. When a high school is on a traditional calendar schedule, its students are competing with neighboring high school and college students for whatever jobs are available. Competition in most communities is intense for all-too-few jobs. 2) They can work during intersessions, including the Christmas-New Year's break of 2 to 5 weeks (depending upon the local calendar chosen).

It is important to remember also that 85% of the nation's student population—those generally age 16 and below—aren't eligible for the kinds of jobs that might be affected by a change of school calendar.

Most jobs for high school students are at fast-food restaurants, grocery stores, and similar establishments. All of these continue all year. So when high school students have vacations of 3 weeks in the autumn, 4 weeks in the winter, 3 weeks in the spring, and 4 weeks in the summer, they are able to work in the seasons other than summer as well as weekends all year. More jobs are actually available to students, and a greater number of year-round students have jobs than before their high schools went year-round.

Question

11. Are there community activities for students during the vacations of a modified calendar?

Answer

Yes, there are activities in many communities for students during their off-track vacation time. Park and recreation departments, boys and girls clubs, YMCA, YWCA, and similar organizations offer all-year programs for youth. In communities without these youth-serving organizations, a long summer of boredom may breed a host of problems, which should encourage responsible adults to rethink the value of the customary long summer vacation.

Question

12. Many children come from divorced families where the custody is shared. How can this work with a year-round calendar?

Answer

Year-round calendars have vacation time scheduled throughout the year, not just summer. Divorced/working parents usually work year-round. A change in the school calendar is welcomed by many parents because of greater time flexibility. In those cases where a court order for visitation allows only summer shared custody and cannot be changed, principals of year-round schools should work with the family to do what is in the best interests of the child and the family situation, within the allowable limits of state law.

Question

13. Who are the biggest opponents of modifying the school year calendar?

Answer

The greatest opposition arises from the summer recreation industry, which has put financial support into an opposition campaign. This group's opposition is clearly wallet-oriented, though publicly there is no admission of this factor. Anti-year-round materials, designed by paid public relations professionals hired by the industry and filled with distortions, half-truths, untruths, and information out of context, have been distributed from coast to coast.

Other opponents surface in local discussions. Some parents fight change because of fears of the unknown about child care, vacation plans, Little League—all of which are quite compatible with year-round schedules. A few teachers will oppose calendar change to protect their perceived fringe benefit of a 2- to 3-month summer vacation. Some opposition will originate with an athletic boosters' club, incorrectly assuming that high school athletics will be damaged by calendar change.

Opposition to change is not consistent from community to community. Factors of opposition are as diverse as people in a community, not unlike any other issue examined in a political context.

Question

14. Why do some schools/school districts revert back to the agriculturally-based traditional calendar?

Answer

There are various reasons given: respect for tradition, love of a long vacation, the costs or bother of having a school or schools out of sync with the routine of other schools in the district, the administrative ease of having all schools alike, opposition from a local business group, particularly those in the summer recreation industry, and sometimes just political infighting.

Most schools have remained on a balanced calendar once a change has been implemented. Indeed some year-round, modified-calendar schools are now in their third decade of operation.

Question

15. Are there examples of year-round schooling not working?

Answer

Yes and no, depending on how one views a particular situation. There are examples of poorly planned or poorly implemented calendar modification, of course. Sometimes districts implement calendar change with little involvement of various stakeholder groups in the discussion. In some cases, the district administration has spent so much time in the discussion phase that little time, effort, or thought has been given to the implementation phase. In still other examples, the effort has been successful in the discussion and implementation phases, but little time and effort has been given to the institutionalization phase.

There are no examples of year-round education harming the learning of students, however. So in that sense, there are no examples of year-round education not working for student learning. Considering that the smallest modified-calendar school has 15 students and the largest has over 5,000—in rural, suburban, and urban areas as well as in lower-, middle-, and upper-income communities—the success rate of schools modifying their calendars has been extraordinarily high.

Question

16. Some states have laws that do not allow school to begin until after Labor Day. How can year-round education work with such a law?

Answer

In a phrase: by being flexible. State laws that will not allow school sessions to begin until after Labor Day are unreasonable and unfortunate. To begin school only after Labor Day throughout a state is to void local and parental control. However, please know that in each state with such a law, year-round education continues. How? Usually, by utilizing state-approved waivers, or by starting school after Labor Day and continuing the instructional year through the following August.

States certainly may require minimum standards to be met and 180 days of schooling each year is quite reasonable, since 180 constitutes fewer than half of the 365 days each year. School districts should be allowed to allocate those 180 days throughout the year as local citizens, through their elected representatives, see fit.

Those few states that have laws limiting the balancing of calendars have done so at the behest of summer recreation businesses. The rationale for the laws are faulty from an educational perspective. Schools were established for optimum learning, not to benefit the summer recreation industry. The irony is that resort/beach/park businesses don't rely very heavily on K–12 student help in any case, so claims that student help wouldn't be available is really a minor issue. How many 8-, 12-, or even 14-year-olds are employed by resorts, for example? Fewer than .1% of the nation's students are employed by the summer recreation industry. The obvious questions, then, are "Why should the educational welfare of the other 99.9% of the students be held hostage to the few who may be employed?" and "Should a state put recreational interests ahead of student learning interests?" States like Colorado, California, Utah, and Nevada are all very much tourist-oriented states, with heavy use of year-round education, at no damage to tourism and the dollars it brings to a state and community.

While the summer resort/recreation industry has cleverly manipulated some state legislatures into believing that the industry's survival depends on an after–Labor Day start for public schools, it is imperative that parents and educators lobby their legislatures to support what is best for students and their learning.

Question

17. Do the proponents of calendar change have a financial interest in the change?

Answer

No. Financial gain is not an important factor in proponents' push for year-round instruction. The NAYRE, the leading voice for calendar change in the nation, is almost wholly self-supporting. Its funding is derived from membership dues, both individual and institutional, registration fees at its conferences and seminars, publications that NAYRE has to offer to its members and constituents, and contributions from individuals who believe in the year-round concept.

NAYRE has no support from the federal or any state government, is not affiliated with any quasi-governmental agency, and does not receive funding from a private foundation. The association proactively steers clear of political settings to avoid being tagged liberal or conservative. NAYRE is a 501c(3) organization, established under Internal Revenue Service regulations.

Question

18. When calendar change is proposed to a community, how much should parents and community members be involved in the discussion?

Answer

A lot. Since calendar change affects a community and its teachers, students, and parents, there should be an open, lengthy, and vigorous discussion of what calendar change can mean for all stakeholders.

Since a school district's responsibility is to educate the community's students to the highest degree possible, the community's professionals (teachers, administrators) should have considerable input into the discussion. However, parents need to endorse generally the decision about calendar implementation to make it fully effective.

Support from the community is also a bonus. The community provides the tax base to fund the school program. General approval of what the local school district is doing is essential for continuing financial support.

Question

19. Many futurists insist that year-round education will be the norm in the future, in that instruction will be available via the Internet, satellite, and cable television nearly 24 hours a day, 365 days a year, if an individual so chooses. Why, then, do some schools return to a traditional schedule after experiencing some kind of modified calendar?

Answer

While indeed some schools have reverted to a traditional schedule after experiencing a modified schedule, the percentage doing so is relatively low. Also, not every school that reverted did so willingly.

There are several reasons that have been given for a return, and often the reasons are quite localized. Sometimes a school board or central administration is irritated by one or two schools following an alternative schedule and order the school's return to a mandated, synchronized district schedule, a circumstance unfortunately experienced by many of the schools that have reverted.

In other instances, the implementation of calendar change was initiated without a measured plan of introduction, rushed into practice without parental and community input, or abandoned with little support after implementation by the central administration or school board.

Sometimes a change of central administration alters the instructional priorities of a district, resulting in a lack of appreciation for the goal of reducing summer learning loss. Sometimes political infighting among elected school board members catches all optional programs in a tug of war among competing political factions.

PROGRAM ISSUES

Question

1. What are the benefits of school calendar modification and year-round schooling?

Answer

The benefits of school calendar modification and year-round education include, but are not limited to:

1. reduction of summer learning loss
2. planned, periodic remediation of learning problems that occur by utilizing vacation breaks (called intersessions) throughout the year
3. better sequencing of work and vacation for both teachers and students
4. better attendance on the part of students and teachers
5. fewer student discipline referrals
6. less student vandalism
7. reduced dropout rate

Question

2. What are the year-round education benefits for students with disabilities or special needs?

Answer

Any student having difficulty learning or requiring repetition, routine, and consistent structure to acquire basic skills and fundamentals is helped by the more continuous schedule of a balanced, year-round calendar. Conversely, that student is hurt by the long summer away from formal instruction because of the traditional calendar.

Since all students lose certain skills, particularly math skills, over the long summer, balancing the calendar is beneficial to all.

Question

3. Which kind of schooling is best for continuous learning?

Answer

The nature of the question provides the answer. If the intent is to have continuous learning, then a school that implements a calendar with more continuous learning is the best schooling. The traditional calendar, with its 10- to 12-week vacation, cannot be said to foster continuous learning. A balanced, year-round calendar acknowledges both the need for vacation (but in smaller time segments) and the need for continuous instruction; thus, the balanced calendar with its learning blocks in all seasons of the year is best for continuous learning.

Question

4. What are *intersessions*?

Answer

An intersession (literally, between sessions) is the vacation period between learning blocks of time. Rather than the "summer" school common in communities utilizing a traditional calendar, intersessions are "summer" school rescheduled when a school moves to a balanced, modified calendar. There may be two intersessions annually (for example, 90/30 and concept 6 calendars), three intersessions (60/20 and 60/15 calendars), or four (45/15, variation calendars).

Question

5. How can intersessions help students to achieve more?

Answer

Intersessions are the periodic short vacations scheduled into a balanced, modified, year-round calendar. During that vacation both enrichment and remedial classes can be held. In effect, intersessions are summer school rescheduled.

When a student begins to have difficulty in mathematics early in the school year (late September or early October), it makes no sense at all to begin the remediation process the following June or July. By then it is too late. Remediation during an intersession in October makes much more sense and is more effective.

Intersession enrichment classes throughout the year strengthen the learning progress of students by building experiential background useful in understanding the approaching unit of subject matter.

Question

6. What effect has balancing the school calendar had on curriculum and school improvement?

Answer

Curricular actions vary from district to district, depending on school board and administrative priorities, the calendar chosen, the kind of intersession programs implemented, the reason calendar modification was implemented (to educate students better or to lessen the impact of overcrowding), or a combination of these factors.

If a district changes the calendar primarily for educational reasons, a review of the curriculum invariably follows. The instructional program is expected to be more continuous, more reflective of the way students actually learn. Intersessions become focused periods of enrichment and remediation. Students become less susceptible to failure and retention in grade.

Calendar balancing offers more opportunities for earlier intervention to struggling students. The planned intersession periods encourage intervention strategies that allow students experiencing difficulty to stay in sync with other students. Because the calendar has been reorganized, or balanced, the long summer vacation is reduced, leading to reduced summer learning loss. This action clearly helps those students experiencing the most difficulty in school, but also helps all students who experience summer learning loss.

Question

7. Is there an impact from year-round education on standard subjects such as history, English, and math at the secondary school level?

Answer

Yes, but to a lesser or greater degree. Calendar modification will have an indirect, rather than direct, impact on the basic secondary curriculum, if a single-track schedule is chosen by the school (which ordinarily secondary schools do). A greater impact will be noticed if a multi-track schedule is implemented.

The basic curriculum will remain essentially the same as it was before balancing of the calendar. What will change are the time sequences of instruction and the provision of remediation/enrichment (intersessions) during vacation periods. While most secondary schools on a traditional schedule utilize a calendar plan of two semesters, single-track year-round schools will more often operate on a quarter, trimester, or continuous basis, although some continue the semester plan, but with two 6-week vacations during the year, rather than one long, 10- to 12-week summer vacation.

Schools using the traditional calendar offer instruction during the three seasons of autumn, winter, and spring. Year-round single-track secondary schools, in contrast, will operate in all four seasons. They will provide as much vacation time to students, but they will distribute that vacation time more evenly all year.

If a secondary school utilizes multi-track to handle overcrowding, the basic curriculum is impacted by having to plan the instructional program so that students in each track have equal access to course offerings. Curriculum designers have to keep in mind the size of each track and essentially plan the curriculum as though each track were a distinct high school of 500, 1,200, or even 1,800 students.

Question

8. Are band, athletics, and extracurricular activities affected by a change of the school calendar?

Answer

Band, athletics, and extracurricular activities continue as before when the school calendar has been modified. There may be altered administrative arrangements and calendar rotations, but the basic programs continue as before.

In schools with single-track schedules, bands still play at scheduled athletic events, hold holiday and spring concerts, and play for commencement exercises. Athletics continue as before on seasonal schedules, with some slight adjustment for early practice, since school may begin in July or early August. Extracurricular activities continue as before.

When a school enters into a multi-track schedule, all activities continue, but with some differences of administrative arrangement. For example, band continues as before, but consideration must be given to the master schedule to allow band members to play together, whether during a regular class period, before school, or after school. If band members choose different tracks, the band director may have to shift to a symphony rehearsal frame of mind. That is, much rehearsal may have to be done individually, by sections, and finally by combined band in a concentrated rehearsal period.

Athletics, to a very large extent, are unaffected by a change to a multi-track calendar. They are seasonal, non-credit, and entered into voluntarily by participants willing to sacrifice much, including vacation time, to be able to play a sport. Some coaches have used intersession time as a chance to hone the playing skills of the athletes. Some athletes have requested and been placed on a track with an intersession period at the height of their favored sport's season.

Extracurricular activities are largely unaffected by a multi-track calendar. The prom continues and is scheduled well in advance. There is just one all-school prom annually and students enrolled on any track are eligible participants. Most multi-track high schools schedule just one graduation ceremony and that, too, is scheduled well in advance.

One significant change at the multi-track secondary level is the operation of student government. Each track elects is own representatives. Class officers are elected by the total student body. Students who choose to stand for a class officer position may also be required to give up some vacation time to serve the needs of the class and governmental operations.

Question

9. Do teachers have to work harder in the autumn than they otherwise would because of the long traditional summer break?

Answer

Yes. Considerable time each autumn (up to 40 school days!) is spent in reintroducing school routines and past teachings that students have forgotten over the summer. This situation curtails instructional time for introduction of new material.

There is ample evidence of summer learning loss. All students lose some ground over the summer, especially in math. Reducing summer vacation can help to reduce summer learning loss. Classroom instruction is more effective with a balanced, modified instructional year.

Question

10. Is there research that shows that year-round education will benefit students coming from homes where English is not the primary language?

Answer

Yes, there is. In his meta-analytic review of 19 studies on the academic results of year-round students, Dr. Walter Winters found several instances where ESL (English as a second language), LEP (limited English proficient) and SLL (second language learners) students were helped by the more continuous instruction in the new language (English). His synopsis, entitled *A Review of Recent Studies Relating to the Achievement of Students Enrolled in Year-Round Education Programs* (1995), confirmed what educators had experienced. His findings have been subsequently confirmed by other studies. A discussion can be found in chapter 5 of this book.

Reports and studies conducted by local school districts such as the Socorro Independent School District, El Paso, Texas, and the San Diego Unified School District, San Diego, California, also confirm Dr. Winters's research.

Question

11. Can the benefits claimed for modified school calendars also be realized by simply reducing class sizes?

Answer

No. The intent and goal of each strategy is different. Both have value, but each in a different way. Calendar modification's primary goal is to reduce summer learning loss, which leads, if the goal is met, to more time for new learning.

Reducing class size substantially can also help students in their learning. (Small reductions have small payoff. Big reductions are required.) Small classes allow more individual attention to personal learning styles. Other programs, such as a focus on reading, a strong arts program, attention to children needing remedial help, and so on, can aid learning as well. Thus, a community's choices should not be limited to reduced class size *or* year-round education; the choices should be reduced class size *and* modification of the school calendar.

Question

12. While calendar modification might be a good idea for urban or at-risk students, wouldn't a year-round calendar be detrimental to gifted and talented students? If a school implemented multi-track year-round education, would the classes gifted students need be offered on each track?

Answer

Gifted and talented students, like other students, learn continuously. They also forget over the long summer, though admittedly to a lesser degree. Of what value is the school's library, science labs, arts rooms, and such to this group if schools are closed for 3 months? A calendar and school designed for optimum learning will be a plus for the gifted and talented student.

In single-track schools, all students and teachers follow the same schedule. The instructional program remains basically the same as that of a traditional calendar, but delivered without the long summer vacation. Students in multi-track schools are assigned to tracks in which they attend classes to meet their instructional needs, whether it is a gifted student who is taking honors classes, English language learners, or others with special needs. No student would be deprived of classes important for their individual talents and abilities by a school's being on a single- or multi-tracked schedule.

Question

13. How does year-round education fit in with other innovative programming, such as block scheduling or multi-age classrooms?

Answer

Quite well. Rethinking the use of time is not exclusively the domain of those rethinking the calendar year. A wider examination of the use of time in school is part of the learning strategies advocated by year-round educators. Both block schedules and multi-age classrooms are widely used with a variety of year-round calendars, as are many other recent educational innovations.

Question

14. Does the year-round calendar interfere with Scholastic Aptitude Test (SAT) or Advanced Placement (AP) testing for high school students?

Answer

Actually a year-round calendar can be supportive of students scheduled for Preliminary Scholastic Aptitude (PSAT), SAT, and AP testing.

Single-track calendars usually provide intersession periods prior to the date of the exam, giving students an opportunity to review seriously for those exams in close proximity of time to taking them. Some schools provide special intersession classes taught by staff members or other professionals to heighten test-taking skills, as well as maintaining constant review for exams such as those for advanced placement.

In some multi-track circumstances students are off-track (on vacation) on scheduled test-taking days and must return for the tests. However, the same study opportunities described above would apply to them also.

Question

15. If a private school, grades 1 through 12, specializing in working with children with learning difficulties/disabilities, were to implement a modified school calendar, what information would help in making this decision?

Answer

The research on summer learning loss is especially applicable to students with learning disabilities/difficulties. Educational leaders need to be so familiar with the research that they can comfortably relay that information to parent and community support groups. Also, there are numerous private and public schools with modified calendars that could share information on changing learning time for the benefit of special needs students. The NAYRE maintains a list of the names and addresses of schools that are both year-round and serving the needs of special students.

Question

16. If a school administration were to put "efficiency" or "simplification" ahead of "better education" in a community's discussion of calendar modification, what should be the reaction?

Answer

If the discussion is centered on what is best for adults and their convenience, rather than what is best for students, then helping to redirect or refine the discussion is important. Adults sometimes forget that the purpose of schooling is to help students to learn the most possible. Calendar modification is an important means to help students forget less and remember more. A major research study has established that there is summer learning loss during the long summer of the traditional school calendar. The loss is true for all students in math and most students in reading, and students having the most difficulty in school suffer the greatest loss. Therefore, it is important to put the reason for calendar modification front and center: better learning, less forgetting.

While redirecting the discussion to emphasize and articulate the purpose of school as maximum possible learning, it is important, however, to recognize adult concerns, particularly those that affect an adult's support of the student, whether financial or emotional.

Question

17. Does multi-tracking have any educational benefit?

Answer

Yes. Summer learning loss can be reduced when the summer vacation of the traditional calendar is shortened. Both single-track and multi-track calendars reduce the long summer vacation. Thus, multi-tracking has educational benefit. Indeed, of the 10 ways suggested to relieve overcrowding, only multi-tracking has an educational component. No research studies of which the authors are aware indicate lower student achievement because of multi-tracking.

Question

18. What arrangements can be made for students transferring into a year-round school, especially multi-track, from a traditional-calendar school?

Answer

When a student transfers into a multi-track school, he or she is usually registered into a track in which there is the greatest number of teaching days available in the remainder of the academic year. One must keep in mind that there is a finite number of days financed by the state, so if the total number of instructional days (former school and new school) exceeds the total average daily attendance/average daily membership limit, that student cannot be included in attendance reports in excess of that limit. Actually, because of having three or four choices of tracks, it is generally easier to place a new student in an appropriate situation than in a traditional school. Also, sometimes principals enroll new transfers into the least-enrolled track to equalize it in numbers with the other tracks. Students transferring from a traditional calendar school to one with a single-track, year-round schedule would notice little difference than any other transfer from one school to another.

Question

19. In actuality, aren't students on a multi-track calendar receiving fewer instructional days than their traditional calendar counterparts? How can this be good for education?

Answer

Most year-round calendar plans provide exactly the same number of instructional days and hours in a school year as the traditional calendar. Students on a multi-track calendar do not receive less instructional time by law, unless a waiver is granted by the state. A few multi-track calendars in use nationwide require a redistribution of instructional minutes that provide for a slightly longer day and fewer days annually of school attendance. However, the total of instructional minutes annually is the same as that of other schools. This circumstance occurs in highly impacted schools with severe overenrollment.

Question

20. If teachers get paid quite low salaries, are required to teach year-round, and receive the same pay as before the calendar modification,

how will all this work out? Teachers need time off. Usually teachers must spend the first 5 to 7 days of their vacations grading papers and then must return to school approximately 3 days before the new term begins. What about teachers with families who want to take a vacation together for more than 1 week? What is this doing to teacher's lives?

Answer

It is important to understand what year-round education is. Specifically, one of its intents is to reduce summer learning loss, an unfortunate reality for most students. An obvious way to reduce summer learning loss is to reduce summer vacation. Modified-calendar schools reduce, but do not eliminate, summer vacation. However, vacation time not scheduled for the summer is redistributed throughout the year.

Thus, for the most part, students are in school exactly the same number of days, and on vacation the same number of days each year, as before. Since teachers follow the same schedule as their students, teachers have the same number of workdays, redistributed.

A majority of teachers favor balancing the calendar to reduce learning loss. They like the idea of teaching 9 to 12 weeks and then having a 3- to 4-week vacation several times a year. A number of districts and school principals have reported that they have waiting lists of teachers wanting to transfer from traditional to year-round.

The questions raised here may be important, but they revolve around self: *my* workload, *my* pay, *my* family life, *my* vacation. Any recognition in the question of what's best for students and their learning is sparse. Education's foremost client is the student, and what's best for students is what a teaching staff should aspire to. Obviously, teacher concerns have to be considered, but the needs of students are paramount.

The public at large understands that teachers are required to work with students only 180 days out of each year's 365, fewer than half of the days. Thus, the public generally thinks of teachers as not working a full year. Most teachers, of course, know that there are actually more teaching and student contact days involved than 180 and think of themselves as at work most of the year. However, other community workers are also in jobs requiring extra time and overtime, sometimes for 48 to 50 weeks a year.

The public at large too often perceives educators as never satisfied with their job circumstances. Educators often talk about hard work and low salaries. The talk falls on deaf ears because most employees feel they are overworked and underpaid.

Education is a noble profession designed to improve the lives of students. It is a privilege and opportunity given to us by the public.

SAVINGS/COSTS

Question

1. What are the savings and costs that modified-calendar, year-round schools place on the annual budget when compared to the costs of the traditional school calendar?

Answer

There are three strands of year-round education, and cost analyses are different for each. A capsule comparison of each strand follows:

1. *Single-track* modified calendars are simply a rearrangement of the instructional days required by the state legislature. Teacher and administrator contracts ordinarily remain the same, or nearly the same, as before. The number of student instructional days will remain the same. So the costs should be the same, or nearly the same, as those in a traditional year school. There may be a very minor uptick in costs in a district with but one stand-alone, single-track, modified-calendar school among many without calendar change. Often the slight uptick is charged solely to the alternative school, an accounting position not supported by all scholars of the matter.
2. *Multi-track* year-round education is designed to provide additional classroom space within existing facilities to relieve overcrowding, or to free rooms for other purposes. There are a number of reliable cost-saving studies on multi-track, and all

indicate that multi-track represents a very significant savings to the community, especially in terms of cost avoidance. When multi-track is implemented, there is less need to build costly new buildings, campuses, or additions. If new construction is avoided, then site preparation costs, bonded indebtedness, and operational costs of new buildings (not built) are also avoided. Multi-track can save a community multi-millions of dollars, or postpone the costs until a more favorable economic climate is present.

3. *Extended year* actually lengthens the instructional year. Students attend from 200 to 240 instructional days annually, rather than the usual 170 to 180 days mandated by most state legislatures. Obviously, it is going to cost more to have an extended year, since teachers and other staff work a 12-month, rather than a 10-month, year. However, the additional costs will be largely in the form of salaries, not benefits, since benefits are already paid on an annual basis.

There are multiple variables and nuances within each of the three strands outlined above. Each of these variables/nuances may affect the budget in either a positive or negative way.

Question

2. Doesn't single-track year-round education cost more to operate than the traditional calendar?

Answer

No, not really. Contractual obligations remain the same. Teachers, administrators, and classified staff work the same number of days as before. The schedule has been modified, but the work day/time have not increased. Thus, the single biggest item in any budget, personnel costs, should remain about the same.

Utility costs should likewise remain pretty much the same. While a modified calendar changes the schedule to include instruction in all four seasons, the total costs of educating in both warmer or cooler seasons will ordinarily be a wash, absent extraordinarily long hot or cold spells.

Transportation costs will remain the same, since school is in session exactly the same number of days as before. Food service costs will remain the same.

A handful of local studies have made the claim that single-track is more expensive. In every such study, however, a close examination revealed that the local district added a feature to the program that was not necessarily year-round education related, but the cost had incorrectly been charged to the costs of the year-round program.

The biggest error some districts make in calculating costs is to incorrectly charge all additional costs of a dual-track program (an option is given to parents to choose between a single-track year-round calendar or a traditional calendar) to year-round education. While offering dual calendar options do raise costs slightly, these additional costs must be shared proportionally by both the traditional and year-round calendars, since both share the benefits and both cause the costs. Many districts incorrectly shift all of the additional costs of dual-track onto year-round education.

Question

3. What is the financial support for intersession programs?

Answer

Intersessions are paid for in the same way as summer school, since intersessions are summer vacation (summer school) rescheduled. Intersessions are ruled by the same financial, educational, and legal considerations as summer school in a traditional-calendar setting. Many balanced calendar schools have developed innovative ways of supplementing the instructional year with intersession programs. Many have used categorical funds, from Title I to gifted and talented funding, to support intersessions. Parent and community groups and individuals have volunteered time to teach intersession classes, discretionary tutorial funds are used to meet special needs, and fee-based programs are also utilized in states that allow them. The opportunity to strengthen student learning throughout the school year often leads to new and creative ways to benefit student learning.

Question

4. What is the savings/cost break-even point for multi-track year-round education?

Answer

There is no precise break-even point, but from school district implementation reports and cost studies, a reasonable estimation can be obtained.

Most schools implement multi-track to reduce overcrowding and to increase the school's capacity within existing facilities. From studies conducted on the savings/costs of multi-track year-round education, it has been determined that the financial break-even point is usually in the 112% to 116% range of rated capacity, while the point at which multi-track clearly saves a district money begins at around 116% of the school's rated capacity. If a school's degree of overcrowding is below 112% of rated capacity, it may be cheaper to utilize temporary classrooms to handle the slight overcrowding.

While the break-even point is around 112% to 116% of rated capacity, and the savings clearly begin at around 116%, it is important to recognize that there are local determinants that may change these percentages slightly, such as school size, age of school, number of specially designated rooms, architectural plan, and the like.

Question

5. Is multi-track a "temporary" solution to overcrowding?

Answer

Multi-track year-round education is implemented to provide additional space and to relieve overcrowding. Usually, it is implemented on a temporary basis. However, temporary can mean a year in one community or a few years in another. Temporary has meaning when compared to the usual life of a school building, which is pegged at 30 or more years.

RESEARCH/HISTORY/RATIONALE

Question

1. What criteria should a school have to meet in order to be considered year-round?

Answer

By definition, a year-round school is one that has altered the school year substantially so that the long summer vacation of the traditional calendar is reduced. The NAYRE has arbitrarily drawn the outer limit of summer vacation at 8 weeks for a school to be included in its national directory of year-round schools. However, heeding the research data about summer learning loss, NAYRE's recommended outer limit of summer vacation is 6 weeks.

Question

2. Schools that have modified their calendars may also have modified other aspects of the curriculum. Can year-round education be factored out as being responsible for any academic gains?

Answer

It's difficult to interpret academic gains as being the result of any single action or activity in a school or district. While educational researchers try to isolate a variable (for example, a modified calendar) and hold constant other factors in order to evaluate the effectiveness of year-round education, it is true that school personnel change, student composition changes, mobility factors rise and fall, priorities in the instructional program come and go, tests change. However, it can be said that similar factors apply to any school, at any time, and in other research endeavors.

Does that mean that school effectiveness cannot be evaluated? Are there not measures by which to judge whether or not a school has achieved and maintained academic gains? If the only significant change is modification of the school calendar, and most everything else remains the same, then generally researchers would ascribe the results to the change, calendar modification.

It should be noted that academic gain, while important, is not the only measure of success for year-round education. Higher teacher and student attendance, reduced staff stress, fewer dropouts, better discipline—all of these have been cited as improved with year-round calendars.

Question

3. Schools say they base their change to a year-round or modified calendar on many factors found within the research. What are those factors and why do they emphasize those particular factors?

Answer

The factors usually emphasized are:

1. summer learning loss, because of the long absence from formal instruction that is a part of the traditional school calendar
2. second language acquisition, which is easier with continuous usage and which is halted by the long summer vacation
3. loss of skills that are improved by regular usage, such as math computation and spelling, two skills not likely to occur over the 10- to 12-week absence from schooling
4. lack of parental/community support of the student for independent learning over the long summer vacation
5. lack of community resources for students living in impoverished neighborhoods to grow academically and emotionally over the long summer
6. reduced rate of dropping out of school on the part of secondary students in year-round high schools

Question

4. Are there any data demonstrating that year-round education improves learning?

Answer

Yes, there is written documentation about year-round education and achievement. Chapter 5 has a full discussion of achievement in modified-calendar schools.

Question

5. Are there any data that modifying the school calendar lowers the crime rate?

Answer

No, there are not compiled data on a lowered crime rate, though we have anecdotal evidence of that. However, there are data on dropout rates at year-round high schools. When compared with traditional calendar schools, the dropout rate for year-round high schools was lower. Since many experts attribute a portion of crime statistics to dropouts, it can be inferred that modified-calendar high schools may help to reduce a community's crime wave.

Question

6. Quotes from *Prisoners of Time* are often used in professional publications. What are the most important quotes from this publication? What is the genesis of *Prisoners of Time* and is it still published?

Answer

There are several thoughtful statements in *Prisoners of Time* that aid in the discussion of time and learning. *Prisoners* was a summary report of the National Education Commission on Time and Learning, published in April 1994. The commission was established by an act of the U.S. Congress. No longer available from the U.S. Government Printing Office, *Prisoners* has been reprinted and is available from the NAYRE, San Diego, California, or Staff Development for Educators, Peterborough, New Hampshire.

The quotes from *Prisoners* cited most frequently are:

1. "Unyielding and relentless, the time available in a uniform six-hour day and a 180-day year is the unacknowledged design flaw in American education."
2. "Our usage of time virtually assures the failure of many students."
3. "(There) is the pretense that because yesterday's calendar was good enough for us, it should be good enough for our children—despite major changes in the larger society."
4. "Our schools and the people involved with them—students, teachers, administrators, parents and staff—are prisoners of time, captives of the school clock and calendar."
5. "The key to liberating learning lies in unlocking time."
6. "The six-hour, 180-day school year should be relegated to museums, an exhibit from our education past."

Question

7. If year-round education is such a great idea, why don't all school districts implement it?

Answer

New ideas take a long time from theory to implementation. Established programs take a long time to give way to new programs. Changing a culture does not happen overnight. There are a variety of examples of how slow change can be.

Democracy is a sound political concept. Democracy's first stirrings occurred at least in the early 13th century. It took another 5 centuries to overtake the idea of divine right of kings and to become well-established in a few countries. Why did it take so long to become established? Answer: there are always powerful forces wanting to maintain the status quo. Consider the world's most populated nation, China, which has not yet experienced democracy. Russia, a major country of the world, has only in the past few years implemented democracy, feeble though it may be. Is democracy therefore not a good idea, given its long history and incomplete acceptance?

Year-round education is a sound concept, even though it may take some time to be fully established. Unfortunately, there are forces that want to maintain the calendar status quo, usually for very limited, personal reasons. However, year-round will someday be very common.

Futurists point out that if indeed the world becomes ever more computer-connected, as it surely will, all education will become year-round, in that students will be able to log into skill-building exercises 24 hours a day, 365 days a year, if they so choose.

Question

8. What percentage of all K–12 students in the United States are enrolled in modified-calendar schools?

Answer

About 4.9% of students in the United States are enrolled in modified-calendar schools. While 4.9% may seem a small percentage to some observers, in context it is larger. At the time of this writing, the number of students enrolled in modified-calendar schools is twice as large as that of the charter school movement; 11 times larger than the Coalition of Essential Schools movement. The 4.9% figure encompasses over 2,000,000 students.

Question

9. Where was the first year-round school in the United States?

Answer

Historically, the first year-round schools appeared in the 1840s. They did not survive. In the 20th century, the first year-round school appeared in Bluffton, Indiana, in 1904, followed over the next 3 decades by a few scattered schools open 12 months, often for the purpose of teaching English quickly to new immigrant children from Europe. All evidence of year-round education had disappeared before the advent of World War II.

In education's modern era (post–World War II), the first year-round school was opened in 1968 at Park Elementary, Hayward, California. It was an extended-year, single-track school, formulated for the purpose of strengthening student learning. The first multi-track in the United States opened the following year, 1969, at Becky-David Elementary School, St. Charles, Missouri. Year-round education in the United States has been continuous since 1968, stretching from coast to coast, into Canada and the Pacific Islands.

From 1968 to the present, the movement to balance the calendar has grown, matured, and organized itself to attain its goal of advancing student learning. Futurists predict that all education will become year-round, since students will receive gradually increasing portions of their class and homework assignments via the Internet, 24 hours a day, 7 days a week and 365 days a year, if they so choose.

Part II

EVALUATING THE PROGRAM

CHAPTER 5

Evaluating the Program and Research Findings

EVALUATION IN EDUCATION

Education is one of the oldest social institutions, yet is often criticized for its short tradition of formal scientific research. There are challenges in the field, for randomized experiments in the educational arena have been controversial and long debated. Consequently, researchers and evaluators in education are quite often left with the option of quasi-experimental research and ex post facto collection of student data.

Comparative measurement on a national scale is difficult as states use different tests and measurement instruments. There is low internal design validity, because there are many extraneous variables in field settings that also influence test scores. Sampling procedures are difficult, and frequently researchers and evaluators must simply use the data available. School districts often need/want findings immediately and length of study is problematic, at best. Often it may be that the implementation of an instructional program is a catalyst for other changes that could impact student achievement. Therefore, due to these often encountered problems/concerns, many maintain that formal experimental designs and inferential data analysis methods should be limited in the field of education (Huberty & Klein, 1996). Given these aforementioned difficulties, descriptive data analysis should/could be utilized instead.

The purpose of *research* is to generate new knowledge or resolve contradictions and inconsistencies in a given body of knowledge. *Evaluation*, on the other hand, is the process of collecting systematic information in order to determine the extent to which educational objectives are actually being realized and to provide answers to significant evaluative questions that are posed. Evaluation is usually initiated to guide and facilitate decision making and to determine effectiveness. It results in a comprehensive description and collection of value statements regarding the various aspects of quality and effectiveness, rendering judgments about the merit or worth of specific educational objects. In short, while research seeks to prove, evaluation seeks to improve.

Although evaluation is not the same as research, the conduct of professional evaluation is usually based on applications of both quantitative and qualitative research methods from the behavioral sciences. Even though the field of research demands experimental design and strict data analysis procedures, evaluation can be stringent as well, given the unit of analysis along with tight controls or matching procedures. The methodology can overlap, and essential activities involving educational research can serve as a basis for program evaluation, by providing an opportunity to subsequently conduct program evaluation. Therefore, in the field of education, in addition to/in lieu of research, school districts increasingly and/or exclusively utilize evaluation. Evaluation, nevertheless, still struggles to gain the status of an independent discipline.

EVALUATING PROGRAMS

Although it is considered one of the youngest fields in education, evaluation within the American educational system has increased since the late 1960s, and even more so because of the mandated federal legislation, No Child Left Behind. The demand has resulted in urgent innovation in schools and higher expectations for performance, which, in turn, resulted in newly implemented offices of research and development, particularly in local school districts.

Program evaluation should be relevant to both the educational system and the life of the school. However, being ranked and either rewarded or sanctioned due to performance results puts high pressure on school districts to maintain/improve that performance. As the political stakes are so important, it is easy to understand why testing has been termed "high stakes" and has become the classic example of winning through intimidation. Although school districts tend to react on the basis of performance, frequently actions do not necessarily lead to improvement or planning processes that generate high-quality decisions or school commitment to implementing change.

The Elementary and Secondary Education Act of 1965 (ESEA) led to a significant shift in focus from students as the objects of educational evaluation to projects, programs, and instructional materials. A major conclusion drawn from recent literature about evaluation objects is the fact that almost everything can be an object of evaluation and should not be limited solely to students or school personnel.

To make evaluation a more insightful and useful tool for education, several principles should be followed at various levels of the process. First, evaluation should be perceived as a process and must be relevant, or stakeholders will lose interest in participating. Second, there must be mutual respect and trust between both parties and an understanding of what is at stake. Finally, both parties should share a sense of joint responsibility for the consequences of the evaluation, especially if both external and internal evaluation is to be utilized.

The relationship between the evaluator and his/her audience should be a two-way relationship and provide a process of mutual learning—in other words, a basis for a dialogue and not just a source of assertive descriptions and authoritative judgments. The evaluator should aspire to become a constructive participant in those dialogues, rather than simply a provider of information. Evaluation has a better opportunity to be utilized by educators if they are involved in its initiation, and are kept informed of its progress by interacting with others throughout the process. Students, teachers, and school administrators should all become active participants in the process, rather than just being passive recipients of descriptions and judgments.

An educational system with a professional conception of teaching will expect its teachers to plan, design, conduct, and evaluate their work, strive to achieve identified goals, and meet defined standards of excellence. In such a system teachers will be perceived as professionals, interested in understanding the problems of their profession, maintaining its standards, and assuring its quality. Teachers will be judged by their portfolios as well as by the standardized test scores of their students. Their districts, to be effective, will have to maintain a consistent focus on currently published educational research, as well as implement program evaluation components based on stringent data collection and analysis procedures.

EVALUATING STUDENT ACADEMIC PERFORMANCE

One of the primary responsibilities of school administrators is to focus on programs that create improvement in learners and demonstrate excellence. And so they turn to/depend upon archival research-based knowledge, normally found in peer-reviewed educational journals, as well as practice-proven research or evaluation reports, in order to help them decide more intelligently about which programs to implement. Although some schools have introduced the year-round calendar program primarily to reflect changing district demographics—in other words, for efficiency or equity purposes—others have modified the calendar to improve the academic performance of students in their schools—in other words, for excellence.

Excellence in student performance is difficult to ascertain in a year-round program, for an issue frequently raised in the literature of year-round education (YRE) has been the sparseness of quality evidence available to synthesize. While the majority of school district reports would be classified as evaluation, relatively few would be considered empirical research. Given the dearth of empirical research, one gathers and reports the best studies/reports published/available, whether considered research or evaluation. But fortunately in the literature base of year-round education it appears that the more recent the reports, the more sophisticated the designs and analyses, and the more positive the findings.

As pointed out previously, quasi-experimental research is generally utilized in the field of education. Although this method allows for the investigation of relationships when true experimental studies are not possible (Borg & Gall, 1989), it does not permit the strength of inference that accompanies random assignment in experimental research. Yet, a matching procedure is most useful in studies where large differences between the two groups are not likely to occur. Sampling errors are reduced by the use of matching, and the small differences that do occur are more likely to be detected (Borg & Gall, 1989).

For example, a study entitled "Evaluating the Achievement of At-Risk Students in Year-Round Education" (Kneese & Knight, 1995) employed an ex post facto, posttest only, control group design with matching. In this study, data were gathered from 10 dual-track schools, meaning that some of the students in the school were on a year-round calendar while others were attending school on a traditional calendar. Of these 10 schools some were classified by the school district as reflecting varying socioeconomic levels—low, middle, or high. The sample included *individual* 4th-, 5th-, and 6th-grade students who had taken reading and math subtests of the Norm-Referenced Assessment Program of Texas (NAPT) in the spring of 1993 and had done so previously in the spring of 1992 as 3rd-, 4th-, or 5th-grade students. From the 3 grades, 311 students from the year-round calendar classes within the dual-calendar schools mentioned previously were *individually* matched on their standard reading and math subtest scores of the NAPT, as well as by gender and ethnicity, if possible, to 311 students on the traditional calendar within the same grades, within the same schools. Students from both calendar classes were exposed to the same curriculum, administered by teachers using identical courses of study adopted by the school district. Students on the year-round calendar were given approximately the same number of days of instruction prior to the administration of the test. Class size was similar and the intersession was not utilized. The year-round comparison group followed a 30/10 year-round calendar, in which 30 days of instruction were followed by 10 days of vacation, except for longer breaks in December and August. The control group classes attended school on the traditional September to June calendar. Numerous other studies in the body of research on year-round education have successfully utilized matching procedures, as well as ANCOVA, a procedure that statistically controls for preexisting differences between groups in comparisons in lieu of matching (see appendix A).

What evidence is needed to define academic performance on a program? One criterion would be repeated consistency of findings and replication of results by other researchers in the field. A research-based consensus should evolve—whether the reports are classified as research or evaluation, whether school district reports or independent research efforts—so as to be able to draw tentative conclusions from the preponderance of evidence. Ideally, performance findings should have been published in refereed (peer-reviewed) educational journals. More and more in educational research, there has been an emphasis on meta-analysis as a way of accumulating data from many studies, combining the performance evidence formally by use of a statistical technique, and thereby synthesizing the findings.

Although measurement of performance—or excellence—is only a part of program evaluation, it should be measured in four ways, according to the Baldridge Award (2004) Criteria for Performance Excellence. First should be a report on current performance. Second should be a cross-sectional (or effectiveness) report of student performance relative to appropriate comparisons. Third, a rate of performance improvement or gains (impact) should be made. And lastly, data should be disaggregated to demonstrate/compare educational improvement by student type.

Effectiveness is defined as substantive change in knowledge or skills, and compares a student's performance to that of a norm group nationally. This comparison is normally over a 1-year time period and referred to as "cross-sectional analysis." Although useful, cross-sectional studies may not provide an accurate representation of effect, as a true increase in achievement probably requires at least 4 years of student exposure to program implementation (Merino, 1983). Because of a possible Hawthorne effect, highs and lows of performance during the first years of program implementation will be found (Kneese, 1996).

A performance report should reflect not only what students know but what they have learned as a result of the program. Therefore, a major determining factor in program evaluation is a report of gain scores, a *longitudinal* report, and, although useful, not simply a 1-year analysis or *cross-sectional* report. This measurement of student performance is termed *impact*—achievement relative to past performance. In other words, impact is defined as the long-term and sustained maintenance and/or improvement of the student performance over time, which is the ultimate goal of measuring student achievement reliably.

For example, some schools/students on the multi-track year-round calendar are initially at low levels of achievement, relative to state standards and national norms, and at levels well below those of other public schools in their communities. The preferred measure of achievement, therefore, should be the multi-year maintenance and/or gain in performance, the measure of change from implementation to present, and not a 1-year comparison unless student data is carefully matched or statistically adjusted. Some researchers concur and report that, by using gain scores as a measure of comparison, year-round education students will perform better than their traditional calendar peers, and for those that report results of year-round education for a period of 4 years or longer demonstrate small but positive gains. Oftentimes, in program evaluation, however, the data is limited to what is available.

Measuring instruments are usually norm-referenced tests, and examples utilized in various states are the Stanford Achievement Test (SAT/9) and Comprehensive Test of Basic Skills (CTBS) and the Iowa Test of Basic Skills (ITBS). In program evaluation, however, it is recommended instead to utilize results from a criterion-referenced test (Popham, 1993), which a school district may not present additionally in a report. Criterion-referenced tests are comparisons between an individual's performance and a defined ability or skill, and are increasingly utilized by states to hold schools accountable. One interprets the test score by determining the percentage correct in the criterion domain that the student can master.

For norm-referenced test results, a criteria of effectiveness must be established in order that judgments can be made in a relatively objective manner. That measure is normally presented as an NCE (normal curve equivalent) score. With the objective of 1 year of gain in 1 year, a student should maintain the same NCE (CTB-McGrawHill, 1976). In other words, from year to year the pretest NCE is the expected posttest NCE. Therefore, any gain of a NCE score from one year to the next is considered an improvement. If one is reporting simply a descriptive report of student performance by NCE scores, one must be careful not to assume that the performance is low or small.

In comparing student performance, however, one may determine a difference in the mean NCE scores of the group in the implemented program to that of a control group. Tests of statistical significance are generally run to determine if there is a difference in performance between the two groups. But the question is—is the difference meaningful? To determine how large or meaningful the difference, one must calculate tests of practical significance (effect size), as well. Effect size analysis reflects the magnitude of the difference between the two groups regardless of the statistical significance. Effect sizes are considered to be small at .2, medium at .5, and large at .8. An effect size of

.33, and at times as small at .25, is generally considered educationally significant (Wolf, 1986).

As mentioned above, both quantitative and qualitative measures should be applied in examining the effectiveness of a program and demonstrating student achievement in the program. In chapter 4 we saw a qualitative component of this review of time and learning. The remainder of this chapter includes presentations of the quantitative research and evaluation findings on student achievement from a perspective of single-track/balanced, multi-track, and extended-year calendars.

THE SINGLE-TRACK/BALANCED CALENDAR

The single-track or balanced calendar is the more common mode of the modified calendars in existence today in North American education. In 2005 the National Association for Year-Round Education (NAYRE) reported that approximately 71% of the modified calendars in use throughout North America were single-track/balanced.

The single-track encompasses a balanced calendar, largely associated with improved learning opportunities, perhaps because it offers a more continuous learning environment for the student. Single-track is normally a cautious first step, usually used at the elementary level and voluntary in effort. The calendar usually consists of 170 to 180 days, equal to that of the traditional calendar, but can have 10 to 12 months of instruction, unlike that of the 9-month traditional calendar. The summer vacation period is rescheduled to be approximately 1.5 to 2.0 months instead of the 3 months of the traditional calendar. Vacation time is interspersed throughout the year into "intersessions," allowing time for immediate remediation, academic enrichment, and/or just vacation time.

There are many single-track/balanced designs available for implementation, as previously detailed in chapter 3, and selected by individual school districts and their stakeholders. All students and teachers follow the same instructional and vacation schedule of the selected design. As compared, however, to the multi-track configuration, it is possible that single-track has a smaller class size and shorter and more frequent intersessions, both of which might be a causal factor in academic performance differences.

This chapter presents findings (both evaluation and research) collected from reports nationwide. The purpose was to determine whether or not students participating in single-track/balanced year-round calendar programs were making adequate academic progress, particularly at-risk students.

Reports from multi-sites are first examined in research syntheses, which includes performance results from all year-round calendars. Next, single-track/balanced studies in the research syntheses are disaggregated and reported. Finally, findings from the most recent single-track statewide evaluation reports are presented.

Meta-Analysis

A meta-analysis by Kneese entitled "Review of Research on Student Learning in Year-Round Education" (1996), published in the *Journal of Research and Development in Education,* was the only known meta-analysis conducted and published on this topic in the 1990s. More recently, one by Cooper, Valentine, Charlton, and Barnett was published in 2003. These have been the only meta-analyses/research syntheses that have interpreted the differences in academic performance between the two types (single-track/balanced and multi-track) of year-round calendars. In the 1980s and early 1990s, there were very few studies available for comparison. Fifteen studies were selected that met strict criteria for inclusion in the Kneese meta-analysis. Subsequently, an effect size was computed for each study reporting mean scores, and then effect sizes were combined across studies.

The weighted overall effect size of the studies, utilizing mean scores, demonstrated a small but positive effect in favor of the year-round calendar. Although there were limited single-track/balanced calendar studies available—Loyd (1991) and Roby (1992)—that met the criteria for inclusion in this study, the result was educationally significant (+.33).

Loyd compared performance of grade 6 students on a single-track (30/10) design to the remaining grade 6 students in the same school on a traditional calendar schedule during the 1989–1990 school year in

Conroe Independent School District in Conroe, Texas. One-year results demonstrated a higher performance in both reading and math for the matched sample of year-round calendar students.

Roby made a comparison of grade 6 students on a single-track (45/15) design to grade 6 students in another school within the West Carrollton School District in Ohio that were on a traditional calendar schedule. Results indicated a higher performance for those on the year-round calendar and male performance was slightly stronger than female.

Research Synthesis

A research synthesis entitled *Year-Round Learning: A Research Synthesis Relating to Student Achievement* (Kneese, 2000a) was published by the NAYRE. The Kneese synthesis updated and expanded two previous syntheses authored by Leslie Six (1993) and Walter Winters (1995).

Individual researcher/evaluation reports on which the 2000 synthesis was based had to meet a set of a priori criteria with respect to methodological adequacy. The specifications for inclusion of any studies in that document were that they had been completed and reported in the 1990s, that the program had been in place for at least 1 year, that there was a reasonable comparison group, and that student achievement was included as a dependent variable, utilizing norm-referenced or criterion-referenced instruments. Studies chosen were of both cross-sectional and longitudinal analyses. For the most part, these specifications were met, although there were a few minor deviations allowed because the study was of general interest.

The studies were from a variety of states including Virginia, Florida, Georgia, Texas, California, Utah, North Carolina, New Jersey, Ohio, and Alabama. Of the 36 studies in the 2000 synthesis, 10 were published in educational journals. Nine were found in Dissertation Abstracts. Several were presented and reviewed at the annual meeting of the American Educational Research Association. Most of the remaining studies were district reports, generally prepared by local school research and development personnel, often as reports to local school boards. Additionally, personal phone calls were made to many districts listed in the membership directory of the NAYRE to seek information regarding achievement data.

From the 36 studies reviewed, 22 studies examining academic performance on the single-track/balanced calendar were subsequently and purposefully disaggregated and reviewed. Seventeen of the 22 studies had been analyzed by inferential statistics. Five more studies had been analyzed by descriptive statistics. The synthesis of sign test findings revealed that results were positive in 54 out of 76 (71%) comparisons, results were negative in 13 out of 76 (17%) comparisons, and 9 (12%) were mixed (see appendix A).

Discussion of Findings

In the studies analyzed by inferential statistics, it is interesting to note that though most of the single-track programs were implemented in elementary schools, one research study was available for review from a high school. While some results were reported by mean scores differences, others were reported in gain scores. The findings were mostly positive in favor of the single-track/balanced calendar, with statistical significance reported in the majority of the studies, as shown in Table 5.1.

In the studies analyzed by descriptive statistics, the findings were generally positive in favor of the single-track/balanced calendar. Although four of the five research reports were from individual school districts, one was from an independent evaluation firm.

One may conclude from this synthesis of research studies that there is an effective maintenance and improvement of the overall academic

Table 5.1. Summary of Vote Count of Positive and Negative Findings in Achievement From Single-Track Year-Round Education Studies Utilizing Inferential Statistics

Effect of Year-Round	Reading	Math	Language	Writing	Total
Positive (+)	20	18	3	2	43
Negative (-)	2	3	2		7
Mixed (+/-)	3	4			7
Level of Significance	.001	.010			.001

(7 results were mixed)

performance of those on the single-track/balanced year-round education program in comparison to those on the traditional calendar.

Meta-Analysis/Research Synthesis

A review entitled "The Effects of Modified School Calendars on Student Achievement and School Community Attitudes: A Research Synthesis" (Cooper et al., 2003) was published in the *Review of Educational Research* and reported the largest body of empirical evidence from multiple national sources, to date, for modified school calendars on both student academic achievement and stakeholder attitudes. Findings revealed, by vote count, that approximately 62% of 58 school districts reported that students in the modified calendar program academically outperformed their counterparts on the traditional calendar schedule.

Additionally, the average weighted effect size for 39 school districts was d = .09 in favor of the overall achievement for students on the modified calendar. Further, Cooper and colleagues found that effect sizes from single-track schools were larger than from multi-track schools and ranged from .17 to .24.

In summary, the researchers reported that the improvement in achievement scores for those on the modified calendar was unlikely to be greater than one tenth of a standard deviation as compared to those on the traditional calendar school. Yet they concluded that the modified calendar program appeared to noticeably improve achievement for disadvantaged students, and that programs more recently implemented were demonstrating considerably improved results.

Statewide and School District Reports of Performance on the Single-Track/Balanced Calendar

Bradley McMillen (2002) of the North Carolina Department of Public Instruction conducted a statewide evaluation of academic achievement in year-round schools. His study compared the academic achievement of students who attended year-round schools and programs during the 1997–1998 school year in North Carolina with their peers on the traditional calendar. McMillen used data of about 350,000 students attending 1,364 schools on a traditional calendar and about 17,000 students attending 106 schools on a modified calendar in a hierarchical linear model analysis. McMillen made comparisons both in schoolwide programs and also in school-within-a-school programs. In the schoolwide analysis, the calendar difference was not statistically significant, but findings favored the students in both math and reading on the modified calendar.

In the school-within-a-school programs, whereby some students in the school are on the year-round calendar while others remain on the traditional calendar, the calendar difference was not statistically significant, but findings in both math and reading favored students on the traditional calendar. The author generated additional regression models in order to examine potential interactions between year-round status and prior achievement, parent educational level, and ethnicity. In the schoolwide data he found significantly higher achievement scores for the lower-achieving students. The relationship was stronger in reading than in math, but the differences were not large (approximately .05 standard deviations).

He also found a small difference favoring Caucasian students in math in the year-round program, compared with their traditional calendar peers. The models for the school-within-a-school yielded no statistically significant interactions. In summary, McMillan stated that the results of this study were fairly consistent with findings from previous studies indicating that achievement of students in year-round schools was equal to that of students in traditional schools and that the year-round calendar may be particularly beneficial for lower-achieving students. He concluded that the effect was too small to be educationally significant, although he admitted that the findings from both single-track and multi-track year-round schools in the study had been commingled. He believed, however, that single-track schools comprised the majority of year-round schools in the state.

Another statewide report was authored by Ann Grooms in 2003 and titled "Study of Year-Round Education in Select Kentucky School Districts." In addition to performance indicators such as student attitudes toward math and reading, dropout rates, attendance, teacher attitudes, and absence rates, student performance data were collected and reported as well. It was reported that the single-track year-round education program appears to have made a difference in mathematics and reading skill acquisition as demonstrated by the Commonwealth Accountability Testing System results over a time period of 1989–1999 through 2001–2002.

A follow-up study was conducted in the fall of 2004 to compare the effect of intersession utilization. Each of the nine Kentucky single-track year-round education school districts included in the original study were matched to traditional or modified-calendar schools with similar demographics in Kentucky, but which had no intersession programs for the students. Tests for the Commonwealth Accountability Testing System were administered for math and reading at the elementary, middle, and high school levels, and performance results indicated that students in the year-round schools exceeded in most cases the performance of their peers in traditional calendar matched schools. For the California Test of Basic Skills, at grades 3, 6, and 9, the select Kentucky year-round school district performance equaled or exceeded that of the traditional calendar matched school district performance in mathematics and reading.

A dissertation authored by Mildred Sexton in 2003 is of particular interest because it is one of the few reports of year-round education at the middle school level. In addition to academic performance, attendance and behavior patterns were compared between the grade 8 single-track year-round students and those on the traditional calendar who had attended the same school for a period of 3 years. The Standards of Learning mean scores of the year-round education students were higher in reading, writing, math, and history than for their peers on the traditional calendar. Ancova results, however, demonstrated no statistically significant differences in year-round education and traditional student attendance nor in the reading, writing, math, history, or science academic performance. Nor were statistically significant differences found in behavior patterns between the two groups.

To summarize, although a school district can fluctuate between multi-track and single-track designs, depending upon the increase or decrease in the student body, the single-track calendar is normally a cautious first step taken by a district, usually at the elementary level and voluntary in effort. The relationship between time spent in school and achievement may be more complex than it appears and certainly can be related to more variables than school schedule alone. In most single-track designs, however, the intersessions are utilized, which may well be a causal factor in increased academic performance. Research on the single-track calendar demonstrates that time can be utilized more effectively and should be spent in the successful completion of learning tasks, where instructional time is not interrupted by lengthy intervals. It may be that a single-track year-round education program is a particularly effective intervention, in particular for the at-risk student in reading, because it sustains student achievement through spaced learning and remedies the retention loss that occurs over the summer in the traditional school calendar.

THE MULTI-TRACK CALENDAR

The implementation of the multi-track calendar is normally precipitated by an immediate need for more physical space in order to alleviate overcrowding. The overcrowding may be temporary (1 to 4 years) or more permanent (5 or more years), due to a fluctuating population of school-age children. While schools operating on the multi-track calendar serve students from all income and academic levels, it is common for them to house the disadvantaged and the academically neediest students of a community due to socioeconomic patterns and factors such as overpopulation in areas of limited housing.

In California there are approximately 1,000 multi-track year-round schools that accommodate over one million students. Half of these students are English language deficient, and the rate of poverty (as measured by AFDC and free and reduced lunch) in these multi-track schools is almost twice the California average (Helfland, 2000). They are staffed by fewer teachers who are fully credentialed and by more teachers with emergency credentials (California Department of Education, 1999). The achievement record of the disadvantaged students in these schools generally begins at low levels relative to state standards and national norms, and at levels below those in comparable public schools in their communities.

And so, the question to be resolved is whether or not the multi-track programs have been effective and successful in maintaining and/or improving student performance over time, and in particular for ESL and/or disadvantaged students. This section's findings were collected from research and evaluation reports nationwide. Results of year-round research/evaluation reports from multi-sites were examined first in research syntheses, which would include performance findings from all year-round calendars. However, only multi-track studies in the research syntheses were disaggregated and reported in this section. Second, statewide and school district findings from the most recent multi-track evaluation/research reports are presented.

Meta-Analysis

In the meta-analysis entitled "Review of Research on Student Learning in Year-Round Education" (Kneese, 1996), it was found that the weighted overall effect size of the studies utilizing mean scores demonstrated a small but positive effect in favor of the year-round calendar. When disaggregating the data, a very small effect size of .08 was determined for the eight multi-track studies. The eight studies utilizing mean scores were Costa, 1987; Gandara and Fish, 1994; Guthrie, 1985; Herman, 1987; Johnson, 1984; Marr, 1989, Van Mondfrans and Moody, 1985; and Van Mondfrans, Moody, and Walters, 1992. There were 3 studies (Kuner-Roth, 1985; Quinlan, George, & Emmett, 1987; Vugrin, 1990) resulting in a negative effect size for all three (−.23), likely due to commingled data from both balanced/single-track and multi-track schools in the districts, a result that might seem surprising only to the uninitiated in research methodology.

As discussed previously, any normal curve equivalent (NCE) gain greater than zero can be considered significant for the program. Results revealed an overall NCE gain of +2.72, with an averaged overall small but positive effect size of +.11. Mean-scaled gain scores were also reported in three of the four studies. By definition, the mean-scaled gain scores were expected to be larger than the NCE gain scores, and the result was +7.39, with an overall positive effect size of +.20.

Although there were limitations in the scope of this 1996 review and in the studies/reports on which it was based, there were several tentative conclusions that could be drawn at that time. The meta-analysis demonstrated that multi-track year-round education has an overall positive, but very small, effect on academic achievement. It is, however, important to note the difference in the Quinlan, George, and Emmett (1987) study between the mean score report (−.59) and the gain score report (+.11), as well as in the Vugrin (1990) study between the mean score report (−.23) and the gain score report (+.11). One must recognize the importance of reporting not just cross-sectional results but also of attempting to report longitudinal results in order to fully understand academic performance. A cross-sectional report of the effects of year-round education on student achievement may not provide an accurate representation of program impact, for a true evaluation of achievement probably requires at least 4 years of program implementation (Merino, 1983; Kneese, 1996).

Research Synthesis

As outlined in the previous section, individual research/evaluation reports on which the synthesis (Kneese, 2000a) was based had to meet a set of a priori criteria with respect to methodological adequacy. The studies were from a variety of states and various sources.

From the 36 studies reviewed in the Kneese research synthesis, 8 studies that solely examined academic performance on the multi-track calendar were subsequently and purposely disaggregated and reviewed. One additional recent study was added, to make a total of nine. The first group of studies had been analyzed by inferential statistics. The second group of five studies had been analyzed by descriptive statistics. The synthesis of sign test findings revealed that results were positive in 19 out of 26 (73%) comparisons, results were negative in 2 out of 26 (8%) comparisons, and 5 (19%) were mixed.

Studies Analyzed by Inferential Statistics

Of the four studies analyzed by inferential statistics (see appendix B), the first was conducted by Dr. Patricia Gandara and Dr. Judy Fish.

1. Dr. Judy Fish and Dr. Patricia Gandara, Palmdale School District, Palmdale, California

This study was an experiment with multiple educational reforms in the context of an extended-year school calendar. Three schools extended their school year to approximately 233 days, utilizing the intersession time. All three schools (grades 1 through 8) were able to demonstrate increases in academic achievement, a high level of parent and teacher satisfaction, and a cost-effective use of existing school facilities. The 60/15 multi-track Orchard Plan resulted in a reduction of class size and utilized team teaching and cooperative learning strategies. Mean scaled scores in both reading and math on the Comprehensive Test of Basic Skills (CTBS) favored year-round education in all three schools. The performance for all year-round education students demonstrated mixed gains, but significant gains for at-risk students were reported.

2. Dr. Bruce Isamu Matsui, Montebello Unified School District, Bell Gardens, California

This study compared grade 8 year-round education students on both balanced and multi-track 45/15 schedules over a period of 8 years to traditional calendar counterparts in the district. Throughout grades 1 through 8, students who attended a year-round education calendar school continuously since grade 1 demonstrated no differences of significance when compared to students who had attended a traditional calendar school since grade 1; nor were differences found when the students had attended a mixed sequence of calendar schedules (some at elementary, some at middle schools) during those 8 years (Matsui, 1990). The researcher found that the results indicated that achievement rates had higher correlations to socioeconomic status (SES) than to school schedules (Matsui, 1990). In other words, he found that SES was highly associated with student achievement and that the student schedules appeared not to adversely effect that association (Matsui, 1990).

3. Dr. Carolyn Shields and Steven Oberg, University of British Columbia, Canada

This study compared the performance of grade 5 elementary students in three multi-track schools to three traditional schools in Utah, matched by SES level. Mean scores on norm-referenced tests (SAT) were analyzed both cross-sectionally and longitudinally. In the first analysis, in 1994, reading scores were found to be significantly higher in multi-track schools. All other differences in all years were found to be non-significant, although the mean scores for year-round education were higher than for traditional schools. In the second analysis, when all scores between 1990 and 1995 were compared with the predicted scores, the year-round performance was greater than for the traditional schools.

4. Dr. Peggy Ann Sorenson, Jordan School District, Sandy, Utah

This study compared grades 4, 5, and 6 of 11 modified 45/15 multi-track year-round schools (172 days of instruction) to that of 11 traditional ones (180 days) in the Jordan School District. Although the year-round schools' scores were higher than traditional schools in each area, no significant difference was found in the main effect for calendar. "This study shows that the year-round education calendar is comparable to the TCS when matched with schools of similar demographics" (Sorenson, 1995, p. 208). However, the interactions of calendar by SES, calendar by grade, and calendar by gender did produce statistically significant differences. "There was evidence to suggest that the lower SES populations benefited most in the year-round calendar" (Sorenson, 1995, p. 92). Chapter 1 year-round education schools also outperformed Chapter 1 traditional schools consistently. The researcher concluded that "there appears to be little evidence to suggest that the eight fewer days of the year-round calendar has adversely affected student achievement" (Sorenson, 1995, p. 92).

Studies Analyzed by Descriptive Statistics

Of the five studies analyzed by descriptive statistics (see appendix B), the first examined is from California.

1. Norman Brekke, Oxnard School District, Oxnard, California

An analysis of the California Assessment Program (CAP) scores representing 9 years of growth in scaled scores for Oxnard School District and the California average indicated that Oxnard's average scores for the subject areas tested in grades 3, 6, and 8 had increased at a rate greater than the California scores in every area except grade 8 reading and history. "While Oxnard continues to fall below the statewide averages, progress has been made through the nine years to close the disparity which existed in the early 1980's. Oxnard's Chapter 1 scores consistently exceeded the statewide averages for those students in every subject area tested" (Brekke, 1992a, p. 8). This was a study of large sample size and one of only a few longitudinal studies of evaluation of year-round education. The multi-track program was mandated systemwide. Additionally, the State of California funded two summer school/intersession programs.

2. William Collins, Mueller Elementary School, Chula Vista District, California

Chula Vista Elementary School District is an urban school district with 31 elementary schools, 20 of which were on traditional calendar at the time of the study. Ten were on a 45/15 balanced calendar. Findings from a 1984–1990 report in the district favored the year-round education students in all instances. In 1990 a multi-track 60/15 (Orchard Plan) school was implemented at Mueller. SAT scores from 1987 (preimplementation) through 1991 (postimplementation) were lower than the district average in all instances. On the other hand, Mueller's gain in math, postimplementation, was 5.2 points higher, while the district average lost 2.8 points. In 1992 Mueller's average on the SAT 8L was 1.7 points higher in math than the district. The intersession was utilized for remediation and enrichment.

3. Dr. Diane Fardig, Dr. Dianne Locker, Orange County Public Schools, Orlando, Florida

This was a formative evaluation designed to provide decision-making information to Orange County Public Schools about three year-round education elementary schools: two multi-track and one balanced calendar. All three were on a 60/15 calendar, with intersessions utilized. Multi-track was implemented at overcrowded schools, and the balanced calendar configuration was implemented at a Chapter 1 school. Surveys, interviews, review of literature, site visits, observation, and achievement data were collected over a period of 4 years. The SAT-8 was administered to grades 2 through 5 during 1990–1992. Cross-sectional analysis of the scores revealed an overall positive change from 1990–1994, although negative from 1990–1992, and positive again in 1992–1993. Cross-sectional means that students tested in one year are a different group than those tested in the next year. On the other hand, longitudinal cohort analysis (same group) revealed the total change on the tests was positive from 1990–1991, negative from 1991–1992, and positive from 1992–1993. Average year-round education test scores were higher than the average test scores for district grades 2 and 4. There was reported a dip in scores in the third year of implementation, referred to as a Hawthorne effect.

4. Bethany Prohm and Nancy Baenen of Wake County Evaluation and Research Department, Wake County Public Schools, North Carolina

Schools had to have implemented year-round education for 3 years to have been in this multi-track study. Attendance at these multi-track year-round education schools was not mandated, but voluntary. The year-round schools had the same number of instructional days as the traditional calendar schools. For descriptive analyses the researchers did a comparison of scale score change and effectiveness index. Findings were that generally student achievement at three multi-track elementary schools was above Wake County Public School System's average and at expected levels relative to achievement of similar students at other schools in the system. Other positive outcomes were that attendance at multi-track schools was higher than system averages and staff and parent attitudes were positive and higher than system averages. This district had a balanced calendar school, but those findings were not included in this study.

5. Dr. Sue Shook, Soccoro Independent School District, El Paso, Texas

This was a district-level year-round education study committee report for Soccorro independent school district (ISD), 1995. In 1993 the entire district went year-round due to overcrowding. The district's student body was almost 90% Hispanic and more than 70% economically disadvantaged. In 1996, five campuses were on the single-track/balanced calendar (three elementary schools and two high schools) and the remainder operated multi-track. The AEIS—Academic Excellence Indicator System of Texas—revealed the following for the district: test scores demonstrated gains in reading grades 3 through 8, math grades 3 through 6, and writing at all grades tested; test scores exceeded state and regional averages in grade 4 reading, writing, and math, and grade 5 reading; all minority group scores improved in all areas of testing at grades 3 through 8 and 10. Based on the 1996 Texas Accountability rating system, all of the district schools met the standards defined as "acceptable," and four exceeded this minimum standard and were identified as "recognized," with one receiving the top recognition of "exemplary." The academic report from each school, whether multi-track or balanced calendar, was published as percent mastery.

In the first analysis, studies analyzed by inferential statistics, the Gandara and Fish (1994) study produced a greater positive effect, which would have been expected, in that the program was implemented for purposes of reform, and there were additional instructional days in the calendar. In two of the three inferential studies there was evidence that the lower SES populations benefited from participation in the year-round calendar.

In the second analysis, studies analyzed by descriptive statistics, the findings were generally positive in all instances in favor of the students attending the multi-track year-round education schools. The findings suggest that the implementation of multi-track year-round education to manage overenrollment and to achieve the potential of cost savings does not affect student achievement adversely. While in some instances multi-track year-round education students were producing approximately the same scores as those on the traditional calendar, they were making better gains. Especially of interest are the districtwide programs such as those of Oxnard School District and Soccorro Independent School District and their findings, rather than a simple comparison of one multi-track year-round school to a traditional calendar school. In these two studies the multi-track year-round programs were found to be especially effective for the economically disadvantaged and Chapter 1 (or Title 1) students.

Meta-Analysis/Research Synthesis

In a review entitled "The Effects of Modified School Calendar on Student Achievement and School Community Attitudes: A Research Synthesis" (Cooper et al., 2003) findings revealed, by vote count, that approximately 62% of 58 school districts reported that students in the modified calendar program academically outperformed their counterparts on the traditional calendar schedule. By disaggregating the data, Cooper's team found that effect sizes from single-track schools were larger than from multi-track schools. The multi-track effect sizes ranged from −.02 to .06, and were minimal. The team noted that there should be little reason to expect that the findings from the two calendars would be different, but did speculate that perhaps multi-tracking adds some uncertainty to school life, which might possibly contribute to the differences found.

Statewide and Districtwide Reports of Performance on the Multi-Track Calendar

The most recent reports have concentrated on achievement differences *within* the multi-track configuration, mainly in California, disaggregating the findings *by design* and *by track*. All California public schools are now ranked based on their Academic Performance Index (API). Schools are ranked first on the basis of their API alone and then divided into decile groupings. Subsequently, schools are required by the Public Schools Accountability Act to be ranked by percent of shared characteristics, such as ethnicity, socioeconomic status as measured by eligibility for reduced or free lunch, teacher credentials, number of English learners, student mobility, class size, and whether the school has a multi-track year-round program. Thus, a new decile ranking for comparison purposes is formed for each school and is called the School Characteristics Index (SCI) (White & Cantrell, 2002).

Stenvall and Stenvall (2001) analyzed California statewide achievement data from 1999 through 2000. The focus of the study, according to the authors, was to assess and interpret school performance based on the newly mandated California ranking by Academic Performance Index (API). The purpose was to determine a minimum expected performance gain of 5% annually from its 1999 base for elementary, middle, and high schools in California districts, and particularly by track differentiation. It was initially determined by multiple regression analyses that all students in modified calendar schools had lower achievement test scores than their peers in regular traditional calendar schools. The researchers suggested that, given higher percentages of limited English proficiency or low SES students in modified calendar schools, lower scores would be expected.

Results by gain scores, however, from 1999 to 2000, demonstrated "that year-round education calendars make a positive difference in raising API scores compared to traditional calendar schools" (Stenvall & Stenvall, 2001, p. 6), although the findings were mixed. At the elementary level, both traditional and modified calendar schools, including single-track and multi-track (three-, four-, and five-track), exceeded the expected performance gain of 5%. For middle schools, the traditional calendar schools did not meet the expected goal, and only the multi-track three-track configuration surpassed that 5% expected gain. At the high school level, the traditional calendar students demonstrated the smallest gain, with the single-track modified calendar students demonstrating the largest gain, and exceeding expectations.

A report published by the Office of Testing and Evaluation, Lodi Unified School District, California, on their Concept 6 (three-track) multi-track schools, was available for examination and was titled "STAR 2002, Results by School." Fifteen of the district elementary schools and one middle school had been on the three-track multi-track year-round calendar. It is important to note that approximately one third of the student population of the multi-track school participation was categorized as compensatory education and limited English proficiency, with an expected initial low academic performance.

A comparison was made between the Concept 6 multi-track school performance in the district to the results of the schools districtwide. The percentile rank of the mean normal curve equivalent score (NCE) was reported. This indicates the performance of a typical student of the group in terms of a percentile rank. Since percentile ranks cannot be averaged, all the percentile ranks in a group of scores were converted to NCEs. The NCEs were averaged, and the mean was converted back to a percentile rank in the same grade's norm group, which took the test at a comparable time.

By examining the chart it is evident that the multi-track school performance in 2002 was comparable to that of the schools districtwide. As mentioned previously, any gain of a NCE score from one year to the next is considered an improvement. However, "while there is no definitive way to say what rates of gain are good or bad, there are guideposts. Federal programs often ask school improvement initiatives to demonstrate gains against national norms of two normal curve equivalents (NCE's) per year, which translates into roughly three national percentiles" (Edison Schools, 2001, p. 22). The average performance for these Concept 6 schools in math was 13.43 over a 3-year time period, which exceeded that goal. The performance in reading and language, however, did not meet that goal (see appendix B).

Vista Unified School District, California, also reported results of their Concept 6 multi-track schools on the Internet, allowing them to be examined. This school district had a different profile from Lodi Unified, reported above. All elementary and middle schools in the district were on the Concept 6 multi-track calendar and reported no compensatory education participation, but a larger Hispanic population.

Vista's districtwide performance was compared to that of California schools statewide. By examining the chart (see appendix B) it is evident that the 2002 performance of Vista Unified was very comparable to the 2002 performance statewide. Again, like Lodi Unified, the math performance average over a 4-year time period was 16.16, which exceeded the expected goal of 12 (or three percentiles per year). The reading and language performance did not meet the goal, however.

The purpose of a research report by Douglas Mitchell and Ross Mitchell, entitled "Year-Round Education: Student Segregation and Achievement Tracking in Year-Round Schools" (1999), was to examine whether or not multi-track year-round education encouraged segmentation of student achievement and educational opportunities through inter-track differences. They questioned whether or not the multi-track program was uniquely related to student achievement and whether inter-track differences in the program were fully accounted for by other student, classroom, or school factors or whether "the school calendar may be viewed as the potential cause for the differences" (Mitchell & Mitchell, 1999, p. 11).

The Mitchells initially documented that school populations were different between the year-round and traditional-calendar schools and also that there were differences in outcomes in both math and reading. When examining differences by track within the year-round education schools in student composition, teacher resources, and academic attainment, they found the C track in the schools studied to be clearly advantaged, and that the B track had the lowest academic attainment. They attributed track B's lowest academic attainment to a higher proportion of students from lower income and Spanish-speaking, limited-English-proficient status homes.

They then sought to determine whether or not student factors and teacher resources were associated with achievement by calendar. For student factors, they found that "ethnicity explains about 11 percent of the total variation in student performance, revealing a gap of more than 19 NCEs between highest and lowest achieving ethnic group in math and nearly a 14 NCEs gap in reading" (Mitchell & Mitchell, 1999, p. 14). For teacher resources, they found that small but significant increases in student achievement could be attributed to greater teacher experience, education, credentials, and contract status.

Although it was determined that for the year-round calendar and the traditional calendar schools the mean achievement difference was very small, the Mitchells subsequently sought to determine whether or not there were inter-track differences within the year-round program in achievement and if so, whether or not they could be explained by student factors and teacher resources. The C track student achievement was found to be substantially higher than all other tracks, with the B track's being significantly lower. They also determined that student demographic factors accounted for a much larger proportion of achievement variance than did teacher resource factors. They concluded that it was not clear "whether inter-track achievement differences should be viewed as entirely the consequence of the sociopolitical process of student and teacher assignment, or as involving significant educational factors as well. It is possible that initial assignment differences create educational inequalities which 'snowball' into substantial achievement differences" (Mitchell & Mitchell, 1999, p. 27).

Finally, they asked whether or not enrollment in the year-round school, over time, predicted achievement differences across the tracks. By examining gain scores, they found that there was no main effect for number of years in year-round education. Yet it was determined that there was a strong effect for years-by-track, and that time exacerbated these effects. In other words, the longer the students were enrolled in year-round schools, the greater the divergence in performance by track. Those on track C in the examined schools continued to outperform those on other tracks and made more significant gains.

The Mitchells stated that while year-round education track assignment among the schools in this study segregated students by achievement levels, other factors such as socioeconomic status, English language proficiency, prior achievement, attendance regularity, among many others influencing student achievement, may actually be responsible for and further compound initial inter-track differences over time. "It is not clear whether these profound differences should be attributed to year-round education instructional program differences or to migration of students and teachers that concentrate resources and opportunities in the C track" (Mitchell & Mitchell, 1999, p. 25). And they concluded by stating that "it is likely that initial differences are compounded by parents and teacher awareness of track differentials which lead them to exercise their choice options in ways that further exacerbate the initial segregation" (Mitchell & Mitchell, 1999, p. 27).

Los Angeles Unified School District has a long history of achievement data, beginning with "Phase I Study of the Concept 6 Calendar, 1987," continuing with "Phase II Study of the Concept 6 Calendar, 1988," and culminating with two more recent studies on student achievement data that were published in 2001 and 2002 by the Program Evaluation and Research Branch and authored by White and Cantrell (2002). In the springs of 1987 and 1988, two studies were conducted investigating the effects of the Concept 6 multi-track school calendar on educational quality. Those studies reported that Concept 6 schools compared favorably to other multi-track year-round calendar schools and demographically similar one-track traditional calendar schools in terms of student outcomes. The authors state that the latter two studies

(2001 and 2002) were a follow-up to the original ones and that much has changed in the intervening years.

By 2000 almost half of the K–12 students in the Los Angeles Unified School District (LAUSD) attended multi-track year-round schools. Seventeen high schools in the district were multi-track, which amounted to all multi-track high schools but one in the state of California (Helfland, 2000). Each of the LAUSD multi-track high schools enrolled between 3,000 and 5,000 students, with only two thirds of the enrolled students on campus at the same time.

Although multi-tracking allows schools to relieve overcrowding without the need to add facilities, it raises several issues to be considered, one of which is academic differentiation. For efficiency reasons, ESL students (who constitute a large proportion of LAUSD students) have frequently been assigned to the same track, an administrative procedure that closely resembles in nature the academic "tracking" found in traditional high schools. An issue to be resolved in these schools is the accessibility of advanced placement classes to students, irrespective of track assignment.

Another concern is that the multi-track calendar can be organized to enhance social inequalities unless steps are taken to prohibit such inequalities. Parents who are better educated can take advantage of school choice plans if careful enrollment procedures are not introduced. Although most principals try to avoid inequality, it has been reported in some instances that advantaged children are more often enrolled in the more popular C track, which is more convenient, or more desirable, for access to specific programs, or most closely aligned to the traditional September to June calendar.

In their 2001 study, White and Cantrell asked the specific questions 1) Do students exhibit similar achievement gains across all school calendar types? and 2) if not, can these differences be explained by SES or track assignment? Presented in the 2001 report are the 1999 and 2000 NCE scores, analyzed through regression analyses. A residual score was calculated that took into account the students' initial performance level. It is the difference between the students' actual 2000 NCE score and what would have been expected for that student, given the initial 1999 performance.

The researchers found that students did not exhibit similar academic gains across all calendar types: one-track/traditional, and multi-track (three-track and four-track designs). It was found that the one-track traditional demonstrated the highest performance, followed by the four-track design, with the three-track performing the lowest. Subsequently, they found "that school demographics explained a considerable portion of the differences in student achievement gains among calendar types" (White & Cantrell, 2001, p. 4). Finally, disaggregating the data by track and after adjusting for student background characteristics performance, they found B track performance was the lowest in both reading and math, across multi-track calendar types, both three-track and four-track, and across school types, elementary, middle, and high schools.

In 2002 the same authors replicated and extended the prior 2001 study in order to investigate differences in student achievement, across and within school calendars, by student and teacher assignment to calendars and tracks. Analyses indicated that the academic performance on the one-track traditional calendar to be the highest; the three-track the next highest in performance; and the four-track the lowest. The researchers stated that the differences could be explained by school demographics, and when comparisons were restricted to similar schools, achievement differences were equalized to within half an NCE point of each other. Variation by track was also evidenced. They found that the clearest pattern of performance was that of the A track, which was clearly the highest in both reading and math, which they attributed to the fact that this track had more experienced and fully credentialed teachers, fewer Hispanic and more African American students, fewer English learners, and slightly fewer meal program participants. And so they concluded that it appeared that student achievement differences were more likely due to the opportunities available to students rather than to the calendar type (White & Cantrell, 2002). Recommendations to the district by the authors urged equalization of opportunity by track to the greatest extent possible, if utilizing various school calendars.

Summary

The question is whether or not there are achievement differences in multi-track year-round education, and if so, whether or not these differences are attributable to student background characteristics or to the program itself. As previously mentioned, no matter what the background characteristics of the student, it is the responsibility of the school to provide educational opportunities, which not only have an improved effect on student achievement, but also have the potential for closing the gap between those advantaged and disadvantaged. Program results must demonstrate performance in student learning beyond that which can be attributed to entry level. To be disadvantaged is to be behind academically, but the question is whether or not the program can improve their performance, and if so, how quickly.

Current data analysis utilizing hierarchical linear regression models, although not implying any causal effects (Kubrin, 1996), does demonstrate association and gives us much interesting information heretofore unknown. From a performance of 1 year only the researchers can estimate expected gains due to extraneous factors. "The most common estimator of school performance uses the predicted mean outcome for each school based on the background and prior ability of students in that school" (Byrk & Raudenbush, 1992, p. 123). "Yet one can never be absolutely sure that all variables have been identified and controlled" (Byrk & Raudenbush, 1992, p. 126).

Much of this recent research utilized cross-sectional analysis, resulting in mixed findings and a fluctuating performance, which would be expected from one year to the next. For example, for *between track performance* Mitchell (2002) found the academic performance by state rank on the single-track year-round education calendar the highest, with the multi-track (other than Concept 6, or three-track) the next highest in performance, with the Concept 6 (or three-track) being the lowest. In 2002 White and Cantrell, on the other hand, found that "three-track schools have a positive effect on student reading performance in elementary schools" (White & Cantrell, 2002, p. 9).

Mitchell (2002) stated that "the Concept 6 MT [multi-track] calendar defines an educational environment that experiences greater academic disadvantages than other multi-track year-round calendars and may be contributing to the continued degradation of educational opportunity by the consolidation of difference through the calendar itself"(p. 30). Mitchell's view may not be sustainable, however, because average academic background, level of support/expectation, parental efficacy, and community environment are likely differential attributes that exist for these students and that the educational system cannot affect.

Conflicting findings were found, as well, for *within track performance* (A, B, C, D). Findings from White and Cantrell and the Mitchells have documented that student groups are segmented and teacher resources unevenly distributed across tracks. Their analyses suggest that there are differences within calendars and across tracks that explain differences in student performance. Mitchell and Mitchell (1999) found the B track to be the lowest-performing track in the school studies. On the other hand, they found the C track achievement to be substantially higher than all other tracks, while White and Cantrell (2002) in their study found the A track performance to be higher.

To date, multi-track year-round education has been an efficient and readily available solution for the dual problems of underfunding and overcrowding of the educational system nationwide. Furthermore, it may be that the multi-track program remedies the very academic deficiencies that exist for the disadvantaged student on the traditional calendar configuration. The purpose of multi-track year-round education is efficiency—to address pressing educational management issues. The implementation of multi-track is *because of* certain factors and not a *cause of* inequitable disadvantage for a certain population. Some deficiencies, unfortunately, may be attributed to improper and/or careless program implementation of the multi-track calendar on top of additional and seemingly unsurmountable preexisting problems.

As for excellence, albeit it a very small effect (nominal), there is recent evidence of improved student performance on the multi-track year-round calendar, particularly for the disadvantaged. Small accumulating gains over time are worthwhile, considering other benefits of the multi-track calendar, as well. According to Levin (1984), as quoted in Aronson, Zimmerman, and Carlos (1998), the increase of time in the educational endeavor appears to result in only modest achievement gains in the short term, yet the cumulative impact of increased time might be considerable. Given the situation under which many educational systems are now operating—severe overcrowding, a large population of non-English-speaking students with likely low SES status and a history of low academic performance, coupled with a shortage of credentialed bilingual teachers—it may be, as Shields and Oberg (2000) have stated: the multi-track calendar, if carefully implemented, has the potential to be an educationally sound reform innovation.

Certainly it can be assumed that other reform initiatives would be/have been utilized in conjunction with the multi-track program, and so it is difficult to claim improved performance, in and by itself, because of specific calendar configuration. Although much continued research is needed, the results demonstrated thus far seem promising for the implementation of multi-track year-round education as an appropriate choice for a public school system faced with difficult realities and increasingly limited resources.

THE EXTENDED-YEAR CALENDAR

Many creative efforts are currently underway in the educational reform movement to extend time in American schools. Richard Riley, former U.S. secretary of education, has stated that there will be continued pressure on school districts to keep their schools open later and longer due to commitment for higher standards of academic performance and issues of accountability. The Southern Illinois University Public Policy Institute in 2001 recommended that legislative bodies, school boards, school administrators, and teacher organizations in all states provide support for modernizing the school calendar, and additionally to create a full-time professional body of teachers. The Institute further urged Congress to provide $900 million a year to schools that reorganize the traditional school calendar by having no more than an 8-week summer break and by redistributing the vacation time to shorter recesses between academic terms that can be used for enrichment opportunities, remediation, and professional development and/or by lengthening the school year to include at least 200 days (Southern Illinois University, 2001).

In many industrialized countries throughout the world the school day lasts up to 8 hours of education daily, 220 days a year. Various states within the United States, however, typically offer 6 hours of education daily, 180 days a year. If change from the traditional American school calendar is forthcoming, possible models are the modified calendar and the extended-year calendar. The extended school year is defined as one in which there is the equivalent of 200 or more instructional days per year mandated for all students, while the modified calendar generally includes the same instructional year of 180 days, but structured with short breaks interspersed throughout the year. These breaks (or intersessions) may be utilized for remediation or enrichment; however, they are likely optional for a small subgroup of the school population and rarely mandated for all students. Therefore, one cannot definitively characterize the modified calendar as being extended, unless the intersession day is a full-day program.

Proponents of the modified calendar recommend shortening the lengthy summer break to reduce summer learning loss. Although research demonstrates that there is a positive but very small effect of the modified calendar on student academic performance, there has been a paucity of research on the academic effect of the extended-year calendar. Therefore, in this section various types of extended-year efforts throughout the United States were identified and described, and findings of student performance in extended-year calendar schools are examined and reported.

The first step in the methodology was to locate extended-year schools nationwide. A broad-based search was conducted from the Internet, nationwide phone calls, the directory of the NAYRE, and the directory of National Charter Schools from the Center for Education Reform. In the United States, 235 schools that have an extended-year calendar were located.

It was subsequently determined that a majority (136 of the 235 extended-year schools) were Edison Schools, managed professionally, and the achievement data for Edison Schools was downloaded from the Internet. Two extended-year schools were subsequently randomly selected from the Edison Schools, one from each type: school district charter or independent charter. One more school was randomly selected from the population of other state charter schools. The remaining extended-year schools were from either public school districts or private schools. Two schools were randomly selected from public school districts, and one from the population of private schools. Requests for achievement data, normally published annual reports, were made by personal phone calls to the research department or principal of the randomly selected schools.

Student achievement can be measured in two ways. One way is relative to national standards or norms, which compare an individual's performance to that of a norm group nationally. Norm-referenced test results, such as the Stanford Achievement Test (SAT/9), the Comprehensive Test of Basic Skills (CTBS), and the Iowa Test of Basic Skills (ITBS), were utilized by the various schools in this study. A second way to measure student performance is relative to past performance—in other words, the improvement of the student performance over time. Results over time is the preferred determinant of measuring student achievement; consequently, multi-year gain scores, the measure of change from pretest to posttest, should be examined over a period of several years in order to evaluate the maintenance and improvement of performance.

How, then, does one define that measure? The percentile rank may be reported, which indicates the relative standing of a student in comparison with other students. In some cases the national percentile rank of the mean normal curve equivalent score (NCE) is reported. This is an indicator of the performance of the typical student in the group in terms of percentile rank. Since percentile ranks cannot be averaged, all the percentile ranks in a group of scores are converted to NCEs, the NCEs are averaged, and the mean is converted back to a percentile rank for those students in the same grade of those in the norm group who took the test at a comparable time.

In some instances schools have reported results from criterion-referenced tests. When criterion-referenced data was available, it was reported but not analyzed for the purpose of this study.

Models of Extended-Year Schools (See Appendix C)

Public and Private Schools—Nonprofit

School 1 was a randomly selected sample from the population of extended-year schools in a public school district located in a major city in the central U.S. Four of the district's elementary schools are engaged in an extended school year program, which encompasses 200 days for the school year for students and 220 days for teachers. These four schools have the same curriculum to be covered as the other elementary schools in the district, but the structure of the day, the number of days, and time spent in areas of difficulty have been reorganized for more effective student achievement. This school district has earned a national reputation as an innovative educational leader and works continually to provide the highest quality instructional program for their students.

School 2 was randomly selected from the population of extended-year schools and is located in a major city in the Southwest. This public school district operated eight campuses in the Elementary Schools Initiative (ESI) during 2000–2001. Each campus offered an extended instructional year of 200 days for students and 212 days for teachers, as well as after-school programs. The goals of ESI were to increase student achievement and to provide timely remediation and enrichment. Six of the eight schools received $104,000 above their usual Title I allotment for funding purposes. School 2 has been a member of the ESI project since the 1996–1997 school year. By the year 1999–2000, School 2 had moved from a rating of acceptable to exemplary in the state accountability system.

School 3 was randomly selected as an example of a private school with an extended-year calendar. Private schools are responsible to the parents who choose and support them by tuition. School 3, located in the West, is a private, non-profit, independent day school, with a mission to educate the whole child through a developmentally responsive, arts-enriched curriculum. School 3 offers the only year-round, truly diverse program for preschool through middle school students in the urban area. It operates 240 days of the year. The school is closed for 2 weeks in December and 1 week in August, as well as for holidays and teacher training day. Parents may take students out of school at almost anytime to accommodate family vacations, special events, and extra-curricular activities. Average student attendance is 210 days. In addition, an enriched after-school program, guided by staff who also work with the students in the classroom, is available until 6:00 p.m.

Charter Schools—Managed for Profit

Charter schools are public schools of choice that operate with freedom from many of the regulations that apply to traditional public schools. The charter established in each school is a performance contract detailing the school's mission, program, goals, students served, methods of assessment, and accountability measures. Charter school laws have been passed in more than 36 states and the District of Columbia, and more than 2,000 public charter schools have opened. Charter schools are accountable to their sponsor—usually a state or local school board—to produce positive academic results and adhere to the charter contract. The basic concept of charter schools is that they exercise increased autonomy in return for accountability to the sponsor, the parents who choose them, and the public that funds them. Charter schools set their own schedules and about one of five report extended day or year schedules (Center for Education Reform, 2005).

Some charter schools are regular public schools that opted out of the school district regulations, some are run by non-profit organizations, parents, or teachers. Fewer than 10% of charters are managed by for-profit organizations, such as Edison. Yet in the 2001–2002 school year, Edison, the nation's largest private provider of public education, operated 136 public schools in 53 cities and 22 states, with the specific goal of raising student achievement. Roughly one third of Edison's schools are charters, some to independent charter boards and some to local school districts. The other two thirds have a direct contract with school districts. Eighty-four percent of Edison schools are achieving at higher levels now than when they opened. On norm-referenced tests, Edison schools have, from 1995–2001, increased the national percentile rank of students by an average of five percentiles every year. This record has occurred even while the students served in Edison's schools have become more disadvantaged and have increased in percentages of students for whom achievement has traditionally lagged (Edison Schools, 2001). Randomly selected, an example of a district charter is *School 4*, located in the West, with an extended-year program of 210 student days. An example of an independent charter is *School 5* which has an extended-year program of 200 student days and is located in the East.

School 6 is another example of a district charter school and is located in the North. This school is an elementary school located in an urban neighborhood and serving a student population largely representative of the mix of students in the city public schools, the sponsor for this charter. In 2000–2001 the school added grade 6, after operating for 4 years as a K–5 school. It operates year-round with an extended number of days: 206 in 1999–2000 and 223 in 2000–2001. The main distinguishing characteristic of School 6 is that it places an emphasis on active learning and individual needs of the students and families. School 6 is professionally managed by Designs for Learning, in the business of educational change since 1987. Founded on the Community Learning Centers model, this firm was created by Minnesota educator Wayne Jennings in response to a request from New American Schools Development Corporation for bold new designs for American Education.

Findings

The purpose of this research was to examine efforts on increasing quantity of time spent (i.e., extending learning), across the nation. Most of the schools that have opted for an extended-year calendar have a history of low levels of achievement. This is the challenge: If these schools/students are at low levels initially relative to state standards and national norms, and at levels well below those of other public schools in their communities, then the appropriate measure of achievement is the multi-year gain in performance. And so, to examine the performance of the schools on the extended-day/year calendar the appropriate measure of achievement is not the level of achievement at one point in time (cross-sectionally), but improvement over time (longitudinally). From the results of the randomly selected extended-year schools, at the end of the 2000–2001 school year, five of the six schools were achieving at levels above the initial achievement point where they started. The clear majority of extended-year schools have improved their student achievement, as shown in Table 5.2.

With the objective of one year of gain in one year, a student should maintain the same percentile/NCE. In other words, from year to year the pretest percentile/NCE is the expected posttest percentile/NCE. Therefore, any gain of a NCE score from one year to the next is considered an improvement. For example, School 1 has increased its average NCE score on the Terra Nova from 39.33 in 1998 to 58.83 in 2001. These accumulating gains are the best way to evaluate the performance of schools. School 3, on the other hand, began with high performance,

Table 5.2. Performance Summary of Extended-Year Schools

Schools	Percentile Rank Gain	Years
School 1	19	4
School 2	17	2
School 3	4	4
School 4	13	3
School 5	18	3
School 6	-13	2

and as such beyond which would be more difficult to extend significant growth. School 6 is one with very low student achievement, including a very high percentage of special education and limited English students in its profile. For this school, perhaps gains will be quite slow and difficult to achieve, as well (see appendix C).

In summary, these six extended-year schools, using norm-referenced tests—tests that gauge the achievement of students relative to their peers nationwide—have increased the national percentile rank of their students by an average gain of 10 percentile points over an average time period of 3 years. Four of these extended-year schools are achieving at higher levels now than when they opened. One has gained minimally. One is down materially. Although it is difficult to define what rate of gain is good or negligible, guidelines from federal programs usually require school improvement initiatives to demonstrate gains, compared to national norms, of two NCEs per year, which translates into roughly three national percentiles. The average performance result of the six randomly selected extended-year schools is within that range. This achievement record has occurred while the students served are quite disadvantaged and are typically the academically neediest students in every community. These students generally begin at low levels, relative to state standards and national norms, and at levels well below those of other public schools in their communities. And so, these schools have been extending the school year, hoping to give these students an extra advantage toward meeting achievement standards.

The goal of school reform is to help students learn. In order to attain the standards that America holds for the student of the future, students need to learn more. More likely than not, if students need to learn more, more time will be needed to learn. Although some report that quality of time spent is more important than quantity of time spent (Aronson, Zimmerman, & Carlos, 1998), it is not a question of either/or, for both are necessary in the schema of school reform. Experiments in creative calendar change (quantity of time) should be considered as a primary step in the restructuring of the educational system; then quality of time can best be explored by layering educational reforms atop.

CHAPTER 6

A Dialogue for School Reform

POLICY IMPLICATIONS

A good map shows where one is, has come from, and is going. It provides a broad context. In the first part of this chapter, the context of the entire educational system is visualized. Current issues in the educational system are reviewed, including growth in the school system due to changing dynamics.

School System Growth Because of Changing Dynamics

In trying to understand current educational issues, educational leaders and the public must consider the impact of demographic factors, which include increases and decreases in student enrollment, the mobility of students/families, and the diversity of the students who attend our schools.

One in eight Americans has been born in another country. Nearly two thirds of the world's immigration is into the United States, 50% of which is flowing into the state of California. Immigrants to the United States are coming from nations closest to our borders and from those that are among the poorest. Since 1960 seven million immigrants have relocated to the United States from Mexico alone (Tarrance, 2000). By 2003 Hispanics represented 13.7% of the nation's population, making them the nation's largest racial or ethnic minority (U.S. Census Bureau, 2004).

Hispanics tend to be concentrated in a limited number of population centers and outnumber African Americans in several large U.S. cities: Los Angeles, Houston, Phoenix, San Antonio, and New York City. Approximately 90% of the U.S. Hispanic population is concentrated in nine states, with California having the highest percentage of population, followed by New York, Texas, and Florida (Tarrance, 2000).

The North American population, including both the United States and Canada, is projected to grow to only 330 million by the middle of the 21st century. Mexico, on the other hand, is projected to grow from today's population of 100 million to nearly 200 million in the same time period, while the entire region of Latin America is to increase to 1 billion in population (the size of China or India today). Thus, the United States will have an exploding population pressing against its southern border in a few decades. This enormous population may well—and some say inevitably—migrate northward, substantially increasing the already surging U.S. Hispanic population. Therefore, the area stretching from Mexico northward and anchored by Los Angeles, Phoenix, Albuquerque, San Antonio, Austin, and Houston may well be termed Mexamerica (Tarrance, 2000).

In many American schools those classified previously as minorities are today the majority. Recent high birth rates and immigration have increased Hispanic school enrollment nationally to 7.5 million, as compared to 8 million African Americans and 2 million Asians. Hispanics are likely to live in segregated neighborhoods, with high population concentrations in metropolitan areas in a few states. Their dropout rate from schooling is also higher than that of any other racial/ethnic group.

The young Hispanic population in the United States largely represents the nation's future workforce, which means that access to educational opportunities is crucial to the economic status of the Hispanic community, the economy of the entire nation, and a workforce qualified to generate quality results and products. Additionally, because high school graduation percentages for the Hispanic population are well below other racial/ethnic subgroups, a lower achievement level overall is plausible, most likely due to English-language deficiency. Therefore, school effectiveness, such as quality and range of educational experiences available to these students, is a more significant issue.

For the educational system, what does this anticipated growth portend? Surrounded by fast-growing communities, many school districts in the United States, led by those in California, have faced, or will face, a recurring problem of overcrowding. The U. S. Department of Education (1999) estimates that in California an additional 1.68 million students will enter classrooms between 1999 and 2009. Further, the growth rate of the student population that is English-language deficient is expected to be 150% or more over the next decade (Boone, 2003).

Overcrowding occurs when the enrollment of a school substantially surpasses the stated student capacity of the school. Thus, overcrowding does not occur simply because of the growth of numbers of enrollees, but rather when the numbers outstrip the capacity of a school to find a seat for each of the students. Ordinarily, a school is considered crowded when capacity is reached, overcrowded when enrollment is 5% to 20% over stated capacity, and severely overcrowded when enrollment soars more than 20% over stated capacity.

When faced with the prospect of overcrowding, decision makers (usually, elected school board members and top level administrators) begin a process of narrowing choices among possible solutions to the problem of overcrowding. Overcrowding is a distinct problem because unfortunate circumstances can arise: 1) limited or tightly spaced seating may not allow all students to sit comfortably during class sessions; and 2) over-capacity enrollment and high daily attendance may impact severely the common areas of the cafeteria, the library, hallways, restrooms, locker areas, and similar areas. Unfortunate student behaviors increase because stress levels increase as people try to function within intensely crowded areas. An unintentional bump in a crowded school hallway can quickly escalade into a shoving match or worse.

Current Issues in the Educational System

Within the politically defined, academically driven educational system, three major areas of concern are warranted: requirements to meet high standards mandated by legislation, a lack of consensus on time needed to learn, and insufficient and/or inefficient financing.

Firmly established in the public's mind as a major problem facing the public schools is lack of financial support, according to the *36th Annual Phi Delta Kappa/Gallup Poll of the Public's Attitudes Toward the Public Schools* (Rose & Gallup, 2004). Twenty-one percent of the respondents claimed finance as the number one problem. Overcrowding was a second at 10%, and other areas trailed further behind.

Since 2000 the poll has asked the public how improvement in

schooling was expected to come about. Respondents have consistently stated that they expect change in the public schools to come through reforming the existing system. In 2004, 66% chose reform of the existing system, instead of any other alternative.

The federal No Child Left Behind (NCLB) Act was designed to boost improvement of overall student achievement while at the same time diminishing the achievement gap that separates Caucasian students from African American, Hispanic, Asian, and other minority students. Eighty-eight percent (88%) of the poll's respondents say that it is important that the achievement gap be closed and 56% say it is the schools' responsibility. The public supports a variety of strategies as possibilities for closing the gap. More than 90% of respondents support the provision of more instructional time and the strengthening of remedial programs for low-performing students.

The advancement of adequate yearly progress (AYP) will determine the effectiveness of NCLB. The purpose is to identify accurately those schools in need of improvement. As pertains to NCLB strategies, the respondents to the poll do not believe that a single statewide test can give a fair picture of a school, do not believe that testing in math and English only can accurately measure school performance, and prefer offering assistance to students in a school in need of improvement over permitting students to transfer out or to receive tutoring from outside. Respondents are also concerned that the emphasis on English and math will diminish attention given to other subjects (Rose & Gallup, 2004), an interesting opinion in light of America's educational history.

As early as the 1890s, the National Education Agency began a push for broadening the purpose of schools. In 1910 approximately two thirds of a high school's curriculum consisted of academic subjects alone. By 1918 courses such as family life, vocation, and the use of leisure time were added to the basic skills of reading and writing. By 1930 the number of academic subjects of a school's curriculum had decreased to one third of the total.

If subjects are added to the curriculum—including perhaps frivolous ones—where is the time to teach the core academics? It is imperative that schools of the 21st century return to their original focus in education: to teach the academic core curriculum, such as reading, writing, math, science, and history, and doing it well, for all students.

While acknowledging that educational issues should be addressed, the public disagrees strongly on such matters as how our schools should be organized, operated, and financed. Although the core issues include meeting higher standards, money and time required to meet the standards, and the responsibility of school leaders to fix many of education's problems, many might argue that the issue is not a shortage of funds but a poor use of funds. Some may contend that the issue is not quantity but quality of time spent in education. If America, however, needs to close the educational achievement gap while maintaining equity, then states must be advised as to a consensus on reform issues and what constitutes adequate resources to ensure the delivery of high-quality education.

While the previously stated shift in student population is taking place, schools must meet new student performance standards, mandated by such measures as the NCLB program. There is a world of difference, however, between standards and expectations. Raising expectations means that the public believes that students can achieve a higher level of success, whether or not resources are available to ensure those expectations. Raising standards, on the other hand, means setting goals for all students to achieve at a higher level, whether or not realistically achievable, and holding the schools accountable for that expected performance.

The NCLB Act was designed with a standards-based reform agenda, including high academic standards for students to meet, a measure of extra support to assist students to meet the proposed standards, increased accountability for the results of student performance on standardized tests, yet providing flexibility for local schools to determine how these standards would be met. The intent was for Title 1 of the Elementary and Secondary Education Act to provide most of the funding for this federal mandate to ensure better educational opportunities for economically disadvantaged students.

While schools are held accountable for higher student performance, some report that they have been restrained in meeting expectations by a lack of funding for the NCLB Act, which requires testing and accountability systems to be developed. With much of the public believing that state and local taxes are already high and refusing to raise taxes further, many school districts find themselves restricted financially. School boards and superintendents are feeling the negative economic impact of this legislation, for they cannot afford the expenditures nor have the resources that NCLB requires. Furthermore, each state is required by NCLB to adopt specific testing and accountability systems, yet is given little or no guidance in matching these educational standards to a uniform standard across the nation. Therefore, there are very possibly 50 different accountability systems in the 50 states, contributing to a concern of validity and reliability issues in data comparisons.

Funding is a real issue for the U.S. federal government, as it increases its role through legislation such as NCLB. Some educational leaders contend that increased federal involvement must be accompanied by significantly increased financial support, particularly since increased standards and accountability have been imposed on schools without resolving existing issues in the school funding system.

Historically, funding considerations have triggered, to a large extent, a struggle of control between local school boards and state legislatures. Correspondingly, the NCLB has triggered a struggle of control between the states and the federal government. For example, in Texas in 2004 the school funding system was declared unconstitutional by a state district court because of insufficient and inequitable funding. The presiding judge ruled that the current system does not provide enough money for schools charged with meeting higher state and federal standards. He further urged Texas to close the educational achievement gap between those economically advantaged and disadvantaged.

Attorney Michael Boone, involved for many years in Texas school finance reform, is concerned that schools have long been underfunded by the state (McKenzie, 2005). As a possible solution to insufficient funding, he has urged state business leaders to commit to his proposal for tax reform in the Texas school finance system (Boone, 2003). His key principle is to draw increased revenues from a new business tax and reduce current property taxes in order to spread the burden over a larger number of taxpayers and to correct current inequities in the state tax system. Boone (2003) has contended that the underfunding by the state tax system in Texas may well be above $1,000 per student, which would necessitate an increase of $4.2 billion for new state revenues.

Alternatively, there are those who doubt that schools require additional funding. For example, Houston businessman Charles Miller (2005) reports that operational spending for education in Texas has increased by 50% from 1996 through 2003, up to a level of $7,116 per student in Texas, which total was close to that of California in 2003, $7,244 per student. He reports that Texas has one of the largest percentages of student population eligible for free or reduced lunch, yet the state ranks very high in the amount of state and local revenue committed to public education relative to each $1,000 in personal income. Miller believes that public education has some serious structural flaws and that major changes are indicated, starting with an urgent need for financial accountability and efficiency, but not necessarily an increase in funding. Davis and Hayes (1990) also determined, 15 years ago, that Texas school districts were only two thirds as efficient as they could be, due to the amount of money spent on non-classroom activities, administrative personnel, excessive regulatory requirements by the state government, and too many school districts.

Increased funding, in and of itself, does not appear to remedy the educational gap either (Spencer, 2005). If indeed current financial support for the educational system is deemed inefficient, however, then it would be warranted to demand a more robust accounting system and hold schools accountable for the use of taxpayer dollars (Governor's Business Council, 2004). If insufficiency, on the other hand, is deemed to be the issue, a large portion of the funds might well be applied toward a long and severely neglected increase in teacher pay scale in order to attract and retain the most qualified full-time professional educators, a key to quality education. Of course, additional resources would be welcomed, indeed, although it would be wise for states to exercise direct oversight over district expenditures and ensure that new state aid improves educational quality. This was done in Massachusetts, where reforms were specifically directed to curricular standards, time spent in schools, and early childhood programs (Dee & Levine, 2004).

Unfortunately, public education is required to do far more than educate, providing multiple social and extended services, and asked to do more and more with less and less, while encumbered with a structural system in severe disorientation/neglect. Until educational professionals in the system specifically delineate what they intend to deliver efficiently in terms of maximum educational outcomes, along with a decision concerning necessary time warranted for student learning, the legislature cannot determine how to best direct the financing that public education necessitates.

The issue foremost in the context of restructuring the school system is a confirmation on time needed to learn, once a decision is made about what is to be learned. The effect of time as an element in school reform is important, for manipulating time is one way to increase student achievement and to alleviate the pressure to attain academic standards. Time in the instructional context has had many meanings in the educational arena, such as allotted time, engaged time, time on task, instructional time, and academic learning time. But the bottom line is time needed to learn, which can be very different for a uniquely diverse student population with a multiplicity of learning styles.

J. B. Carroll (1963) proposed a model for time needed to learn that took this concept into account. His model demonstrated that learning is a function of the extent to which a student actually has allotted time and spends the amount of time he or she needs in order to learn, due to aptitude for learning. Neither insufficient time nor more time than is needed, however, will produce optimal results. Nor will time needed to learn suffice unless the student is focused on learning. Nevertheless, Carroll's model is brilliant, for it converts aptitude/intelligence into a simple time variable (Gandara, 2000).

According to Anderson (2000), the Carroll model is an inverse relationship of poor quality of instruction and difficulty understanding instruction to an increase in the amount of time a student will need to spend in order to learn beyond that of the student's natural aptitude. For example, a student with a lower ability to understand instruction will require a higher quality of instruction. Alternatively, students will need a great deal of ability to understand low-quality instruction. Time needed to learn, therefore, is the amount of time needed because of the student's aptitude for learning, adjusted, as necessary, for the student's ability to understand instruction and the quality of the instruction provided.

There are differences of opinion, however, about time needed to learn for those who are English-deficient. Although "most immigrant students learn conversational English relatively quickly, they generally need four to ten years to become fluent enough to really comprehend the language and use it as a medium of academic learning" (Olsen & Jaramillo, as cited in Anderson, 2000, p. 17). Today, however, because students are more linguistically diverse than ever, it is a near impossible task to teach immigrants in their native languages/dialects. For example, a high school in Dallas, Texas, reports having a student population representative of 36 different nationalities in the 2004–2005 school year.

Lorin Anderson concludes that the Carroll model of time not only demonstrates an important role in increasing student achievement, but also impacts school reform. Although many may acknowledge that the time variable is important in education, most have not yet conceptualized that manipulation of time (i.e., restructuring the school calendar) should be considered a primary school reform, as long as time spent is equal to time needed and that time is differentiated for different learners. Although major reform will necessitate concerted direction/focus and take time, there are measures that can be taken immediately that will provide positive results to meet the agenda for schools, as outlined next.

MEETING THE AGENDA OF SCHOOL REFORM

The agenda of school reform is to emphasize excellence, equity, and efficiency. All three characteristics should be considered when evaluating educational systems. Excellence is judged by educational outcomes for all students, and includes consideration of socioeconomic factors upon the learning processes while at the same time recognizing the impact of achievement upon socioeconomic mobility. Equity should provide equality of opportunity to learn and the individual freedom to learn in one's own way. Efficiency is considered important for educating well-trained workers with the required skills and attitudes for efficient production in the workplace. It also relates to prudent resource allocation so as to avoid waste of time and money.

Because of the dynamics of political interest groups and social movements, however, an educational system that supports one set of requirements of the agenda may be inversely related to the other. The educational thrust of the 1950s and 1960s was toward equity, in the

1970s and 1980s toward efficiency (Carnoy & Levin, 1985). In the 1990s, however, emphasis was shifted toward efficiency with respect to excellence, an outcome considered important for the economy. Today the most important thrust in education is equity in excellence. *All* students must have the opportunity for an excellent education. Recognizing that educational reforms with the potential to meet all three criteria are not common, the intent of this chapter is to examine whether or not restructuring the school calendar holds promise to meet these criteria.

Excellence

Excellence relates not only to standards for school performance, but also to quality of educational services available to students. National calls for reform to raise educational standards have been stressed in various reports, such as *Prisoners of Time: Schools and Programs Making Time Work for Students and Teachers* by the National Education Commission on Time and Learning (1994). In the 1980s reports such as *A Nation At Risk*, from the National Commission on Excellence in Education (1983) and *Action for Excellence*, by the Task Force on Education for Economic Growth of the Education Commission of the States (1983) mentioned the need for more effective use of instruction time and more time spent on instruction through longer annual school sessions and school days (Carnoy & Levin, 1985).

More recently, the passage of the NCLB Act is the most far-reaching reform—in terms of standards, accountability, and excellence in national educational policy—than any other federal legislation. The success or failure of the current standards movement in American education is directly linked to the use of time (Urbanski & Goodling, 2000). Although *all* students are now required to meet higher standards, not all are able to meet that expectation without additional help. Thus, schools will need more time or more efficient use of existing time to help those who are less likely to attain the higher standards now demanded of them. More time may come from additional classes, extra tutoring, after-school programs, or summer sessions (Urbanski & Goodling, 2000). More efficient use of existing time can come from modifying the usual school year calendar to balance the time students are in and out of school.

The challenge for the school administrator is to demonstrate a strategic program model, supported by practice-proven research, the goal of which should be to improve academic performance for *all* students. And because increased academic performance is being required, Congress, school boards, school administrators, and teacher organizations have been urged to consider reforms in the calendar year, whether balanced or extended, through careful planning and discussion (Southern Illinois University Public Policy Institute, 2001). For those who may question the wisdom of the Policy Institute's recommendation or the academic justification of the year-round schedule, a discussion follows on research findings of a modified or year-round schedule.

Evaluating Excellence in Year-Round Education

Schools say they base their change to year-round education and calendar modification on several factors, including that of student academics. Although over the last 3 decades there have been both positive and negative perceptions of student achievement on the year-round calendar, recent research has reported that year-round education is producing a student academic performance generally equal to and in many cases better than that of the traditional calendar structure (Chen, 1993; Curry, Washington, & Zyskowski, 1997; Grotjohn & Banks, 1993; Haenn, 1996; Six, 1993; Winters, 1995), albeit a differential effect by subject and by varying student demographics when the data is disaggregated. Additionally, as would be expected, there is a differential effect by calendar type. While the findings of student academic achievement, reported below, are positive, one would assume that other quality endeavors would be in effect and contribute to the results, as well. It seems reasonable to expect, however, that small academic gains on the year-round calendar would, given time, demonstrate results.

Achievement on the Year-Round Calendar Reported by Research Syntheses

There have been eight research syntheses published, reviewing a range of 12 to 39 studies on the topic of year-round education and student achievement by either vote-count and/or meta-analysis, and including both balanced (or single-track) and multi-track configurations (Cooper et al., 2003; DeJarnett, 1994; Grotjohn & Banks, 1993; Kneese, 1996; Kneese, 2000a; Palmer & Bemis, 1999; Six, 1993; Winters, 1995).

To date, syntheses have reported by vote count a greater percentage of positive academic gains than mixed or negative results on overall academic performance when a year-round calendar is adopted (Cooper et al., 2003; DeJarnett, 1994; Kneese, 2000a; Palmer & Bemis, 1999; Six, 1993; Winters, 1995). Cooper and colleagues (2003) found that overall approximately 62% of 58 school districts reported students in the modified calendar program academically outperformed their counterparts on the traditional calendar. Kneese (2000a) found that, for studies utilizing inferential statistics, results were positive in 40 out of 61 (66%) comparisons, while for studies utilizing descriptive statistics, results were positive in 21 out of 29 (72%) comparisons. Although results of the meta-analyses demonstrate a positive effect of the year-round calendar on student achievement it is very small, an effect size of less than .25 (Cooper et al., 2003; Kneese, 1996).

Achievement on the Balanced/Single-Track Configuration

When disaggregating the data, it has been determined that effect sizes are larger for student achievement on the balanced (or single-track calendar), than on the multi-track configuration (Cooper et al., 2003; Kneese, 1996). Research by Kneese (1996, 2000b; Kneese & Knight, 1995) has consistently found an effect size for the balanced (or single-track calendar) in the range of .30 to .33 for all students in all grades tested, which would be considered educationally significant. Cooper and colleagues (2003) found a small effect in the range of .17 to.24 for the single-track/balanced calendar.

And so, although one might conclude that both types of year-round calendars would perform in an identical manner, given an equal opportunity to learn, we see a variance in performance one from the other, perhaps due to a difference in implementation purposes. And, further, in some research reports, findings of the two types of year-round education (balanced/single-track and multi-track) have been commingled, evidenced both in the individual studies and in the syntheses, which may be a likely explanation for negative or mixed results.

Achievement on the Multi-Track Configuration

Reports of academic achievement solely on the multi-track calendar are generally positive, but very small. Kneese (1996) found an effect of .08 for the multi-track studies reporting results by mean scores and .11 by gain scores. Cooper and colleagues (2003) found an effect in the range of −.02 to .06, which included reports from studies utilizing both mean and gain scores. As mentioned previously, a multi-track performance report would be more meaningful if reported by gains. Although quite small, accumulating gains on the multi-track calendar over time may prove very beneficial in terms of academic performance and in times when underfunding/overcrowding does not permit adequate facilities.

There is research to support conclusions that suggest greater gains on standardized achievements tests in year-round schools from both first-year and longitudinal evaluations of students (Southwest Educational Development Laboratory, 1993). Further, the greatest gains are found in multi-track year-round schools when compared to the total performance of all year-round schools (Southwest Educational Development Laboratory, 1993).

Achievement Findings Disaggregated by SES Level

One question to be addressed is whether the school calendar has a differential effect on different demographic groups. Although it is believed that there are educational benefits in particular for those who are educationally disadvantaged (Gandara & Fish, 1994; Kneese & Knight, 1995; Willis, 1993), some research has demonstrated that high SES year-round students outperform their traditional counterparts (Kneese, 2000c; Ritter, 1992; Van Mondfrans & Moody, 1985). So, although the year-round education program demonstrates positive results for all student populations when disaggregated by socioeconomic level, a consistent pattern in the research findings is that for the disadvantaged student population greater academic gains are made in the year-round program than on the traditional calendar (Kneese & Knight, 1995).

It is reported that for disadvantaged learners, learning loss is most severe in reading (Cooper et al., 1996; Goren & Carriedo, 1986), yet for students "at-risk" or economically disadvantaged, the year-round program appears to be most advantageous in reading with effect sizes ranging from medium to large (Kneese & Knight, 1995). Cooper's team (2003) reports that their "findings strongly suggest, as proponents have argued, that the modified (or year-round) calendar will have its greatest impact on students struggling in school or from disadvantaged homes" (p. 60). McMillen (2002), in his statewide assessment in North Carolina, also found that lower achieving students in modified calendar schools had significantly higher achievement scores than the lower achieving students in traditional calendar schools.

Research on the Extended-Year Calendar

There are those who believe that small increases in the duration of time allocated to schooling would not likely impact student achievement (Glass, 2002). Nor would changing the calendar, with an equal amount of 180 days, be likely to yield a higher level of student academic performance (Glass, 2002). Others claim that adding more time to the calendar will result in improved academic performance for all students, but only if time is used more effectively (Aronson, Zimmerman, & Carlos, 1998). The alternative viewpoint is that modifying and/or increasing the number of days of the current schedule would contribute to increased student academic achievement, due to more continuous instruction and less time for forgetting, particularly for the disadvantaged students.

Much research has been reported on the 3-month summer effect on achievement. The most recent and extensive study, entitled "The Effect of Summer Vacation on Achievement Test Scores: A Narrative and Meta-Analytic Review," authored by Cooper and colleagues and published in 1996 in the *Review of Education Research*, raised several important issues in the research findings that relate to the discussion concerning the restructured calendar and student achievement. Among the findings of the study were that all students lost math computational skills, disadvantaged students lost reading skills, and summer vacation increased the disparities between middle-class and disadvantaged students' reading scores. The detrimental effect of summer vacation on student achievement appeared to increase as grade level increased.

These findings correspond to the findings of other researchers (Entwisle & Alexander, 1992; Parsley & Powell, 1962). Kneese (2000b) also found a demonstrated decrease in performance (learning loss) for traditional calendar elementary students over a 1-year time period as compared to year-round students who demonstrated a sustained performance. It can be inferred from these studies that diminishing the length of any vacation period might aid in reducing forgetting. Additionally, those with limited English proficiency may experience a loss in acquisition of English language skills over the extended vacation period and need more exposure to educational opportunities than the extended-year calendar offers.

Although, to date, there has been little research on the extended-year calendar, Julie Frazier-Gustafson in 1998 examined the impact of adding 30 mandatory days to the school year on the achievement of K–3 students. Overall, it was found that the impact of the extended-year school on the child's cognitive development was a key reform in improving academic performance in early childhood. In 1999 James Bradford, superintendent of Buena Vista City Schools in Virginia, reported positive longitudinal findings on Parry McCluer High School, a nationally recognized high school with a very successful extended school year program. A mandate by the Buena Vista school board, effective in 1990, required all students scoring below the 25 percentile on standardized achievement tests to attend school year-round.

If allocation of time is a particularly important issue for all students, and not only those disadvantaged, as research has determined, students should be exposed to additional and more frequent learning opportunities. Cooper's team states that those who oppose the way time is currently utilized in school should address a way to "remedy the inequities in learning opportunities, and the consequent difference in achievement, that summer vacation creates for children from different economic backgrounds. They must also state why an optimal pedagogical strategy ought not include both an alternative calendar and more efficient use of time" (Cooper et al., 1996, p. 263). Efforts for extended learning opportunities have not gone unnoticed, for in 2002 Mayor

Rudolf Giuliani of New York City proposed Saturday classes and New York's Governor George Pataki suggested longer school days. California Governor Gray Davis recommended adding 30 days of instruction for middle schools to address academic deficiencies.

Equity

Equity is probably the most discussed but least understood concept in the educational arena; therefore, there is no universal agreement on its breadth or importance. Nevertheless, equity regularly appears in discussions of educational goals and resources. In educational finance, one might define equity as equal treatment of persons in equal circumstances with equal distribution of available financial resources. In the matter of student achievement, one might define equity as the provision of equal access to education for all students, with sufficient funding sources to guarantee the equity.

Moreover, equity can be horizontal or vertical. *Horizontal equity* assumes that all individuals are similar and should be treated in the same manner. *Vertical equity* assumes, on the other hand, that individuals are different and should be treated differently, because all students do not have identical educational needs. With their different aptitudes/capabilities, as well as the different expectations from adults, all of which affect the content and level of education required, the time and financial support needed for students to learn become crucial factors in the educational enterprise.

The concern about equity particularly involves the inclusion of different racial and ethnic peoples, perspectives, and cultures in American educational policy. In all states, with California and Texas in the forefront, Hispanic students are expected to become, if not they are not already, the majority. These students, often from economically disadvantaged backgrounds, have special educational or service needs that simply cannot be ignored by the educational system, whose responsibility it is to educate to the students' potential for learning.

A correlation between a student's socioeconomic level and the degree of academic achievement attained in school has long been acknowledged in research. While it is commonly perceived by many educators that students from a low socioeconomic background are generally at a disadvantage when they enter school, according to research reported by Marr (1989) and Cooper and colleagues (1996), once these students were in school, they appeared to learn at the same rate as their higher SES peers.

Moreover, a study in England conducted in the 1980s measured differences in outcome achievement, after taking into account differences in background and prior attainment of children. The question posed was whether some schools had more effective results than others in helping ethnic minority pupils to achieve. The study determined that the school a child attends is a greater determining factor for achievement than the group to which he or she belongs. This research finding partially shifts the focus from individual, family, and background characteristics to a sharper focus on policies and practices in schools, which can aid all children to achieve at higher levels than heretofore and demands professional responsibility from educators to ensure that no groups of children underachieve (Tomlinson, 1992).

For the at-risk student, school effectiveness is a more urgent issue, for he or she most likely begins schooling at a disadvantage in terms of attainment. In order to enhance the learning opportunities of the growing disadvantaged student population, the most effective school policies must be enacted.

Until recently, equity in American education has been defined as the extent to which peripheral students were offered educational opportunities designed for the needs and characteristics of "mainstream" students (Northwest Regional Educational Laboratory, 2004). Today there is a new educational mainstream—racially, culturally, ethnically, linguistically, and economically diverse—within which all must be given the opportunity to develop knowledge, skills, and understanding at the highest possible level.

If equity as uniformity is an outdated concept, it follows that extra help must be provided to students by implementing quality instructional programs. Schools in which only some students—or no students—now achieve educational excellence will require substantial restructuring and must be transformed to abide by principles of equity (Northwest Regional Educational Laboratory, 2004). High-quality education must be advanced by 1) skilled educators with ability to draw from a repertoire of educational strategies for differentiated learning styles; 2) expert administrators/school board officials with knowledge of what actions to take to ensure educational opportunity; 3) strong public support for this flexibility required in the organizational structure of the educational system; and 4) restructured time sequences.

Evaluating Equity in Year-Round Education

Access to equity is, in part, determined by the structure of learning time. Students in districts and schools with a high concentration of poverty and limited-English speakers should have the access to extra help and the opportunity to have more time on task, provided by such arrangements as the extended-year calendar and the balanced calendar (when intersession is available and utilized). The educational community must recognize that equity is inseparable from excellence; for excellence without equity is not excellence—it is privilege (Urbanski & Goodling, 2000).

At least one third of elementary and secondary students in the United States can be identified as high risk, and for this particular student population the effect of the traditional calendar schedule on *learning retention* should be of particular concern to educators. Many studies have found that the gains made during the school year are not sustained over the summer vacation and that this loss is greater for at-risk students (Cooper et al., 1996; Pelavin & David, 1977). As Jamar (1994) stated, "Higher [socioeconomic status] students may return to school in the fall with a considerable educational advantage over their less advantaged peers as a result of either additional school-related learning, or lower levels of forgetting, over the summer months" (p. 1). A 1978 study, commissioned by the New York State Board of Regents, found that advantaged students advance academically an average of 1 year and 3 months in school and then learn 1 additional month's worth during the summer, whereas disadvantaged students advance an average of 1 year and 1 month during the year and then lose 3 to 4 months during the summer (Brekke, 1992a; Thomas, 1978).

Limited English proficiency (LEP) is one indicator of an at-risk student. For most of these students, the language of summer is the language of the family, which would be a language other than English. As an increasing number of students come from homes where English is not the primary language, 3 months away from formal instruction in second language acquisition is detrimental. Furthermore, those who have difficulty learning in a traditional calendar structure could experience 9 months of failure and frustration before attending summer school, which is far too late for effective remediation to occur. In contrast, the intermittent intersession periods of the year-round education calendar can accommodate frequent remediation.

It has been consistently found in the research that a modified year-round program is especially effective for the disadvantaged student and, in fact, may very well remedy the very deficiencies that exist in the traditional calendar schools for this population. Researchers have determined that the extended vacation period within the traditional structure may result in minimized retention of academic material for all students, the greatest loss being in skill subjects, such as math computation (Cooper et al.,1996), while for disadvantaged learners, the loss for this same group is more severe in reading (Goren & Carriedo, 1986; Cooper et al., 1996). On the other hand, for students at-risk or economically disadvantaged, a year-round program appears to be most advantageous in reading. And so, the modified school calendar can offer many academic opportunities, fulfilling the need for outcomes in terms of equity, in particular (Kneese & Knight, 1995).

Educational equity can be routinely available for all. Schools can be restructured to be arenas where one balances and efficiently accommodates the needs of all, which includes students of diverse cultures and with differentiated learning needs. There are those who have opposed year-round education, contending that the disadvantaged student population appears to be consolidated/isolated on one track of one of the multi-track calendars (Oakes, 2004). However, if multi-tracking is implemented/utilized appropriately, this could be considered an advantage, as it appears that many types of students cannot be "mainstreamed" and need specialized accommodation and highly credentialed teachers in the field. So, this calendar modification would likely translate into extending to at least some, if not all, a more efficient/effective time to learn with longer days and/or a longer school year, along with shorter and more frequent breaks for more continuous learning. This is vertical equity and opportunity for equity in excellence.

Efficiency

A major enterprise in many communities is public education, and it is in itself a large economic system. Twenty percent of the nation's population either attends or is employed in American public schools. The educational system nationwide serves more than 40 million students in about 15,000 districts that include more than 80,000 schools (Jordan & Lyons, 1992).

Expenditures for American public schools currently exceed $200 billion annually, and we rank at the top of international spending on education, according to Hess (2004). Sources of revenue come from a combination of local, state, and federal sources. The majority of this revenue comes from state and local taxes, with approximately 7% of the total budget coming from federal sources. These revenues support the day-to-day operation of schools and represent the largest single item in the budgets of most state and local governments.

Funding public schools varies among states, and spending levels per pupil differ both within and between states. Citizen interest in providing adequate funding for public schools is high, for America's concern is producing an educated workforce in order to remain competitive within the international economy. Another concern is changes occurring in the family, which has led to increasing duties expected of the schools. Interest in extended day programs in schools has increased because of the increasing number of single-parent households and latch-key children. Moreover, providing adequate funding to provide quality education is becoming increasingly difficult because of recent social and economic developments.

For example, in the 1990s there was an increased amount of funds targeted for special needs students above the average allotted to educate most other students. Additionally, state school finance programs have been required by courts to reduce the disparities in educational opportunity among districts and provide a more adequately funded program that was equitably available for all students. Because of academic accountability issues focused on the schools, some voices have advocated that funding be based on pupil performance. However, under such a policy, underachieving school districts would have even less to spend, although demonstrating greater need for financial support.

Given the issue of major population growth in urban areas, adequate funding for education becomes ever more complex, for many of the nation's largest cities face a declining tax base, while needing to replace an aging infrastructure, combined with expanding social needs and a deterioration of social services (Jordan & Lyons, 1992).

A responsibility of schools is to provide quality of instruction and to do so efficiently. Efficiency in the public school arena means maximizing outcomes for a given level of spending. Additionally, efficiency relates to prudent resource allocation so as not to waste *time and money*. In the views of Hess (2004) and Miller (2005), however, the nation's taxpayers are investing dollars with inadequate return for the investment.

Evaluating Efficiency in Year-Round Education

Knowledge of the extent to which programs have been implemented successfully and the degree to which they have the desired outcomes is indispensable to school district stakeholders and policy makers. In almost all cases, however, it is equally crucial to be informed about how program costs compare to their outcomes. Whether accomplished impressionistically, as in most everyday life decisions, or by formal procedures, comparison of the costs and benefits of social programs, including education, is one of the most important considerations in deciding whether to expand, continue, trim, or terminate them.

The application of economic principles to the educational enterprise received little attention until about 1960. Today, again and again, decision makers must constantly determine how to allocate scarce resources and to put them to optimal use. A school district would be negligent not to examine the cost-effectiveness of any program implemented, new or established, and any evaluator would be deemed unprofessional not to compare outcomes with monetary costs. For the evaluator, there are four efficiency assessments—*cost-feasibility analysis, cost-effectiveness analysis, cost-benefit analysis, and cost-utility analysis*—which provide a frame of reference for relating costs to program results and are useful to political constituencies who determine the level of acceptance of programs.

How does one assess efficiency? Educational investment decisions can be evaluated by the same techniques used to assess other public projects. Cost-benefit and cost-effectiveness analyses are the best means of judging efficiency of programs; however, "the question of 'correct' procedures for actually conducting cost-benefit and cost-effective analysis of social programs remains an area of considerable controversy" (Rossi, Freeman, & Lipsey, 1999, p. 366).

Cost-effectiveness evaluation is indicated, more likely than not, to evaluate single-track initiatives, as most single-track programs are implemented for the sole purpose of effectiveness. *Cost-effectiveness analysis* refers to the appraisal of programs on the basis of their costs and their effects with regard to producing a given performance outcome. The evaluator determines a year-round program's cost, given the fact that there is a common index of effectiveness, such as normal curve equivalent (NCE) scores on a test of mathematics achievement or frequency of school attendance, and compares that cost and performance to that of the traditional calendar. The purpose of this analysis is to provide decision makers with data necessary to choose among alternatives on the basis of least cost and greatest effectiveness. It can be used not only to compare different programs, but also to determine relative effectiveness of a particular program over time, or for different student populations. Outputs in this analysis need not be expressed in monetary terms; since most educational objectives are not economic, this is a major consideration.

Cost-benefit analysis, which translates the cost of the program into program effects in terms of monetary values and not performance effects, is most likely indicated for evaluation of multi-track initiatives. *Cost-benefit analysis* systematically compares the costs and benefits of a project in order to evaluate its economic productivity. The purpose is to assess costs and benefits associated with alternatives for achieving a goal or an objective. In education, it is often used for comparing projects such as dropout prevention, compensatory education, or preschool programs.

In any analysis, the quality of information gleaned for purposes of decision making depends to a great degree on the quality of the means and extent of obtaining the data, as well as the validity of the data examined. Because there may be a number of variables to be considered when moving toward a conclusion, the omission or avoidance of any of them may alter or skew the final results. An understanding of this principle is especially important when reviewing cost studies of year-round education.

Given the identical allotment of time and personnel in *single-track* schools as that of the traditional calendar, it would be reasonable to assume similar costs. While implementation costs might be expected to contribute to a small increase in expenditures in the initial years, such an expectation might not be realistic. For example, there is considerable discussion in the profession about how implementation costs should be enumerated and distributed. District A might indicate that implementation of a new program would cost $50,000, with a major portion of that cost allocated to the time spent by an administrator in implementing the program. District B, on the other hand, would indicate that the administrator assigned to implementation was merely substituting this task for other tasks under the job description notation of "other duties as assigned." For District B, then, implementation costs might be negligible to nil under that district's accounting methodology.

Also in dispute is the notion of putting 100% of implementation costs, if any, on the back of the new program. If the program has arrived with a considerable degree of political insistence and resistance, this position holds, then much of the cost of administrator time should be shared equally between the new program and the old.

Another example of accounting differences among districts involves transportation of students. If a school district has both modified calendar and traditional schools there will be, in many cases, an overlap of 6 to 8 weeks annually where one or the other calendar schools are not in session. School buses, however, continue to transport students who are still in session. To which of the calendars should the transportation costs of those few weeks be allocated. All to one? Shared equally? Shared proportionally?

Accordingly, there are conflicting reports. Quinlan, George, and Emmett (1987) after a statewide study have noted that operating costs for single-track year-round education programs are about the same as those for traditional schools. Worthen and Zsiray (1994) report that single-track programs would be expected to cost approximately the same, or perhaps more, than traditional programs. In examining the literature, to date, only one *cost-effectiveness study* was found (Dossett & Munoz,

2000), which reported that a district's *single-track* year-round schools were less cost-effective than traditional calendar schools in both reading and math. In each of these studies, however, there was insufficient information available to judge the extent to which variables were included/excluded in the analysis, thereby diminishing study validity. It is recommended, therefore, that further cost-effective analyses be investigated over time, evaluated school by school and district by district, and constructed very carefully to include as many variables as could conceivably influence final results.

The remaining literature search revealed *cost-benefit analyses*, although often termed *cost-effectiveness analyses* by the reports' authors. One might assume that *cost-benefit analyses for multi-track year-round education* would reveal considerable savings, given that there would be avoided large capital costs, despite some increased operational costs. It has been reported that in implementing multi-track year-round programs, cost savings can be estimated to be in the range of 8% to 51%. Yet determining costs and savings can be a multifaceted exercise, as many researchers and economists have pointed out.

Hough, Zykowski, and Dick (1990) analyzed data from a California sample in a feasibility study and found that one key factor in determining efficiency was a district's operating expenses. They further determined that a school district could save money by utilizing the multi-track version of year-round education, though taxpayers could potentially realize either a saving or incur a cost, long-term, depending upon a host of factors. In fact, most districts implementing multi-track year-round education have reported a decrease in operational costs per pupil.

Operational costs per pupil reach a break-even point when a school's enrollment is increased to 20% over a school's rated capacity, according to a study by officials in San Diego City Schools, with per-pupil operational costs decreased by $8.92 if the student population exceeds 20% of stated capacity. Socorro Independent School District, Texas, determined a similar savings in per-pupil operating expenses after exceeding that 20% enrollment increase (Minnesota Department of Children, Families, and Learning, 1999). Brekke (1990) reported that Visalia Unified found a similar reduction in operational costs per student of $9 annually, given an increase of 15% student enrollment. But a 30% enrollment increase generated a 51% reduction in operational costs per student.

Another study (Coleman & Freebern, 1993) compared costs of relocatables to that of multi-track year-round education when considering solutions to overcrowding. When enrollment was up approximately 10% over rated capacity, use of relocatables to reduce overcrowding was found to be less expensive. As enrollment got closer to 20% over capacity, however, multi-track year-round education was deemed the fiscally prudent choice. To put the above-mentioned savings/costs in perspective, an interesting study by White (1991) reported on 100 Jefferson County schools in Colorado, which had been on the multi-track calendar for 14 years. It was not until new schools were built, and expenses compared, that district administrators recognized/realized that expenditures for new construction exceeded $116 million, while saving but $3.56 million annually in operating costs after converting back to a traditional schedule.

In all of these studies, however, a more extensive description of how costs were determined would help validate the conclusions. In thinking about cost implications of moving to multi-track year-round education, one would need to consider capital expenses or costs avoided, operating expenses, transition expenses, special funding and incentive revenues, as well as incidental factors. After factoring these criteria into the equation, what, to date, have been some models utilized for determining cost-benefit? There are likely three possible models: 1) a single-school comparison whereby the year-round education budget is compared with its own prior traditional calendar budget; 2) a matched-school comparison; or 3) a simulation model estimating costs of a newly implemented year-round education program as compared to that of the traditional calendar in same year in same school.

Price Waterhouse (1991) developed a cost analysis model, which included cost-avoidance and cost-savings statistics for Cherry Creek School District in Colorado. The study found that overall operational savings would be achieved by implementing three multi-track year-round schools that would house as many students as four traditional schools.

By 1993 Zykowski, Mitchell, and Dick reported on the cost implications of year-round education in a study conducted by the California

Educational Research Cooperative. A cost model was developed as follows: operational costs + capital costs + transition costs + incentive revenues = increased year-round education cost/savings. Data were collected from four school districts and costs were then compared to avoided costs of new construction. Results demonstrated a range of total savings per student per year from $73.98 to $201.89.

Also in 1993 Denton and Walenta determined that the optimal approach for analyzing cost-savings of multi-track year-round education was to develop a simulation cost model. They built upon the Quinlan and colleagues (1987) model, which suggested that cost analysis categories be distinguished as avoided costs, transition costs, projected operating costs, and incidental costs. From all of the reviews of cost analyses, however, it is clear that a more extensive list of variables need to be included.

Of course, educational administrators search desperately for ways to demonstrate how funds can be used more efficiently. If overcrowding is present, an immediate resolution is for school districts to implement multi-track year-round education—or some other cost-benefit alternative of the district's choice—and utilize existing and additional funds, if available, to update aging infrastructure until a long-term solution to overcrowding is resolved. Decision makers will always be faced with the issue of facility replacement and whether additional and newer construction might or might not prove to be of more cost-benefit than maintaining older buildings with limited service. Yet an over-riding problem is that population growth is rarely sustained, and there are examples of districts overcompensating for student enrollment growth that abated after a relatively short period.

Interviews with public school administrators in both rural and urban school districts in Texas revealed that the greatest problems they faced were lack of *time and money.* As mentioned previously, the definition of efficiency is prudent use of *time and money.* Given the desperate need for *time and money*, why is it that a system as large as that of American public education is so inefficient in utilizing its facilities and time to educate? Why is it that a school building/facility is utilized for learning only 6 to 7 hours a day, 5 days a week, and 9 months of the year?

A new configuration of the school calendar can meet the goal for efficiency, whether short-term or long-term. The traditional 9-month calendar commonly followed in most of our nation's schools today may be deemed inefficient, both academically and economically. For in addition to being faced with rising costs for operations, maintenance, and updating of current facilities, as well as new construction, educational facilities are currently underutilized during the long summer vacation. More important, during those approximately 3 months, time is wasted for educational opportunity and the instructional learning patterns of our students are interrupted. Summer learning loss subsequently becomes a reality.

CHAPTER 7

Conclusion: A Promising Solution

The authors of this book have discussed in depth the matter of summer learning loss, which Bracey (2002) refers to as the phenomenon no one wants to deal with. The problem is real; it impacts achievement levels and must be minimized.

A constructive approach to improving the use of school time would be modification of the school calendar, for the current calendar structure does not respond to requisites of time upon learning. Indeed, dismissing students from formal instruction for up to 3 months at a time is hardly an award-winning prescription for improving test scores or for satisfactory student learning. Is it not self-evident that a method to reduce summer learning loss might be the reduction of American education's long summer vacation? The start of a community's discussion of minimizing summer learning loss might be the asking of this question: How long should summer vacation be?

Despite media stories that purport to demonstrate a decline in the quality of American education and suggest a need to hasten change, school reform occurs very slowly. Decline or not, the quality of education will only improve as educational stakeholders demand it. Initially, the nation's citizenry must focus on the importance of education and be willing to accept change as required to improve the overall learning of students. Correspondingly, the American educational system must focus on the impact of time as a crucial element in school reform. In addition to calendar reform, education needs spend larger portion of students' allotted school time on instruction in core subjects.

To illustrate this latter point, data indicate that in 1998 students in the United States spent 980 hours annually in school, while students in Japan spent but 875 hours in school (Ministry of Education, Culture, Sports, Science and Technology, 2004). In contrast, the instructional time in core coursework—math, science, language, and social studies—during the final 4 years of schooling in the United States were estimated to be only 1,462 hours (an average of 365 hours annually) as compared to 3,190 hours (an average of 797 hours annually) in Japan (Bainbridge, 2005).

The strongest factor identified in a meta-analysis conducted by Scheerens and Bosker in 1997 was the effect of time, which demonstrated an increase in student achievement by 15 percentile points (Marzano, 2000). The researchers determined that time allocated for instruction should be maximized and that the amount of instructional time lost to absenteeism and unproductive extracurricular activities should be minimized (Marzano, 2000).

Although many educators, policy makers, legal theorists, and scholars concur that education would do well to reform on a large scale, they disagree on the means and methods to improve education in the United States. Consequently, America has experienced many educational reform movements that emphasize differing and sometimes conflicting values. In a nation of 50 states and approximately 15,000 local school districts, there is bound to be a multitude of different concepts of improving educational quality.

As a result of this disagreement/fragmentation, professional discussion arises about how the United States should attempt to reach a national consensus on improving the quality of education. The recent involvement of the U.S. Congress in education through Goals 2000 and the No Child Left Behind legislation adds an additional dimension to the question of who should define education. In this context, the issue is not whether there is need for educational reform, but who has the power to define it. According to the U.S. Constitution, unenumerated power remains with the states. In turn, most state constitutions offer some limited details concerning state/local educational powers but leave it to the legislatures to determine the level of local authority for school operation. Because of the complex/conflicting relationship among the various levels of the American educational system, local school districts are often stymied into inaction.

Figure 7.1 outlines 1) the issues warranting change in the educational system; 2) the subsequent policy discussions to be taken to address/implement public school reform; and 3) the performance of

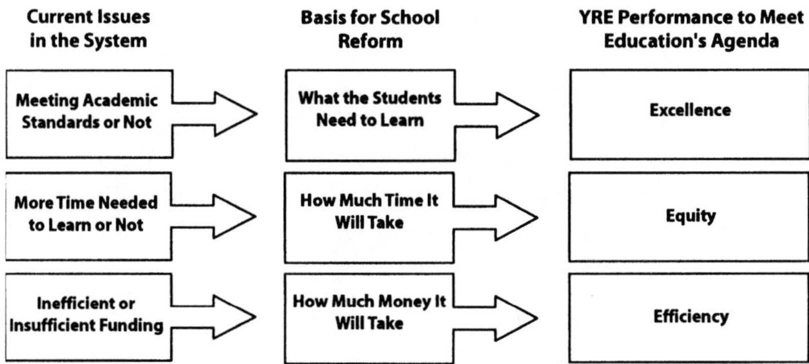

Figure 7.1. *Action for School Reform*

and results from year-round education in meeting the requirements of the educational agenda:

There is tension within the K–12 educational system to meet academic standards, while there is too little instructional time in academic core subjects, stellar performance in which is desired on standardized tests. How time is distributed in education (i.e., the school calendar) in the 50 states is flexible and should be differentiated, because of the needs of diverse student populations. Modifying and/or extending the school calendar should be considered a primary reform effort that meets not only the academic agenda of the schools, but additionally responds to the current issues apparent in American education today. Despite what may be inefficient and/or insufficient funding, the amount of money needed for a student to learn cannot be determined until the focus and time allotted to instruction are established.

Agreed, there are many issues to be resolved in school reform endeavors. The goal is a top performing, perfectly structured/organized educational system, which will not necessarily be attained through insistence upon more and more accountability. A prescriptive future for quality American education should include and prioritize a confirmation of the importance/value of learning, a thoughtful and comprehensive restructuring of the educational system, a determination of the time and sequence needed for knowledge retention, and the money required for the educational endeavor.

A quality education requires hiring the best teachers at the top dollars, lowering the pupil-teacher ratios, and implementing the most innovative instructional methods and materials. At the same time, public service entities are consistently pressured to be cost-effective/efficient. Education, delivered effectively and efficiently, should be viewed as the best investment in the future of America—our children—for the gift of adequate and well-sequenced learning time can make a difference with respect to academic performance.

Conceptualizing time in the context of school reform was the impetus for the authors to write this book. The goal was to synthesize the research findings about, and to evaluate the potential of, education year-round to aid students in their learning. A final decision is left to the reader, and ultimately to the public, to determine whether or not a case has been made for the significance of modifying the school calendar.

APPENDIXES

Appendix A - Single-Track Calendar

Comparison of Achievement of Year-Round and Traditional Calendars: By Inferential Statistics

School/District Author	Calendar Plan **	Population Studied	Comparison Group	Years Of Study	Tests Used	Results ***	Comments
Alabama, Florida, Mississippi School Districts Cason, C.B. Dr.	45/15 ST	4th grade in YRE elementary	4th grade in matched TCS elementary within same district	1990-1994	SAT	Read + * Math +/- Statistically significant differences	The average number of days by students and teachers and the average number of suspensions were analyzed.
Alameda USD Kneese, Carolyn Calvin Dr.	60/15 ST	Gr.ades 5, 7 in 3 YRE schools N=1110	Grades 5, 7 in 3 schools matched by SES	1993-1995	District Level	Grade 5 read + Grade 5 Math + * Grade 7 Read + Grade 7 Math + Statistically significant difference. Practical signifiance	Mean Gain scores favored the YRE in every comparison, albeit only slightly for the low SES and mid SES schools. YRE appeared to be particularly beneficial for higher SES in both read and math.
Austin ISD, Conroe ISD, Waxahachie ISD, TX Dunn, Eddie R Dr.	60/20 30/10 45/15 ST	YRE elementary. campuses N=615	TCS students matched within district on several variables	1993-1995	TAAS	Read + Math -	Examined gain scores. Data disaggregated by student type, gender, race, SES level. Statistical significance was found in minor comparisons.
College Park Elementary, College Park, GA Consolle, Pam Dr.	45/15 ST	Grade 5 YRE students N=58	Grade 5 TC students in school matched on SES & minority N=101	1997-1998	ITBS	Read + * Math + * Statistically significant differences	Attendance & out of school suspensions were evaluated as well.

*** With the substitution of + for 0, this grading of results follows a pattern first suggested by Barbara Merino (1983)
+ The overall study favors year-round education
+/- The overall study indicates a mixed pattern of results, some favoring YRE, some traditional calendar (TC)
- The overall study favors traditional calendar education

* Statistically significant differences
** ST=Single-Track Year-Round Education,
MT= Multi-Track,
TC= Traditional Calendar School

Continued on Next Page

Appendix A - Single-Track Calendar

Comparison of Achievement of Year-Round and Traditional Calendars: By Inferential Statistics

School/District Author	Calendar Plan **	Population Studied	Comparison Group	Years Of Study	Tests Used	Results ***	Comments
Collins Intermediate School Conroe ISD Conroe, TX Ritter, C.	45/15 ST	YRE 6th graders N=48	TCS 6th graders	1991-1992	Midterm Chap Tests End of Year Chap Tests, Trans. Math	Math at midterm +* Math at end of year +/- Statistically significant differences	This is perhaps the only study that has examined the impact of YRE on gifted and talented students.
Conroe ISD Conroe TX Kneese, Carolyn Dr.	30/10 ST	Grades 4, 5, 6 N=933	TC matched sample	1992-1993	NAPT	All students Read + * All students Math + * At-Risk students Read + * At-Risk students Math + Statistically significant differences. Practical significance	Data disaggregated by student type and years of program implementation. Examined gain scores.
Friendswood ISD Friendswood, TX Owens, Michael Dr.	ST	Grades 4-6 N=180	TC random selection	1993-1994	ITBS	Grade 4 Read + Grade 5 Read + Grade 6 Read + Grade 4 Math + Grade 5 Math + Grade 6 Math + Grade 4 Lang + Grade 5 Lang - Grade 6 Lang +	Intersession were non-instructional breaks but could be utilized as enrichment.

*** With the substitution of + for 0, this grading of results follows a pattern first suggested by Barbara Merino (1983)

+ The overall study favors year-round education

+/- The overall study indicates a mixed pattern of results, some favoring YRE, some traditional calendar (TC)

- The overall study favors traditional calendar education

* Statistically significant differences

** ST=Single-Track Year-Round Education, MT= Multi-Track, TC= Traditional Calendar School

Continued on Next Page

Appendix A - Single-Track Calendar

Comparison of Achievement of Year-Round and Traditional Calendars: By Inferential Statistics

School/District Author	Calendar Plan **	Population Studied	Comparison Group	Years Of Study	Tests Used	Results ***	Comments
Conroe ISD **Conroe, TX** Kneese, Carolyn Dr.	30/10 ST	Grades 4-6 N=933	TC matched sample	1993	Norm referenced Assessment Program of Texas (NAPT) of IOWA test of basic skills (ITBS)	Grade 4 Read +* Grade 5 Read +* Grade 6 Read +* Grade 4 Math +* Grade 5 Math +* Grade 6 Math +* Statistically significant differences Practical significance	Data disaggregated by SES level of schools and student type: all and at-risk. Examined post test scores only.
Durham Public School **Durham, NC** Haenn, Joseph Dr.	ST 45/15	Grades 4-5 N=c.153 2 Schools	1) YRE students transferred to TCS 2) State expected gain	1994-1995	NC End of Grade (EOG) Tests	Read +/- Math +/-	Although each of the two groups of school A & school B YRS students (Stayers and Transfers in) did not significantly outperform the TCS (Transfers Out) students on read and math posttest scores, they did show significant pre/post gains in both which was greater than state expected gain.
Rockingham CC Schools, Eden, NC Frye, Fay H.	45/15/ST	Grade 5 on YRE in 4 elementary school N=154	Grade 5 in TC in District matched on Cogat	1993-1996	End of course test	Read +* Math +* Statistically significant differences	Additional data for Kindergarten 1st and 2nd grade students as well as survey data were presented but not included in this review.
San Diego City School, CA Fass-Holmes, B. Dr. Gates, K.E. Dr.	45/15/ST	Grade 2-6-9 elem. school Grade 6-8 1 middle school N=c.6,740	10 TC schools matched on SES & other variables	1990-1993	ASAT for FES APRENDA for LEP students	Read + elem. level Read - middle Math + elem. Lang. + elem.	Authors caution that data is for non-mobile students only & not generalizable to all students at all STYR schools in district. Statistically significant differences were found in minor comparisons.

*** With the substitution of + for 0, this grading of results follows a pattern first suggested by Barbara Merino (1983)
+ The overall study favors year-round education
+/- The overall study indicates a mixed pattern of results, some favoring YRE, some traditional calendar (TC)
- The overall study favors traditional calendar education

* Statistically significant differences
** ST=Single-Track Year-Round Education,
MT= Multi-Track,
TC= Traditional Calendar School

Continued on Next Page

Appendix A - Single-Track Calendar

Comparison of Achievement of Year-Round and Traditional Calendars: By Inferential Statistics

School/District Author	Calendar Plan **	Population Studied	Comparison Group	Years Of Study	Tests Used	Results ***	Comments
San Ysidro SD **San Ysidro, CA** Barron, Ruben Dr.	60/20 ST	Grades 2 & 5, 1 YRE elementary	Grades 2 & 5, 1 TC school	1988-1992	CTBS - Grade 5 SABE - Grade 2	Grade 5 Read -* Grade 5 Math -* Grade 5 Lang. -* Grade 2 Read +/- Grade 2 Math +/- Statistically significant	Students in grade 5 were tested in English. Students in grade 2 were tested in Spanish. Student & teacher attendance were evaluated.
Sweetwater Union High School, **National City, CA** Chen, Zengshu Dr.	45/15 ST	Grades 9-12 N=4000 (approximately)	Southwest High School	1984-1993	CTBS (7 Years) Stanford Achievement (3 Years) CAP (3 Years) SAT (5 Years)	CTBS + * Stanford Achiev. +/-* CAP - SAT - Statistically significant differences	Additional survey data constituted the second half of this study but not reported here.
Waco ISD **Waco, TX** Elsberry, James Stanton Dr.	60/20 ST N=c.300	YRE students Grades 3 & 5 in 2 elementary schools	TC in same schools	1990-1992	TAAS	Grade 3 Writing + * Grade 3 Read + Grade 3 Math + Grade 5 Writing + * Grade 5 Read + * Grade 5 Math + * Statistically significant differences	Data were gathered from student, teacher, and parent sources concerning the relationship between YRE and TCS achievement and attendance and attendance and perceptions of effectiveness.

*** With the substitution of + for 0, this grading of results follows a pattern first suggested by Barbara Merino (1983)

+ The overall study favors year-round education

+/- The overall study indicates a mixed pattern of results, some favoring YRE, some traditional calendar (TC)

- The overall study favors traditional calendar education

* Statistically significant differences

** ST=Single-Track Year-Round Education,
MT= Multi-Track,
TC= Traditional Calendar School

Continued on Next Page

Appendix A - Single-Track Calendar

Comparison of Achievement of Year-Round and Traditional Calendars: By Inferential Statistics

School/District Author	Calendar Plan **	Population Studied	Comparison Group	Years Of Study	Tests Used	Results ***	Comments
Waco ISD, Waco, TX Stripling, Rosanne Dr. Stanley, Diane	60/20 ST	Grades 4, 5 at 8 YRE elementary schools Grades 6, 7, 8 from 1 YRE middle school N=c.2350	Grades 4, 5 from 8 TC elementary schools Grades 6, 7, 8 matched to students from 4 TCS middle schools	1994-1995 for Grades 4, 5, 7, 8 1993-1995 for Grade 6	TAAS	Grades 4, 5, 7, 8 Math +* Grades 4, 5, 7, 8 Read + Grade 6 Math -* Grade 6 Read - Statistically significant differences	Mixed results. Data available from years 1992, 93, 94 but studied and reported separately each year. Mean TLI gain was positive in Read & Math for YRE grades 4, 5, 7, 8 and negative for TC grades 4, 5, 7, 8. At 6th grade, TC students outperformed YRE students in both Read & Math.
West Carrollton Schools, OH Roby, Douglas E. Dr.	45/15 ST	Grade 6 Schnell Elementary N=52	Grade 6 Russell Elementary N=45	1991-1992	ITBS	Read + * Math + * Statistically significant differences Practical significance	With the verbal cognitive ability covariate held constant, statistically significant differences were found in favor of the YRE in both Math & Read. Differences in gender data suggest that YRE is more beneficial for male than female.
West Carrollton Schools, OH Campbell, Wallace, D. Dr	45/15 ST	At-Risk students, Grade 2 N=30	Matched pairs at TC schools in district	1991-1992	Gates-MacGintie Reading Test	Read +	Outcomes were measured by basic skill gains in reading, absences, promotion rates, no. of books read, & reading levels completed. Qualitative analysis examined the perceptions of students, administrators, teachers, & parents relating to the outcomes.

*** With the substitution of + for 0, this grading of results follows a pattern first suggested by Barbara Merino (1983)

+ The overall study favors year-round education

+/- The overall study indicates a mixed pattern of results, some favoring YRE, some traditional calendar (TC)

- The overall study favors traditional calendar education

* Statistically significant differences

** ST=Single-Track Year-Round Education,
MT= Multi-Track,
TC= Traditional Calendar School

Continued on Next Page

Appendix A - Single-Track Calendar

Comparison of Achievement of Year-Round and Traditional Calendars: By Descriptive Statistics

School/District Author	Calendar Plan **	Population Studied	Comparison Group	Years Of Study	Tests Used	Results ***	Comments
Austin ISD **Austin, TX** Curry, J. Washington, W. Zyskowski, G., Ph.D.	60/20 ST	11 Schools elementary 1 middle school N=7,000 (approx.)	The District, Title I, and the District by disaggregated groups	1996-1997	TAAS	Read + Math + Writing +	TAAS is a criterion-referenced assessment mandated by state for public school students in grades 3-12. Passing std is 70% for math and read. Scale score is 1,500 for minimum expectation standard. The Texas Learning Index (TLI) correlates a student's grade level and results necessary on TAAS to pass exit-level exam in H.S.
College Park Elementary School Fulton County School System Russell, C.	45/15 ST	1 YRE elementary school	2 TCS matched schools	1991-1992	ITBS	Read +/- Math +/-	Parents, Staff and students were surveyed as well.
Ft. Worth ISD **Ft. Worth , TX** Brinson, Paul, Dr.	45/15 ST	28 YRE campuses	Comparable TC campuses selected from TEA 1993-1999 Accountability Manual	1994-1997	TAAS	Elem. Read + Elem. Math + Elem. Writing + Middle Read - Middle Math - Middle Writing -	Six issues evaluated in this report concerning YRE were student performance, cost, parent & school personnel satisfaction, student attendance, enrollment, & discipline.

*** With the substitution of + for 0, this grading of results follows a pattern first suggested by Barbara Merino (1983)

+ The overall study favors year-round education

+/- The overall study indicates a mixed pattern of results, some favoring YRE, some traditional calendar (TC)

- The overall study favors traditional calendar education

Continued on Next Page

* Statistically significant differences

** ST=Single-Track Year-Round Education,
MT= Multi-Track,
TC= Traditional Calendar School

Appendix A - Single-Track Calendar

Comparison of Achievement of Year-Round and Traditional Calendars: By Descriptive Statistics

School/District Author	Calendar Plan **	Population Studied	Comparison Group	Years Of Study	Tests Used	Results ***	Comments
Texarkana ISD **Texarkana, TX** Paslay, Bobbie	60/20 ST	K-1 4 elementary schools N=500 (approx.)	TC same grades in same schools	1991-1992	CAT	Math+ Read+	1990-1991 was the pilot year at the Kindergarten Center. Some students are voluntary but all students at one elementary follow the year-round calendar.
Trenton Public School **Trenton, NJ** Management & Evaluation Association	50/10 ST 70/10 ST	Grades K-5 at 2 elementary schools	All TCS in district except those at 2 YRE schools	1995-1996	Metropolitan Achievement Test (7th ed)	Read+ Math+	Additional data was collected on attendance, mobility, retention and student, teacher, administrator and parent attitudes. Informal observations and interviews were conducted as well.

*** With the substitution of + for 0, this grading of results follows a pattern first suggested by Barbara Merino (1983)

+ The overall study favors year-round education

+/- The overall study indicates a mixed pattern of results, some favoring YRE, some traditional calendar (TC)

- The overall study favors traditional calendar education

* Statistically significant differences

** ST=Single-Track Year-Round Education,
MT= Multi-Track,
TC= Traditional Calendar School

Appendix B - Multi-Track Calendar

Comparison of Achievement of Year-Round and Traditional Calendars: By Inferential Statistics

School/District Author	Calendar Plan **	Population Studied	Comparison Group	Years Of Study	Tests Used	Results ***	Comments
Palmdale,CA **Palmdale School District** Fish, Judy Dr. & Gandara, Patricia Dr.	3-60/15 MT Orchard Plan	Grades 1-8 N=c.1,000	3-TC schools in district matched on ethnicity, baseline scores	1988 - 1992	CTBS	Read + Math + At-Risk Read +* At-Risk Math + Statistically significant differences	Mean Scale Scores favored YRE in all 3 schools. Demonstrated increase in gain scores for whole student body in 1 school. All schools offered at least 50 hrs of additional instructions via intersession for at-risk students.
Montebello USD **Bell Gardens, CA** Matsui, Bruce Isamu Dr.	45/15 MT	Grade 8 Year-Round students N=142	Grade 8 TC students N=144	1989-1990	CAT	Read +/- Math +/-	A comparison between YR students who have attended 8 continuous years on a YR 45/15/schedule & TC students in the same district over the same time period. Various subgroups examined by disaggregated data.
Jordan School District **Sandy, Utah** Sorenson, Peggy Ann Dr.	45/15/MT	Grades 4, 5, 6 in 11 YRE schools N=8,500	Grades 4, 5, 6 in 11 TC schools	1991-1994	SAT	Read +/- Math +/- Lang. +/-	No significant difference was found in main effect yet significant results were found in interactions of calendars with SES, grade, and gender.

*** With the substitution of + for 0, this grading of results follows a pattern first suggested by Barbara Merino (1983)

+ The overall study favors year-round education

+/- The overall study indicates a mixed pattern of results, some favoring YRE, some traditional calendar (TC)

- The overall study favors traditional calendar education

* Statistically significant differences

** ST=Single-Track Year-Round Education,
MT= Multi-Track,
TC= Traditional Calendar School

Continued on Next Page

Appendix B - Multi-Track Calendar

Comparison of Achievement of Year-Round and Traditional Calendars: By Inferential Statistics

School/District Author	Calendar Plan **	Population Studied	Comparison Group	Years Of Study	Tests Used	Results ***	Comments
School District in an urban area of Utah, Shields, Carolyn M. Oberg, Steven L.	MT	Grade 5, YR students 3 schools	Grade 5, traditional students 3 schools Matched on SES & administrator background	1990-1995	SAT	Read+* in 1994 only Math+ Lang+ Total Battery+ Science+ SS+	An additional analysis compared actual scores of each school for each test & subtest with predicted band of achievement as determined by SOE. Over 6 years 21% of traditional student scores fell below predicted range where 4% from MTYRE in non–transitional years fell below.

*** With the substitution of + for 0, this grading of results follows a pattern first suggested by Barbara Merino (1983)
+ The overall study favors year-round education
+/- The overall study indicates a mixed pattern of results, some favoring YRE, some traditional calendar (TC)
- The overall study favors traditional calendar education

* Statistically significant differences
** ST=Single-Track Year-Round Education,
MT= Multi-Track,
TC= Traditional Calendar School

Continued on Next Page

Appendix B - Multi-Track Calendar

Comparison of Achievement of Year-Round and Traditional Calendars: By Descriptive Statistics

School/District Author	Calendar Plan **	Population Studied	Comparison Group	Years Of Study	Tests Used	Results ***	Comments
Oxnard School District Oxnard, CA Brekke, N.R., Supt.	60/20 MT	Total District K-8 N=c. 12,300	State Average on CAP Grades 3, 6, 8	1982-1990	CAP	Scale scores - Gain scores +	A consensus from the teachers, parents, and administrators is, after 13 years of experience with YRE, that all students, in particular those that are educationally disadvantaged, experience less learning loss than in the traditional calendar setting.
Mueller Elem. School Chula Vista District, CA Bill Collins, Principal	60/15 MT	Grade1-6 YRE School N=c.600	Schools in the district	1987-1989 pre scores 1990-1992 post implementa-tion	SAT	Read - Math +	Additional data were collected by survey. Intercession is utilized for remediation and enrichment.

*** With the substitution of + for 0, this grading of results follows a pattern first suggested by Barbara Merino (1983)
+ The overall study favors year-round education
+/- The overall study indicates a mixed pattern of results, some favoring YRE, some traditional calendar (TC)
- The overall study favors traditional calendar education

* Statistically significant differences
** ST=Single-Track Year-Round Education,
MT= Multi-Track,
TC= Traditional Calendar School

Continued on Next Page

Appendix B - Multi-Track Calendar

Comparison of Achievement of Year-Round and Traditional Calendars: By Descriptive Statistics

School/District Author	Calendar Plan **	Population Studied	Comparison Group	Years Of Study	Tests Used	Results ***	Comments
Orange County P.S. Orlando, FL Fardig, Diane Locker, Dianne	60/15 2 MT schools 1 ST school	Grades K-5 Test results for Grades 2-5	District averages for TC schools	1990-1993	SAT (8)	Read Comp + Total Math +	Other evaluation questions included that of the environment, costs, activities, attendance, curriculum, instructional methods, student conduct, attitudes of students and parents pre and post implementation, and program goals.
Wake County Public Schools NC Prohm, B., & Baenen, N.	45/15 MT	3 YRE elementary schools	All elementary schools in district	1992-1995	NC End of Grade Tests	Read + Math +	Additional data collected included attendance and parent and staff attitude survey.
Socorro ISD El Paso, TX Shook, Sue	60/20 ST & MT	3 ST elementary schools, 2 ST high schools, all other schools MT	District, Region, State average	1994-1995	TAAS	Read + Math + Writing +	Positive gains, but factors other than the YR calendar were not controlled.

*** With the substitution of + for 0, this grading of results follows a pattern first suggested by Barbara Merino (1983)

+ The overall study favors year-round education

+/- The overall study indicates a mixed pattern of results, some favoring YRE, some traditional calendar (TC)

- The overall study favors traditional calendar education

* Statistically significant differences

** ST=Single-Track Year-Round Education, MT= Multi-Track, TC= Traditional Calendar School

Appendix B

Concept 6 Annual Data Report (2000–2001)
Lodi Unified School District

Program Profile (2000-2001)
Established in 1996
Serving grades: K-8
Enrollment: 15 Elementary Schools, 1 Middle
Program, Type: Multi-Track, Concept 6
StudentTeacher Ratio: 19.6:1
Calendar Days: 163

Ethnicity
41.4% White
27.8% Hispanic
18.8% Asian
7.2% African American
4.4% Other

Program Participation
29.4% Limited English
52.2% Free/Reduced Lunch
34.2% Compensatory Ed.

SAT 9

National Percentile Rank of Mean NCE Scores

Grade	1999	2000	2001	2002	Gain		2002
READING					1 Yr. Same	Multi-Yr. Successive	District
2	38	40	41	39	N/A	1	41
3	29	35	35	38	-3	9	38
4	37	36	40	42	7	5	42
5	35	37	35	39	-1	4	39
6	41	40	43	42	7	1	43
7	41	36	43	41	-4	0	43
8	41	44	43	45	2	1	47
LANGUAGE							
2	40	42	43	47	N/A	7	43
3	31	39	42	45	2	14	46
4	42	41	47	49	7	7	49
5	38	40	42	47	0	9	46
6	44	44	49	50	8	6	49
7	47	50	56	49	1	2	54
8	49	49	51	47	-9	-2	51
MATH							
2	40	46	51	52	N/A	12	53
3	32	46	53	58	7	26	57
4	37	40	44	45	-8	8	51
5	34	41	43	50	6	16	49
6	43	45	48	57	14	14	57
7	38	38	41	48	0	10	51
8	42	42	41	50	9	8	50

Continued on Next Page

Appendix B

Concept 6 Annual Data Report (2000–2001)
Vista Unified School District

Program Profile (2000-2001)
Established in 1989
Serving grades: K-7
Enrollment: 28 Schools
Program, Type: Multi-Track, Concept 6
StudentTeacher Ratio: 26.8:1
Calendar Days: 163

Ethnicity
45.2% White
41.2% Hispanic
6.1% African American
2.5% Asian
3.7% Other

Program Participation
23.9% Limited English
41.6% Free/Reduced Lunch
0% Compensatory Ed.

SAT 9

National Percentile Rank of Mean NCE Scores

Grade	1998	1999	2000	2001	2002	Gain		2002
						1 Yr. Same	Multi-Yr. Successive	State
READING								
2	42	46	51	50	51	N/A	9	52
3	41	44	47	47	48	-2	7	47
4	45	46	50	50	52	5	7	50
5	44	47	48	50	49	-1	5	47
6	47	50	50	50	50	0	3	49
7	50	48	52	53	49	-1	-1	46
LANGUAGE								
2	46	52	54	52	54	N/A	8	53
3	41	46	50	52	54	2	13	55
4	47	48	53	54	56	4	9	55
5	47	50	51	56	56	2	9	54
6	47	50	52	54	55	-1	8	55
7	53	53	59	59	57	3	4	57
MATH								
2	47	57	71	71	70	N/A	23	63
3	48	53	64	67	66	-5	18	64
4	43	48	57	59	61	3	18	58
5	44	50	54	60	61	2	17	58
6	48	56	58	60	61	1	13	62
7	46	55	51	56	54	-6	8	54

Appendix C - Extended Year Calendar

Annual Data Report (2000–2001)
School 1

Program Profile (2000-2001)
Established in 1998
Serving grades: K-6
Enrollment: 221
Program, Type: Public School District
StudentTeacher Ratio: 20.1:1
Average Daily Att.: 94.7%
Calendar Days: 200
Professionally Managed: No

Ethnicity
12% Caucasian
1% Asian
87% African American

Program Participation
0% Limited English
85% Free/Reduced Lunch
10% Special Ed.

TERRA NOVA

National Percentile Rank of Mean NCE Scores

Grade	1998	1999	2000	2001	Gain	
READING					1 Yr. Same	Multi-Yr. Successive
2	35	56	78	65	N/A	29
3	*	*	*	*	N/A	N/A
4	46	59	51	53	N/A	7
5	46	57	62	62	11	16
6	35	60	61	61	-1	26
LANGUAGE						
2	36	57	82	59	N/A	23
3	*	*	*	*	N/A	N/A
4	48	51	53	56	N/A	8
5	42	56	55	56	3	14
6	37	57	57	71	16	34
MATH						
2	41	52	84	57	N/A	16
3	45	63	56	63	-21	18
4	*	*	*	*	*	*
5	35	44	53	48	N/A	13
6	26	49	56	55	2	29
* Not Tested						

Continued on Next Page

Appendix C

Annual Data Report (2000–2001)
School 2

Program Profile (2000-2001)
Established in 1997-1998
Serving grades: K-5
Enrollment: 432
Program Type: Public School District
StudentTeacher Ratio: 18.2:1
Average Daily Att.: 95.6%
Calendar Days: 200
Professionally Managed: No

Ethnicity
4 Caucasian
16 Asian/Pacific
376 African American
34 Hispanic
2 Native American

Program Participation
369 Economically Disadvantaged

SAT 9

National Percentile Rank of Mean NCE Scores

Grade	Fall 99	Spr 00	Spr 01	Gain	
READING				1 Yr. Same	Multi-Yr. Successive
K	59	80	78	N/A	19
1	49	61	72	-8	23
2	35	37	66	5	31

Grade	Fall 99	Fall 00	Fall 01	Gain	
READING				1 Yr. Same	Multi-Yr. Successive
3	30	44	52	N/A	22
4	31	13	31	-13	0
5	17	31	24	11	7
LANGUAGE					
3	22	26	61	N/A	39
4	38	33	36	-10	-2
5	26	58	32	-1	6
MATH					
3	21	53	69	N/A	48
4	44	42	44	-9	0
5	26	48	33	-9	7

Continued on Next Page

Appendix C

Annual Data Report (2000–2001)
School 3

Program Profile (2000-2001)

Established in 1982
Serving grades: PreSchool - 8
Enrollment: 250
Program Type: Private School
Instructional Staff: 24
Calendar Days: 240
Professionally Managed: No

Ethnicity

A wide variety of income, ethnic, and cultural background, family composition, and personal skills. Definition of minority constitutes more than 35% of local population

Program Participation

Students with learning disabilities included in test mean

CTBS/4

National Percentile Rank of Mean NCE Scores

Grade	1999	2000	2001	2002	Gain	
READING					1 Yr. Same	Multi-Yr. Successive
4	71	58	60	58	N/A	-13
5	61	82	70	72	12	11
6	70	50	77	69	-1	-1
7	73	74	82	88	11	15
8	70	76	78	76	-6	6
LANGUAGE						
4	66	54	47	60	N/A	-6
5	55	72	65	69	22	14
6	63	47	70	63	2	0
7	66	65	71	79	-9	13
8	65	67	65	67	3	2
MATH						
4	60	52	55	50	N/A	-10
5	54	60	61	68	-13	14
6	57	49	59	61	0	4
7	70	58	79	85	26	15
8	70	78	65	61	-18	-9

Continued on Next Page

Appendix C

Annual Data Report (2000–2001)

School 4

Program Profile (2000-2001)
Established in 1998
Serving grades: K-6
Enrollment: 965
Program Type: District Charter
Student/Staff Ratio: 17:1
Calendar Days: 210
Professionally Managed: Yes

Ethnicity
9% African American
17% Asian Pacific
16% Caucasian
58% Hispanic
0% Other

Program Participation
6% ESL
2% Special Ed.
36% Free/Reduced Lunch

SAT 9

National Percentile Rank of Mean NCE Scores

Grade	Fall 99	Spr 00	Spr 01	Gain	
READING				1 Yr. Same	Multi-Yr. Successive
2	47	61	59	N/A	12
3	40	56	62	1	22
4	51	45	54	-2	3
5	53	52	47	2	-6
6	N/A	56	49	-3	N/A
7	N/A	N/A	55	-1	N/A
MATH					
2	57	76	72	N/A	15
3	43	75	81	5	38
4	51	48	63	-12	12
5	54	57	55	7	1
6	N/A	64	64	7	N/A
7	N/A	N/A	66	2	N/A
LANGUAGE					
2	53	73	66	N/A	13
3	38	65	71	-2	33
4	52	52	59	-6	7
5	51	60	55	3	4
6	N/A	57	58	-2	N/A
7	N/A	N/A	67	10	N/A
SPELLING					
2	50	61	63	N/A	13
3	43	63	69	8	26
4	54	50	59	-4	5
5	48	56	53	3	5
6	N/A	54	53	-3	N/A
7	N/A	N/A	61	7	N/A

Continued on Next Page

Appendix C

Annual Data Report (2000–2001)

School 5

Program Profile (2000-2001)
Established in 1998
Serving grades: K-5
Enrollment: 404
Program Type: Ind. Charter
Student/Staff Ratio: 16.2:1
Calendar Days: 200
Professionally Managed: Yes

Ethnicity
99% African American
0% Asian Pacific
1% Caucasian
0% Hispanic

Program Participation
0% ESL
7% Special Ed.
56% Free/Reduced Lunch

SAT 9

National Percentile Rank of Mean NCE Scores

Grade	Fall 00	Spr 01	Gain
READING			1 Yr. Same
1	58	63	**5**
2	42	44	**2**
3	37	48	**11**
4	28	44	**16**
5	24	36	**12**
MATH			
1	46	63	**17**
2	37	48	**11**
3	34	38	**4**
4	37	41	**4**
5	32	34	**2**

Grade	Fall 98	Spr 01	Gain
READING			Multi-Yr. Successive
1	42	63	**21**
2	33	44	**11**
3	26	48	**12**
4	27	44	**17**
5	21	36	**15**
MATH			
1	29	63	**34**
2	27	48	**21**
3	22	38	**16**
4	33	41	**8**
5	19	34	**15**

Continued on Next Page

Appendix C

Annual Data Report (2000–2001)
School 6

Program Profile (2000-2001)
Established in 1996-1997
Serving grades: K-6
Enrollment: 140
Program Type: District Charter
Average Daily Att.: 91%
Student/Staff Ratio: 15:1
Calendar Days: 223
Professionally Managed: Yes

Ethnicity
46% African American
27% Asian Pacific
28% Caucasian
9% Hispanic

Program Participation
33-40% Limited English
20% Special Ed.

Iowa Test of Basic Skills

National Percentile Rank of Mean NCE Scores

Grade	Fall 99	Sp 00	Gain	Fall 02	Spr 01	Gain	
READING			1 Yr. Same			1 Yr. Same	Multi-Yr. Successive
2	16	19	3	25	25	0	
3	41	31	-10	18	14	-4	-9
4	53	49	-4	21	20	-1	-27
5	25	40	15	35	47	12	-33
6				28	29	1	22
LANGUAGE							
2	16	17	1	20	18	-2	-2
3	27	20	-7	12	8	-4	-19
4	27	39	12	19	16	-3	-9
5	14	19	5	28	27	-1	-13
6				21	28	7	
MATH							
2	22	36	14	25	28	3	-6
3	31	33	2	16	19	3	-12
4	59	39	-20	20	23	3	-36
5	36	33	-3	33	30	-3	-6
6				37	45	8	

Minnesota Comprehensive Assessment

Same Students-Successive Gain

	MATH 1998	MATH 2000		READING 1998	READING 2000
Level	1.44	1.78		1.33	1.56
Scale Score	1166	1349		1216	1278

References

American College Testing. www.act.org/news/data/04/states.html.

Anderson, L. (2000). Time, learning, and school reform: A conceptual framework. In P. Gandara (Ed.), *The dimension of time and the challenge of school reform* (pp. 13–27). Albany, NY: SUNY Press.

Aronson, J., Zimmerman, J., & Carlos, L. (1998). *Improving student achievement by extending school: Is it just a matter of time?* San Francisco, CA: West Ed Regional Educational Laboratory. http://web.wested.org/online_pubs/timeandlearning/3_research.html.

Austin, B. W. (Ed.). (1996). *Repairing the breach: Key ways to support family life, reclaim our streets, and rebuild civil society in America's communities.* Report of the National Task Force on African-American Men and Boys. Dillon, CO: Alpine Guild, Inc.

Bainbridge, W. L. (2005, March 27). *U.S. students get short shrift.* www.schoolmatch.com/articles/SPMAR05.htm.

Baldridge Education Criteria for Performance Excellence (2004). www.quality.nist.gov/Education_Criteria.htm.

Ballinger, C. (1987). Unleashing the school calendar. *Thrust for Educational Leadership, 16*(1), 16–18.

Ballinger, C. (1988, February). Rethinking the school calendar. *Educational Leadership, 45*(5), 57–61.

Ballinger, C. (1995, November). Prisoners no more. *Educational Leadership, 53*(3), 28–31.

Ballinger, C., Kirschenbaum, N., & Poimbeauf, R. (1987). *The year-round school: Where learning never stops.* Bloomington, IN: Phi Delta Kappa Fastback # 259.

Barron, R. (1993). *The effects of year-round education on achievement, attendance and teacher attendance in bilingual schools.* Unpublished doctoral dissertation, Northern Arizona University.

Bechtel, R. (1991). *A study of academic growth in third grade students and its relationship to year-round education.* (Doctoral dissertation, Pepperdine University, 1991). *Dissertation Abstracts International, 52,* 2404.

Boone, M. M. (2003, December 18). The time is now, the need is urgent. *Park Cities People*. Editorials, 10–11A.

Borg, W., & Gall, M. (1989). *Education research: An introduction* (5th ed.). White Plains, NY: Longman.

Bracey, G. W. (2002, September). Summer loss: The phenomenon no one wants to deal with. *Phi Delta Kappan, 84*(1), 12–13.

Bradford, J. C. (1999). *Year-round schooling, Buena Vista City Public Schools, Buena Vista, Virginia: A nationally recognized high school program, over 20 years of experience, an extended school year program that really works*. Buena Vista, VA: Buena Vista City Public Schools.

Brekke, N. R. (1990). *YRE: A break from tradition that makes educational and economic sense.* Oxnard, CA: Oxnard School District. (ERIC Document Reproduction Service. ED 324 818).

Brekke, N. R. (1992a). *What YRE can do to enhance academic achievement and to enrich the lives of students that the traditional calendar cannot do.* Oxnard, CA: Oxnard School District.

Brekke, N. R. (1992b, May). Year-round schools: An efficient and effective use of resources. *School Business Affairs,* 26–37.

Brekke, N. R. (1993, December). *Year-Round Education Calendars*. Oxnard, CA: Oxnard School District.

Brinson, P., & Coulter, S. (1997). *Year-Round Schools Reports, 1996–1997, Ft. Worth ISD.* Ft. Worth, TX: Department of Research and Evaluation.

Byrk, A. S., & Raudenbush, S. W. (1992). *Hierarchical linear models: Applications and data analysis methods.* Newbury Park, CA: Sage Publications, Inc.

Cabat, S. (1996). *Student satisfaction related to year-round education and block scheduling.* Hitchcock, TX: Hitchcock Independent School District.

California Department of Education. (1999). *Construction of California's 1999 school characteristics index and similar school ranks.* Sacramento, CA: Office of Policy and Evaluation.

Campbell, W. D. (1993). *Year-round schooling for academically at-risk students: Outcomes in reading scores for grade 2 students in West Carrollton Schools, Ohio.* Unpublished doctoral dissertation, University of Dayton, Ohio.

Carnoy, M., & Levin, H. (1985). *Schooling and work in the democratic state.* Stanford, CA: Stanford University Press.

Carroll, J. B. (1963). A model of school learning. *Teachers College Record, 64*, 723–733.

Cason, C. B. (1995). *The impact of year-round school of student achievement, student/teacher attendance, and discipline.* Unpublished doctoral dissertation, University of Alabama, Birmingham.

Center for Education Reform. (2005). Retrieved December 21, 2005, from http://edreform.com/charter_schools/.

Chen, Z. (1993). *Year-round education: High school student achievement and teacher/administrator attitudes.* Unpublished doctoral dissertation, United States International University.

Coleman, R. W., & Freebern, C. L. (1993). *A comparative study of multi-track year-round education and the use of relocatables.* San Diego, CA: The National Association for Year-Round Education.

Collins, W. (1993). *Evaluation report of Mueller school multi-track program.* Chula Vista, CA: Chula Vista School District.

Consolie, P. (1999). *Achievement, attendance, and discipline in a year-round elementary school.* Unpublished doctoral dissertation, University of Georgia.

Cooper, H., Nye, B., Charlton, K., Lindsay, J., & Greathouse, S. (1996). The effects of summer vacation on achievement test scores: A narrative and meta-analytic review. *Review of Educational Research, 66*(3), 227–268.

Cooper, H., Valentine, J. C., Charlton, K., & Barnett, A. (2003). The effects of modified school calendars on student achievement and school community attitudes: A research synthesis. *Review of Educational Research, 73*(1), 1–52.

Costa, J. S. (1987). Comparative outcomes of the Clark County School District year-round and nine-month schools. (Doctoral dissertation, University of Nevada, 1987). *Dissertation Abstracts International, 48,* 2495.

CTB-McGrawHill. (1976). *Technical paper No. 2, interpreting NCE's.* Mountain View, CA: Research Management Corporation.

Curry, J., Washington, W., & Zyskowski, G. (1997). *Year-round school evaluation report, 1996–1997, Austin Independent School District.* Austin, TX: Austin Independent School District.

Davis, M., & Hayes, K. (1990, March). *Efficiency and inefficiency in Texas public schools.* Austin, TX and Washington, DC: Texas Public Policy Foundation and The National Center for Policy Analysis. Retrieved December 21, 2005, from www.texaspolicy.com/pdf/1990-03-sf-efficiency.pdf.

Dee, T. S., & Levine, J. (2004, Fall). The fate of new funding: Evidence from Massachusetts' education finance reforms. *Educational Evaluation and Policy Analysis, 26*(3), 199–215.

DeJarnett, S. W. (1994). *Year-round education: A synthesis of research.* Unpublished doctoral dissertation, University of Georgia.

Denton, J. J., & Walenta, B. (1993, April). *Cost analysis of year round schools: Variables and algorithms.* College Station, TX: Texas A&M University. (ERIC Document Reproduction Service: ED 358 515).

Dossett, D., & Munoz, M. (2000, July 6). *Year-round education in a reform environment: The impact on student achievement and cost-effectiveness analysis.* Louisville, KY, University of Louisville. (ERIC Document Reproduction Service: ED 464 424).

Dunn, E. R. (1996). *The effect of calendar configuration on elementary students' achievement gains.* Unpublished doctoral dissertation. Houston, TX: Baylor University.

Eames, A., Sharp, C., & Benefield, P. (2004, September). *Review of the evidence relating to the introduction of a standard school year.* Berkshire, UK: National Foundation for Educational Research.

Edison Schools. (2001, September). *Fourth Annual Report on School Performance.* Retrieved on July 1, 2002, from www.edisonschools.com/design/d23.html.

Elsberry, J. S. (1992). *An evaluation of the implementation of year-round education.* Unpublished doctoral dissertation, University of Texas, Austin.

Entwisle, D. R., & Alexander, K. L. (1992). Summer setback: Race, poverty, school composition, and mathematics achievement in the first two years of school. *American Sociological Review, 57,* 72–84.

Eurydice European Unit. (2004, September). *Organization of school time in Europe. School Year 2004–2005.* Brussels, Belgium: Eurydice.

Fardig, D., & Locker, D. (1992). *Year-round education, program evaluation report, Orange County Public Schools, Orlando, Florida.* Orlando, FL: Office of Educational Research, Educational Improvement.

Fass-Holmes, B., & Gates, K. E. (1994). *Report on single-track year-round education in San Diego Unified School District.* San Diego, CA: Planning, Assessment Accountability Division, San Diego Unified School District.

Frazier-Gustafson, J. A. (1998). *Longterm influences of extended year schooling on academic achievement.* Retrieved December 20, 2005, from www.nayre.org.

Frye, F. H. (1996). *YRE-what is the real truth?* Eden, NC: Rockingham County Consolidated Schools.

Gandara, P. (2000). *The dimensions of time and the challenge of school reform.* Albany, NY: SUNY Press.

Gandara, P., (Ed.) & Fish, J. (1994). Year-round schooling as an avenue to major structural reform. *Educational Evaluation and Policy Analysis, 16*(1), 67–85.

Glass, G. (2002). *Time for school: Its duration and allocation.* www.asu.edu/educ/epsl/EPRU/documents.

Glines, D. (1994). *Year-round calendar and enrollment plans.* San Diego, CA: National Association for Year-Round Education.

Glines, D. (2002). *National Association for Year-Round Education: A historical perspective.* San Diego, CA: National Association for Year-Round Education.

Gold, K. M. (2002). *School's in: The history of summer education in American public schools.* New York: Peter Lang.

Goren, P., & Carriedo, R. (1986). *Policy analysis on the implementation of an expanded multitrack year-round school program.* San Diego, CA: San Diego City Schools Planning, Research and Evaluation Division.

Governor's Business Council. (2004, November). *From good to great: The next phase in improving Texas public schools.* www.texasgbc.org/GBC-From Good to Great.pdf.

Grooms, A. (2003, April). *Study of year-round education in select Kentucky school districts.* Cincinnati, OH: Educational Services Institute, Inc.

Grooms, A. (2004). *Findings obtained from year-round research in Kentucky schools from two separate studies.* Cincinnati, OH: Educational Services Institute, Inc.

Grotjohn, D., & Banks, K. (1993, April). *An evaluation synthesis: Year-round schools and achievement.* Paper presented at the Annual Meeting of the American Educational Research Association, Atlanta, GA.

Guthrie, T. (1985). *Final evaluation report, year-round school 1984–1985.* Houston, TX: Houston Independent School District.

Haenn, J. (1996, April). *Evaluating the promise of single-track year round schools.* Paper presented at the Annual Meeting of the American Educational Research Association, Atlanta, GA.

Helfland, D. (2000). Year-round discontent at Hollywood High. *Los Angeles Times*, p. 1.

Helfland, D. (2001, June 9). A lonely battler for students. *Los Angeles Times*, p. 1.

Herman, J. (1987). *Los Angeles experience: Evaluating the results of Concept 6.* Los Angeles, CA: Los Angeles Unified School District.

Hess, F. (1999). *Spinning wheels: The politics of urban school reform.* Washington, DC: Brookings Institution Press.

Hess, F. (2004, April 14). Status quo vs. common sense: Constructing a culture of competence in schools. *Education Week, 23*(31), 43–56. www.edweek.org/ew/articles/2004/04/14/3/hess.h23.htm.

Hough, D., Zykowski, J., & Dick, J. (1990, April 20). *Cost analysis of year-round education programs.* Paper presented to the American Educational Research Association Annual Meeting, Boston, MA.

Huberty, C. J., & Klein, G. A. (1996, Winter). On evaluating the impact of an innovative educational project. *Journal of Research and Development in Education, 29*(2), 89–93.

Jamar, I. (1994). *Fall testing: Are some students differentially disadvantaged?* Pittsburg, PA: University of Pittsburgh, Learning Research and Development Center.

Johnson, N. (1984). *The effects of year-round school programs on pupil achievement in selected schools in the Los Angeles Unified Public School District.* (Doctoral dissertation, Pepperdine University, 1984). *Dissertation Abstracts International, 45,* 3061.

Jordan, K. F., & Lyons, T. S. (1992). *Financing public education in an era of change.* Bloomington: IN: Phi Delta Kappa Educational Foundation.

Kneese, C. C. (1996). Review of research on student learning in year-round education. *Journal of Research and Development in Education, 29*(2), 60–72.

Kneese, C. C. (2000a). *Year-round learning: A research synthesis relating to student achievement.* San Diego, CA: NAYRE.

Kneese, C. (2000b). Increasing achievement for elementary students, including those at-risk, through the manipulation of time and the school calendar. In P. Gandara (Ed.), *The dimension of time and the challenge of school reform* (pp. 89–102). Albany, NY: SUNY Press.

Kneese, C. (2000c, Winter). The impact of year round education on student learning: A study of six elementary schools. *ERS Spectrum, 18*(1), 20–26.

Kneese, C., & Knight, S. (1995, Spring/Summer). Evaluating the achievement of at-risk students in year-round education. *Planning & Changing, 26*(1/2), 71–90.

Kubrin, C. (1996). *Hierarchical linear models.* Retrieved February 12, 2003, from www.stat.washington.edu/raftery/Courses/Soc528/Comments/HLM/helm.kubrin.html.

Kuner-Roth, B. (1985). A comparison of academic achievement of students in a year-round school district with a conventional school year district. (Doctoral dissertation, Temple University, 1985). *Dissertation Abstracts International, 45,* 3061.

Levin, H. (1984). *Clocking instruction: A reform whose time has come?* Palo

Alto, CA: Stanford University, the California Institute for Research on Educational Finance and Governance.

Levin, H. (1987). Accelerated schools for disadvantaged students. *Educational Leadership, 44*(6), 19–21.

Loyd, C. R. (1991). Impact of year-round education on retention of learning and other aspects of the school experience. (Doctoral dissertation, Texas A&M University, 1991). *Dissertation Abstracts International, 52*, 3514.

Management & Evaluation Associates, Inc. (1996). *Evaluation report: Year-Round Education Program, Year 1, 1995–1996.* Trenton, NJ.

Marr, C. (1989). Year-round school and student achievement. (Doctoral dissertation, Northern Arizona University, 1989). *Dissertation Abstracts International, 51,* 124.

Marzano, R. J. (2000). *A new era of school reform: Going where research takes us*. Aurora, CO: Mid-Continent Research for Education and Learning.

Matsui, B. I. (1990). *Comparison of year-round vs. traditional sequences on selected achievement variables.* Unpublished doctoral dissertation, University of Southern California.

McKenzie, W. (2005, January 30). More money or tighter control? *Dallas Morning News,* Viewpoint, 5H.

McMillen, B. J. (2002). A statewide evaluation of academic achievement in year-round Schools. *Journal of Educational Research, 95, 67–74.*

Merino, B. J. (1983). The impact of year-round schooling: A review. *Urban Education, 19*, 298–316.

Miller, C. (2005, January 19). Kick judges out of school. *Houston Chronicle.* Section E1.

Ministry of Education, Culture, Sports, Science and Technology. (2004). *Japan's education at a glance.* www.mext.go.jp/english/statist/04120801/005.pdf.

Minnesota Department of Children, Families, and Learning. (1999). Working group alternative calendars: Report to the legislature. San Diego, CA: Minnesota Department of Children, Families, and Learning.

Mitchell, R. (2002). Segregation in California's K–12 public schools: Biases in implementation, assignment, and achievement with the multi-track year-round calendar. *Williams, et al. v. State of California, et al.* Superior Court, San Francisco, CA.

Mitchell R. E., & Mitchell, D. E. (1999). *Student segregation and achievement tracking in year-round schools.* Paper presented at the 94th Annual Meeting of the American Sociological Association. Retrieved December 20, 2002, from www.geocities.com/weswalker99/rmitchell/MTYRE_Paper1_Chicago_Formatted.htm.

National Commission on Excellence in Education. (1983). *A nation at risk: The imperative for educational reform.* Washington, DC: U.S. Department of Education.

National Education Commission on Time and Learning. (1994). *Prisoners of time: Schools and programs making time work for students and teachers.* Washington, DC: Government Printing. ED 366115.

Northwest Regional Educational Laboratory. (2004). *Educate America: A call for equity in school reform.* www.nsrel.org/cnorse/booklets/educate/index .html

Oakes, J. (2002). Exhibit C. Paper. *Williams, et al. v. State of California, et. al.* Superior Court, San Francisco, CA.

Oakes, J. (2004). The inequality of concept 6 schools: A response to Charles Ballinger. Responding to state expert reports. *Williams, et al. v. State of California, et. al.* Superior Court, San Francisco, CA.

Owens, M. (1994, November). *Report to the school board on student performance in Friendswood ISD: Program for traditional and alternative calendar students enrolled for 2 years from grades 4, 5, 6 during the years 1992–1993 and 1993–1994.* Friendswood, TX: Friendswood I.S.D. Curriculum & Instruction Department.

Pallas, A., Natriello, G., & McDill, E. (1989). *The changing nature of the disadvantaged population: Current dimension and future trends.* (Report No. 36). Baltimore, MD: Center for Research on Elementary and Middle Schools. (ERIC Document Reproduction Service No. 320 655).

Palmer, E. A., & Bemis, A. (1999). *Year-round education.* Retrieved November 3, 2004, from www.extension.umn.edu.

Parsley, K. M., & Powell, M. (1962). Achievement gains or losses during the academic year and over the summer vacation period: A study of trends in achievement by sex and grade level among students of average intelligence. *Genetic Psychology Monographs, 66,* 285–342.

Pasley, B. (1992). *Conventional and year-round program (60/20 Plan) comparison.* Texarkana, TX: Texarkana Independent School District.

Pelavin, S., & David, J. (1977). *Research on the effectiveness of compensatory education programs: A reanalysis of data.* (ERIC Document Reproduction Service, No. ED 147 386.)

Popham, W. J. (1993). *Educational Evaluation* (3rd ed.). Boston: Allyn & Bacon.

Price Waterhouse, Inc. (1991). *Cherry Creek school district selected cost analysis of year-round education versus nine-month education.* Cherry Creek, CA: Cherry Creek School District.

Prohm, B., & Baenen, N. (1996). *Are multi-track year-round schools effective?* Wake County Public Schools, Raleigh, NC: Evaluation and Research Department, Wake County Public School System, NC.

Quinlan, C., George, C., & Emmett, T. (1987). *Year-round education: Year-round opportunities. A study of year-round education in California.* Sacramento, CA: California State Department of Education.

Ready, D. D., Lee, V. E., & Weiner, K. G. (2004). Educational equity and school structure: School size, overcrowding, and schools-within-schools. *The Teachers College Record, 106*(10), 1989–2019.

Ritter, C. (1992). *The effects of year-round school calendar on gifted and talented students*. Unpublished master's thesis, Sam Houston State University, San Antonio, TX. (ERIC Document Reproduction Service No. 350 739).

Roby, D. E. (1992). *Comparison of reading and math achievement in West Carrollton School District under two types of school structure—YR vs. TC.* Unpublished doctoral dissertation, University of Dayton, Ohio.

Rose, L. C., & Gallup, A. M. (2004, September). The 36th annual Phi Delta Kappa/Gallup poll of the public's attitudes toward the public schools. *Phi Delta Kappan, 86*(1), 41–52.

Rossi, P. H., Freeman, H. E., & Lipsey, M. W. (1999). *Evaluation: A systematic approach* (6th ed.). Thousand Oaks, CA: Sage Publications.

Russell, C. (1992). *College Park elementary school: Year-round school evaluation.* College Park, GA: Fulton County Board of Education, Office of Planning, Research, and Development.

Sexton, M. B. (2003). *A case study of the effect of year round education on attendance, academic performance, and behavior patterns.* Unpublished doctoral dissertation, Virginia Polytechnic Institute and State University, Blacksburg, VA.

Shields, C. M., & Oberg, S. L. (1999). What can we learn from the data? Toward a better understanding of the effects of multitrack year-round schooling. *Urban Education, 34*(2), 125–154.

Shields, C. M., & Oberg, S. L. (2000). *Year-round schooling: Promises and pitfalls*. Lanham, MD: Scarecrow Press.

Shook, S. (1995). *Year-round education in Socorro ISD.* El Paso, TX: Department of Strategic Planning, Socorro Independent School District.

Six, L. (1993). *A review of recent studies relating to the achievement of students enrolled in year-round education programs.* San Diego, CA: NAYRE.

Sizer, T. (1994). *Reinventing our schools: A conversation with Ted Sizer.* www.ed.psu.edu/nsys/ESD/sizer/Edvs.Sch.html.

Sorensen, P. A. (1995). *A study comparing 23 modified 45/15 year-round and traditional schools in Jordan School District on Stanford Achievement Test scores for years 1991–1993*. Unpublished doctoral dissertation, Brigham Young University.

Southern Illinois University Public Policy Institute (2001, April). *Year round schools: New century, new ideas.* [Brochure] Carbondale, IL: Author.

Southwest Educational Development Laboratory, 2. (1993, March). *Year-round education.* Retrieved January 17, 2003, from www.sedl.org/policy/insights/yearround9303.html.

Spencer, J. (2005, March 6). Low performance goes beyond funding. *Houston Chronicle*, A1.

Stenvall, J. T., & Stenvall, M. J. (2001). *An analysis of 2000 API scores for California public schools on traditional and year-round calendars at elementary, middle and high school levels.* San Diego, CA: National Association for Year-Round Education.

Stenvall, M. (1996). Year-round science: Shorter year-end breaks plus longer classes equals success. *Science Teacher, 34*(2), 32–34.

Stripling, R., & Stanley, D. (1995). *The effectiveness and efficiency of year-round education in the Waco Independent School District, 1994–1995.* Waco, TX: Waco Independent School District.

Tarrance, V. L. (2000). *The new Hispanic migration and the dream for the new America.* Paper presented to the Raleigh Tavern Philosophical Society, Houston, TX.

Task Force on Education for Economic Growth. (1983). *Action for excellence.* Denver, CO: Education Commission of States. (ERIC Document Reproduction Service No. ED 235 588).

Thomas, G. (1978). *Learning, Retention, Forgetting.* Research Division, State Department of Education, Albany, NY.

Tomlinson, S. (1992). Achievement, assessment, and the school effect. In J. Lynch, C. Modgil, & S. Modgil (Eds.), *Education for cultural diversity convergence and divergence: Cultural diversity and the schools* (vol. 1, pp. 389–399). London: The Falmer Press.

Urbanski, A., & Goodling, B. (2000, May–June). Should we extend the school year? *American Teacher Speakout.* www.aft.org/pubs-reports/american-teacher/may_jun00/speakout.html.

U.S. Census Bureau. (2004, September 4). *Facts for features.* www.census.gov/Press-Release/www.releases.archives/facts-for_features_special_editions/002210.html.

U.S. Department of Education. (1999). *A back to school special report on the baby boom echo: No end in sight.* Washington, DC: Author, Office of Educational Research and Improvement.

Van Mondfrans, A., & Moody, J. (1985). *Provo's year-round education program second year evaluation.* Logan, UT: Provo City School District.

Van Mondfrans, A., Moody, J., & Walters, L. (1992). *Evaluation of year-round education in the Jordan School District: 1988–1989 school year.* Sandy, UT: Jordan School District.

Vugrin, J. F. (1990). *Feasibility study for growth planning, 1990–1991 school year.* San Diego, CA: Chula Vista Elementary School District.

White, J. A., & Cantrell, S. M. (2001, March). *Comparison of study outcomes in multi-track year-round and single-track traditional school calendars.* Program Evaluation and Research Branch Policy Analysis Unit. Los Angeles, CA: Los Angeles Unified School District.

White, J. A., & Cantrell, S. M. (2002, July). *Comparison of student achievement and teacher and student characteristics in multi-track year-round and single-track traditional school calendars: Update 2002–2001.* Program Evaluation and Research Branch Los Angeles Unified School District, Planning, Assessment and Research Division Publication No. 130. Los Angeles, CA: Los Angeles Unified School District.

White, W. D. (1991, February). *Year-round schools—from beginning to end.* Paper presented at the 22nd Annual Meeting of the National Association for Year Round Education, San Diego, CA.

Willis, B. (1993). *YRE pilot project at Cypress-Fairbanks Independent School District, Student achievement on Texas Normative Assessment Instruments.* Houston, TX: Cypress-Fairbanks Independent School District.

Winters, W. L. (1995). *A review of recent studies relating to the achievement of students enrolled in year-round education programs.* San Diego, CA: NAYRE.

Wolf, F. M. (1986). *Meta-analysis: Quantitative methods for research synthesis.* London: Sage Publications.

Worthen, B. R., & Zsiray, S. W. (1994). *What twenty years of educational studies reveal about year-round education.* Chapel Hill, NC: North Carolina Educational Policy Research Center.

Zykowski, J., Hough, D., Mitchell, D., and Gavin S. (1991). *A review of year-round education research.* Riverside, CA: University of California, California Educational Research Cooperative. (ERIC Document Reproduction Service No. ED 330 040).

About the Authors

Charles Ballinger has been involved with school calendar modification for over 3 decades, both as coordinator and director of year-round education and modified school calendars for the San Diego County Office of Education and as executive director of the National Association for Year-Round Education. Over the years, Dr. Ballinger has witnessed growth in the calendar modification movement to encompass more than 2,000,000 student participants. During his tenure he also saw the expansion of the philosophy and terminology of year-round education to include a variety of ways to curb the significant learning loss experienced by many students during the extensive summer vacation allowed by numerous North American school districts.

Carolyn Kneese recently retired as associate professor of educational administration at Texas A&M University, Commerce, Texas, and is an educational consultant. She has taught for 10 years in public schools and universities, in addition to 12 years of research experience, particularly in the area of program evaluation. The majority of her time in program evaluation was spent investigating issues related to the impact of the balanced (or single-track) calendar on student achievement, including at-risk and disadvantaged student populations. She has had many opportunities through the years to speak about this topic at conferences and to consult with school districts nationwide. Additionally, she has had time in the field with administrative interns in urban, rural, and suburban Texas school districts. Some of these districts had year-round programs, which afforded her the opportunity to observe the year-round experience in the natural environment.